The
Running Injury
Recovery Program

For Healthy Running!

Bruce Wilk

The

Running Injury Recovery Program

Bruce R. Wilk, P.T., O.C.S.

ORTHO CONCEPTS
MIAMI, FLORIDA

The Running Injury Recovery Program
First Edition (paperbound)
Revised July 2013
Published by Ortho Concepts, Inc.

This book is intended to provide information about health issues in general, but not to provide specific professional advice to any particular reader about his or her medical condition. Any such information is not intended to replace or substitute for professional medical advice. Readers are advised to consult their own physicians for specific medical advice and treatment. Every effort has been made to ensure that the information in this book is accurate. Neither the author nor the publisher shall be liable or responsible for any loss incurred allegedly as a consequence of the use and application of any information or suggestions contained in this book.

ISBN-13 (paperbound) 978-0-9883603-0-3

Acknowledgements

This book and the accompanying *Running Injury Recovery Program Workbook* are the culmination of thirty years of personal experience and professional development. For their content, I owe thanks to every friend, colleague, teacher, patient, coach, and running partner who has contributed to my knowledge and insight during that time – only a few of whom can be mentioned here.

The first and most important person who has made these books possible is my wife Sherry, who has always been my inspiration in good times and my strength in hard times. Our two daughters, Rachel and Tracy, are an eternal source of motivation and life-affirmation.

Byron Kibort, my friend and business partner at *The Runner's High*, helped me research facts about the shoe industry for this book, and also provides a daily example of the benefits of a positive attitude.

This book could not have been written without the support of my coworkers at *Orthopedic Rehabilitation Specialists (ORS)* in Miami, who worked alongside me as the protocols in this book were developed, and who encouraged me to share them with others. These include some of the finest manual therapists anywhere: Jeff Stenback, P.T., O.C.S.; Cynthia Gonzalez, D.P.T., O.C.S., A.T.C.; Christopher Jagessar, P.T., O.C.S., A.T.C.; Natalie Barzana, M.S.P.T.; and special thanks to Annmarie Garis, D.P.T. and Sokunthea Nau, D.P.T., who also served as expert models in many of the exercise photos.

Outside of our practice, Chris Johnson, P.T., helped me review the physical therapy literature related to this book, and shared my enthusiasm for treating running injuries.

Many thanks go to my office staff at *ORS*, including Nancy Branco, Sandra Smith, and Annabel Navarro, who always keep me organized and well-prepared.

Over the years, many runners have encouraged me to write this book. Foremost among these, I thank Amby Burfoot, Editor at Large of *Runner's World Magazine*, for his motivation and support; and my longtime training partners, David Rosenblatt and Frank Zomerfeld, for their many years as sounding boards for my ideas, and for their detailed reviews of the manuscript.

Special thanks also go to Tammy Foster, a great professional runner and coach who helped me research the history of running and coaching for this book, and who modeled for the photos of our most difficult exercises. Others who contributed their running skills to model for photos include Corina Velazco, Bernardo Valero, and Daniel Ruiz, who were active in the Miami Runner's Club and have gone through the recovery program at my P.T. office. Additional thanks to all of the photographic models, and to the photographer, Gary Mercer, for the hours spent getting each exercise just right; and to Ana Abele of Professional Press for preparing the photos for these books and for the website.

Finally, I thank my editor, Albia Dugger, who took this entire project from dream to reality.

* * *

HOW TO CONTACT THE AUTHOR

Bruce R. Wilk, P.T., O.C.S., MTC
Orthopedic Board Certified Physical Therapist
RRCA Running Coach Specializing in Prevention
& Management of Musculoskeletal Injuries

Ortho Concepts, LLC
Online support for *The Running Injury Recovery Program*
and *The Running Injury Recovery Program Workbook*
www.postinjuryrunning.com

Director
Orthopedic Rehabilitation Specialists
8720 N. Kendall Drive
Suite 206
Miami, Fl. 33176
Office (305)595-9425
www.wilkpt.com

President
The Runner's High
11209 S. Dixie Hwy
Pinecrest, FL 33156
(305)255-1500
www.therunnershigh.com

Running Coach
Miami Runners Club
(305)227-1500
www.miamirunnersclub.com

Table of Contents

Chapter 13 213
Entering Phase Three:
Training Programs and Habits

13.1 Running Habits and Running Injuries • 13.2 Elements of a Good Post-Injury Training Program • 13.3 About Training Programs and Stress • 13.4 Introduction to Phase Three • 13.5 Phase Three Groups and Regions

SIDE TRACKS: Biking and Stress Fractures: "The Sports Medicine Idiot Test"

Chapter 14 235
Closed-Chain Exercises for
Strength and Balance

14.1 Neuromuscular Re-education and Body Awareness • 14.2 Muscle Imbalance • 14.3 Closed-Chain and Open-Chain Exercises • 14.4 Closed-Chain Exercises for Balance and Strength • 14.5 Goals for Closed-Chain Exercises • 14.6 Techniques for Closed-Chain Exercises • 14.7 Timing for Closed-Chain Exercises • 14.8 Closed-Chain Exercises through the Phases

BOX 14-1 *SIDE TRACKS:* Pros and Cons
BOX 14-2 *HOW TO:* Closed-Chain Exercises
BOX 14-3 *GUIDELINES:* Basic Closed-Chain
BOX 14-4 *GUIDELINES:* Regional Closed-Chain

Chapter 15 301
Fitness Walking and Glides

15.1 Establishing Your Base Schedule • 15.2 Post-Injury Running Posture • 15.3 Focus on Stride and Technique • 15.4 Biomechanics: From Foot-Strike to Pushoff • 15.5 Two Recovery Groups • 15.6 Fitness Walking • 15.7 Glides • 15.8 Glide Drills for Balance • 15.9 Moving Ahead

BOX 15-1 *HOW TO:* Build Your Walk/Glide Program
BOX 15-2 *HOW TO:* Fitness Walking
BOX 15-3 *HOW TO:* Glides
BOX 15-4 *HOW TO:* Glide Drills

List of Tables

Preface

The Education of
an Injury-Prone Runner

This book is for all runners who have ever suffered a running injury, and for the families, coaches, and healthcare professionals who care for them. As a physical therapist who specializes in running injuries, and who is also a lifelong runner and triathlete, my goal is to help you understand and treat some of your own running injuries, and to guide you around some of the many pitfalls you may have already encountered in the modern maze of professional running-injury management.

It's true that some elite runners have bodies like machines that are perfectly designed for running. They can run forever over any terrain, in any type of shoe, and never seem to get injured. That's their good luck. I myself am not one of those runners. I've always been injury prone. In fact, the main reason I became a physical therapist was to learn more about my own running injuries and figure out how to avoid them – or at least to learn how to get over them as quickly as possible and get back to running.

Unfortunately, it turns out that physical therapists and other healthcare professionals, including medical doctors, are not specifically trained to identify and manage the types of injuries that are unique to runners.

When we graduate from our respective colleges, we have a wealth of medical knowledge, but no practical application to runners. My own education as a physical therapist (more than thirty years ago) didn't include the study of running injuries, and today the situation hasn't changed – the newly-graduated young therapists coming into my practice this year haven't been trained in running injuries either.

As a physical therapist and runner, I tried to educate myself about running injuries. I talked to my professors and other physical therapists. I went to medical specialists and searched the medical literature. I attended professional conferences and asked questions, but I got very few answers. When I got frustrated with the lack of scientific information, I started making my own observations and writing my own publications. The fact is, there is still no good database for healthcare professionals to build a solid foundation on. There are no standard medical protocols for defining, diagnosing, or treating runners' injuries. As a result, runners often end up with faulty diagnoses and all kinds of treatments that never correctly address their problem, ranging from drugs to fad treatments to unnecessary surgery. Those are major pitfalls!

So, if doctors and physical therapists (or P.T.s, as we call ourselves) are not trained to treat running injuries, what happens to us runners? We usually end up looking to other runners for anecdotal advice, or searching through running magazines and the Internet. Sometimes these sources have helped me, but often their advice is generic, or doesn't fit my specific problems. At worst, some of the advice I've seen has been useless or downright harmful. That's another pitfall.

Here's yet another pitfall: What if you unknowingly buy a defective running shoe that *causes* a running injury? According to the manufacturers themselves, three percent of all running shoes sold are defective. Defective or poorly-designed shoes are a real problem – I know from personal experience. When I was practically crippled by running a triathlon in a defective running shoe, I started seriously studying the science and function of running shoes, and ended up opening my own running specialty store – in addition to my physical therapy clinic.

Over my many years of study, coaching, and treating running injuries as a physical therapist, I've developed what I think is a pretty good system for identifying, evaluating, and treating running injuries. However, the course of the injured runner is not a straight line, and the treatment is not one-size-fits-all. The main problem I have with almost every bit of published advice is that it's written for the running population at large. Everyone gets the same advice.

I'm convinced that, to be effective, a physical therapy program must have two things: One, it must be custom-tailored to you as an individual and, two, it must include hands-on manual therapy. If you just point to where it hurts and somebody just massages it, that's not physical therapy in my book. Hands-on means that a qualified medical professional physically examines you and finds your specific structural and functional problem, and treats that dysfunction. If there is one key to success in a P.T. practice, I'd have to say that's it. Your body is individual, your injury is individual, and in my clinic, everybody get individualized, hands-on diagnosis and treatment.

Some running books, written by great runners and coaches, promise that if you follow their particular style or method you'll never get a running injury. I find two things wrong with that. First, that particular style or method may work fine for the author, but it's not guaranteed to work for *your* individual combination of bone, tendon, muscle structure, and goals. Second – and as a physical therapist who specializes in running injuries, I'm not going to lie to you – at vulnerable moments, runners are going to get injured. It's practically unavoidable (unless you're one of those few, rare, injury-proof running machines).

I think it's valuable to point this out because, when it comes to running injuries, as in life, attitude is important. If I'd become discouraged every time I had an injury, I would have quit running long ago. I'd rather my patients understand that, if they do get an injury, we're going to figure out the problem and learn from it, and that they actually can come out on the other side running better than they did before.

In this book and the accompanying *Workbook*, I'll teach you two approaches to managing your running injuries. First, you can learn how to be your own physical therapist for most running injuries – after all, when it comes right down to it, no one knows your body and your running injuries better than you do! Second, and more seriously, you should know when to seek good, qualified, professional help; how to find it; and what to expect from your P.T. or other healthcare professional when you do get it. Then you can use the principles in this book to get back to running.

For me, running has always been an important part of my life. It keeps me focused and balanced, and it rewards me in all aspects of my life. It led me to my profession, where I get to work with all kinds of runners, from fitness runners to elite racers. I truly love figuring out the real root of their problem, designing an individual and effective course of therapy, and seeing them leave my office as a better runner.

In the end, the most important lessons I've learned have come from countless miles of running, from more than my fair share of running injuries, and from more than thirty years of experience treating many fine people in my physical therapy clinic. As a lifelong runner, I still enjoy challenging myself at races – as do my wife and two daughters. I encourage you to keep running, and to be the best (and healthiest) runner you can be.

* * *

Introduction
The Running Injury
Recovery Program

When a physical therapist treats you for an injury, he or she has already put in many years of hard work to acquire expert knowledge, learn professional skills, and develop injury-management protocols. They diagnose your injury, explore the causes, develop your recovery plan, determine your schedule, assign your exercises, and make sure you are doing them correctly. They do your manual therapy, keep your records, evaluate your progress, and write your progress reports.

In *The Running Injury Recovery Program* you become your own physical therapist, so you'll have to learn to do all of these things for yourself. In other words, you'll be taking a condensed course in physical therapy for runners.

Like any technical education, your course will be divided into two parts: theory and practice. These are covered in two separate books: *The Running Injury Recovery Program* (this book) and *The Running Injury Recovery Program Workbook*. If you only want to learn about the theory, then read this book. If you have a running injury and need to treat it, then you'll need both books.

The Running Injury Recovery Program will be your primary textbook. It contains everything you need to learn, the skills you need to acquire, and the exercises that you need become familiar with before you can actually begin treating your running injury.

The companion book, *The Running Injury Recovery Program Workbook*, is like the lab manual for your course. It contains all the step-by-step instructions that will guide you through the day-to-day work of your recovery program. The *Workbook* is made up of a series of Self-Assessments with Worksheets that will help you determine your recovery group, your exercise schedule, and which exercises you will be doing. Some Self-Assessments will instruct you to prepare individualized Log Forms before you begin your exercises. Others will help you evaluate your Log Forms after you do your exercises, or clear you to move on to the next level in your recovery program. Do NOT try to use *The Running Injury Recovery Program Workbook* until you have read all of the chapters in *The Running Injury Recovery Program*.

You can find some of the main elements of the *Workbook* in the Guidelines tables in this book (in Chapters 5, 11, 13 and 16), which summarize the recovery groups, exercise assignments, and clearance goals for each of the four phases of the recovery program. You won't actually be able to follow these Guidelines until you have completed the Self-Assessments in your *Workbook*.

At the end of this book you'll find a Course Map which covers the entire *Running Injury Recovery Program* from education to treatment and recovery. When you start your *Workbook*, you'll use the Course Map along with your *Workbook* to keep you on track from start to finish. The Course Map follows the chapters in this book, and lets you check off each of your accomplishments as you complete them.

As you read through this book, you'll be able to check off many of the lines related to education in the white boxes on your Course Map. You won't be able to check off the action lines (light-shaded boxes) or checkpoints (dark-shaded boxes) on your Course Map until you start your *Running Injury Recovery Program Workbook*.

If the *Running Injury Recovery Program* sounds a bit complicated – well, it is. However, the *Workbook* is designed to take you through your recovery program in small, easy steps. If you follow the Course Map and the Guidelines for your group, they'll keep you on track.

That said; when you start your *Workbook*, try to do your best. The closer you follow the *Running Injury Recovery Program*, the faster you will recover and the better you will run. I personally use all of the techniques described in this program every day in my P.T. clinic to treat injured runners, and I see how well they work. I know that, if you follow your individualized recovery program, you can overcome your running injury, correct the underlying causes, and improve your running habits – and you will become a better runner.

To learn more about *The Running Injury Recovery Program*, you can check out our website at www.postinjuryrunning.com where you'll find lots of current information, references, educational programs, access to personal coaching and exercise equipment, and answers to some Frequently Asked Questions (FAQs).

* * *

Chapter 1
Do I Really Have
a Running Injury?

All runners have pain sometimes – but not all pain comes from running. For example, a patient came to my P.T. clinic recently because her doctor had diagnosed her swollen knee as a running injury. When I examined her knee, I found an insect bite surrounded by a red rash and inflammation. She had an infection, not a running injury – so I sent her to an urgent care center for antibiotics. The doctor who had seen her less than an hour earlier had diagnosed her based only on the fact that she was a runner, without ever looking at her knee!

Of course not all cases are quite so obvious, but you get the idea. Since runners are generally healthy, it's easy to assume that when you have a pain it must come from running. So, the first question you should always ask yourself is, "Do I really have a running injury?"

1.1 Is It a Running Injury?

There are many types of running injuries, but they all have one thing in common – they all result from running. The rules for identifying a running injury are very simple and specific: A running injury happens *when* you run. The injury gets worse *while* you are running. And it settles down after you *stop* running.

Here's an example of how these rules can be applied: One of my patients is a long-distance runner who has run many marathons. I had been his physical therapist for 15 years when he came in complaining of a new problem – a "strain" in the groin area. He told me that his pain was continuous and worsening; it did not calm down after rest; and it did not get worse when he ran.

Since pain from a running injury does get worse while running, and decreases with rest, I quickly realized that his pain couldn't be due to a running injury and sent him to see his medical doctor. It turned out that his pain was due to a tumor in the lower part of his lung. He had surgery to remove the tumor and, after rehabilitation, he successfully returned to running marathons. He also learned the rules for identifying running injuries!

All running injuries are caused by **dysfunctional running** – a pattern of impaired movement that is repeated during running. The source of a dysfunctional running pattern can be almost any combination of internal and external factors that affect your normal running movement. It might include your footwear, your environment, fatigue, stress, erratic training habits, or a number of other factors – but the end result is that something goes wrong with your running. Running injuries occur when you run long enough or hard enough in that dysfunctional running pattern to damage something. In other words, to be a running injury, it must come from running!

1.2 Runners are Different

As runners, we know we're different from non-runners. We have different lifestyles, different eating habits, different schedules – and our injuries are different too! In general, runners' injuries differ from those in the general population because they're caused by different physical dynamics. A runner and a non-runner may be diagnosed with the same *type* of injury, but the clinical presentations of those injuries are different, and so are the ways we have to manage them.

For example, one injury that I often see in my P.T. clinic in both runners and non-runners is plantar fasciitis – an injury caused by overstretching the strong ligament that forms the arch on the bottom of the foot, which causes severe pain in the foot and heel. However, the plantar fasciitis that most healthcare professionals see is not plantar fasciitis from a runner, it's plantar fasciitis from a person who is overweight or who regularly carries heavy loads. It's a different type of plantar fasciitis.

As an illustration of how this works, let's look at two of my patients: "Joe" and "Greg" each came to my P.T. office with very severe pain typical of plantar fasciitis. Before I could start treating them, I had to discover what caused their injuries. The first step is always to take a complete medical history and make a thorough physical examination.

Joe was not a runner. His job required him to spend a lot of time on his feet. He had to carry heavy loads, and he'd put on some extra weight over the years. He showed me his old, worn-out work shoes and explained that he was having crippling pain in his foot when he put his weight on it. When he first stood in the morning, his whole body was generally stiff and achy. On examining Joe, I found that he had generalized stiffness and weakness.

Greg was just the opposite. He was a fit and active top-notch runner who worked on a boat and spent a lot of time barefoot. Greg had recently started running in a pair of unsupportive "barefoot technology" shoes, and had suddenly developed crippling foot pain. He was now completely unable to run in any shoe, and unable to walk barefoot during work. When he first stood in the morning, he noticed a specific, sharp pain in his heel. On examining Greg, I found a very specific stiffness and weakness associated with his injury.

Joe and Greg both had plantar fasciitis, but their injuries were completely different. Greg's plantar fasciitis was caused by running; Joe's was not. Because their injuries were *caused* in different ways, each of them got a different rehabilitation plan that was suited to his individual needs.

1.3 Traumatic versus Nontraumatic Injuries

Another important thing to know is that not all injuries that happen while running are running injuries. For example, if you're running and you stumble on an uneven surface and twist your ankle, that's a traumatic injury, not a running injury.

Running is a **nontraumatic activity** – a mid-range activity that is performed well within your normal range of motion. It doesn't require moving joints and muscles in an extreme direction or with an awkward movement.

On the other hand, a **traumatic activity** is something that happens outside your normal range of motion. A traumatic injury such as a sprained ankle or twisted knee is not a running injury because it doesn't occur within your normal running movement.

Most running injuries are caused by repetitive wear and tear resulting from a problem within your habitual running pattern. So, a non-traumatic running injury is one that develops over time from dysfunctional use, poor technique, or a combination of other factors.

1.4 Factors that Contribute to Nontraumatic Running Injuries

Many different factors can contribute to nontraumatic running injuries, but they are generally grouped into two categories: things that are caused by you (**intrinsic factors**), and things that are caused by outside influences (**extrinsic factors**).

When we're trying to identify the cause of a particular running injury, it's important to sort out the main contributing factors and try to correct them. If an extrinsic factor is overwhelming your intrinsic factors, we want to identify that. If your problem is an intrinsic factor, we can try to modify that with extrinsic factors.

Here are some examples of *intrinsic* factors that can contribute to running injuries:

- *Mobility and stability*: A lack of sufficient **mobility** (range of motion) and **stability** (balanced muscle strength) increases your risk of running injuries.

Running requires greater mobility and stability than walking.

- *Motivation:* A lack of alertness or control can affect your running form and opens the door to mistakes that can cause a running injury.

- *History of previous injuries:* Runners have an increased risk of injury if they have been injured during the previous 12 months, or if they have a history of injuries that have not been resolved.

- *Pre-existing medical conditions:* Any pre-existing medical condition that affects your running ability – including previous traumatic injury, surgery, and some chronic diseases – is a risk factor for running injuries.

- *Inexperience:* Runners who have not been running consistently for at least three years have not fully developed their muscle and bone strength for running, and are more prone to injury.

Now let's look at some examples of *extrinsic* factors that contribute to running injuries:

- *Training habits:* How much and how hard you train affects your risk of injury. That includes either too much or too little of factors such as speed, distance, frequency, and duration of training.

- *Equipment:* Any equipment that affects your running performance can contribute to an injury. That includes shoes, socks, inserts, and other accessories that cause discomfort or blisters; clothing that restricts or chafes (including running bras that are too tight or not supportive enough);

hydration systems that increase your load or change your balance points; and heart-rate monitors that distract you or over-motivate you.

- *Environment:* Any sudden change in your environment can affect your running performance and contribute to an injury. That includes changes in the external environment (such as running surface, temperature, weather conditions, or elevation) and changes in your internal environment (such as fatigue, illness, poor nutritional status, dehydration, and electrolyte imbalance).

We'll be discussing some of these factors in detail throughout this book because they are an important part of understanding and overcoming your running injury. As you assess your injury, consider your own various intrinsic and extrinsic factors, and how they might have contributed to that specific injury.

1.5 Getting Started

Once you have determined that you actually have a running injury, you can proceed to the first step in your recovery, which is education. In the following chapters, you'll learn about running injuries and how they are assessed and treated, as well as a lot of other related information you'll need to know when managing your running injuries.

After you have learned the basics, you'll be guided through the process of developing a self-management program that is specific to your injury, and to you as an individual. The ultimate goals of your recovery program are to overcome the dysfunctions involved in your injury; to improve and balance your running strength and efficiency; and to return you to running as a better, safer, and healthier runner.

* * *

Chapter 2
An Introduction to the
Four Phases of Recovery

Sometimes a running injury can make you feel like your world is coming to an end. Your problem keeps growing until it seems way too big or too complicated to deal with, and it just keeps getting worse. Your journeys into the world of medical management and running "advice" have turned into a dark maze that leads you in circles. You're scared, you're frustrated, and you don't know what to do next.

You need a plan – and not just any plan; you need one that is clear and manageable, with step-by-step instructions. Most importantly, it has to lead you out of this maze and into the clear light of recovery.

I assure you, it can be done. In my P.T. office, I've worked with many, many despairing runners who have come back out of the depths of overwhelming injuries. I always think of one patient in particular, "Will," who was also a training buddy. Will was a talented runner who grew as an athlete much faster than I ever did. He only ran his first 10K because he lost a bet while drinking with his brother-in-law, and I freely admit that he beat my best time by ten minutes.

During Will's first marathon, a nagging hamstring injury turned severe and crippled him, and he ended up in my P.T. office. Our professional relationship began literally with the first step – by teaching him how to walk. Will showed me the true value of an individualized training plan, the importance of developing proper technique, and that hard work really does pay off. Step by step, Will returned to healthy and functional running, and I continued as his running coach and P.T. for many years. I'm just saying that, even in the darkness, there is always light at the end of the tunnel.

2.1 A Proper Injury Recovery Program

Running injuries don't just occur randomly, out of the blue. We have to recognize that running injuries are really caused by problems (**dysfunctions**) in our running. It's all about *how* you run, and how that affects your body. Many pre-existing factors can predispose you to an injury, ranging from imbalances in muscle strength to lack of awareness when you're fatigued, or even shoe failure. When we're treating a running injury, it's important to address not only your physical dysfunction, but also the dysfunctions in your training habits, technique, and equipment selection. Think of it as an integrated approach to running injury management.

Any injury-management program must be carefully planned and executed. Although physical therapists don't have agreed-upon protocols for managing running injuries, we do have well-designed protocols for disorders in walking (**gait disorders**), and we can use those protocols as a framework on which to build an injury-management program for running injuries. Your running should be evaluated, the dysfunctions in your running should be identified, and those dysfunctions should be managed through a progressive program of functional exercises, each with clear **functional goals**.

Sometimes you need a skilled healthcare professional to help you identify your running dysfunctions, manage your injury, and supervise your injury recovery program. There are other times when you can do the same thing for yourself. The goal of this book is to share what I've learned over more than thirty years of treating running injuries as a physical therapist, and to give you the tools you need to develop your own injury recovery program. A proper injury recovery program has two requirements: it should always be individualized to your specific needs, and it should always be divided into phases, each with objective requirements for clearance.

2.2 The Four Phases of Recovery

Your injury recovery program will be divided into four phases, each with very specific goals:

- *Phase One*: Education and Self-Help
- *Phase Two*: Regaining Mobility
- *Phase Three (Part One and Part Two)*: Improving Strength and Balance
- *Phase Four*: Return to Functional Running

Phase One is the **acute phase** immediately after an injury, when there is pain, swelling, and inflammation. Your goals in Phase One are (1) to treat your injury symptoms, (2) to protect the injured area to prevent further injury, and (3) to learn about the many factors involved in a successful injury recovery program.

In Phase One, you'll use the PRICE method of treatment (protect, recover, ice, compression, and elevation). You'll work to reduce any swelling with ice, compression, and elevation. You'll reduce or take a temporary rest from running to prevent further damage. And, you'll protect the injured area until you've regained full range of motion.

Moving from Phase One to Phase Two, you'll start using **self-mobilization techniques** and **stretching exercises** as tools to identify and assess your specific injury. The goals of **self-assessment** are to locate the areas of tightness, stiffness, and weakness that are signs of **muscle imbalance**; and to focus your attention as specifically as possible on the injured region.

In Phase Two, you'll also use self-mobilization techniques and stretching exercises to begin directly addressing the problems caused by (or that caused) your injury. Your recovery goals in Phase Two are to regain **mobility** (full range of motion), correct muscle imbalance (tightness, stiffness, and weakness) and work on **body awareness** (postural control and biomechanical factors).

Phase Three continues with the self-mobilizations and stretching exercises you learned in Phase Two, and adds more challenging exercises that concentrate on strengthening the dysfunctional components of your running. These **functional strengthening** tasks will be harder than those you did in Phase Two, but easier than those you'll find in Phase Four.

In Phase Three Part One, you'll learn **Basic Closed-Chain Exercises** that will be used as a self-assessment tool to prepare you for Phase Three Part Two. Closed-chain exercises, such as stepping and hopping, form a direct chain of balance from the feet upward through the body. In addition to strengthening your muscles, these exercises will help develop balance and body awareness, decrease undesirable side-to side movements (**shear forces**), and help promote a functional movement pattern for running.

In the Phase Three Part Two, you'll advance to **Regional Closed-Chain Exercises** to address your specific injury regions, and begin building up your running time through an individualized **walk/glide program**. The walk/glide program is a progressive series of **fitness walking** and controlled running (**gliding**) drills which begin a period of recovery that we call **post-injury running**.

Phase Four pulls together all the skills you have learned in the previous phases and adds more difficult exercises that will help you build endurance, power, and running **efficiency**. The goal of this final phase is to return you to **functional post-recovery running**. In this phase, minimally reaching your goal will not be enough. These exercises will actually be more challenging to your balance and control than the ones you might encounter in your regular training program.

Phase Four exercises include drills in accelerations, hills, and plyometrics. **Plyometrics** are specialized, high-intensity training techniques used to develop athletic power (strength and speed), and to improve the responsiveness of your nervous system. By the time you finish plyometrics, you will have developed all the skills required to return to *functional post-recovery* *running*, including improved mental focus, strength, balance, endurance, and neuromuscular coordination.

2.3 The Individualized Plan

What makes this a self-help book and not just a running "advice" book is that the methods we use here are not "one size fits all." In my P.T. office, no two patients ever follow the exact same pathway to recovery. When an injured runner comes to me for treatment, I learn about their individual history and running goals, evaluate their injury, and develop an individualized injury-management plan specifically for that patient.

This book will show you how to develop your own individualized recovery plan, just as we do in my office. When you start *The Running Injury Recovery Program Workbook*, you'll be guided step-by-step through a comprehensive series of **Self-Assessments** that will determine where you begin, and put together a customized injury recovery program, using six specific criteria:

1. Your running *history*.
2. Any *pre-existing conditions* that affect your running – including pre-existing medical conditions, injuries, or surgeries.
3. The *severity* of your running injury.
4. Whether your injury is *simple or complex*.
5. The specific *region* of your injury.
6. Your individual running *goals*.

The time-frame required for you to complete your injury-management program will vary depending upon your individual plan, and upon your ability to successfully meet the requirements for clearance through each phase of recovery.

2.4 Using These Books

Recovering from an injury involves a lot more than waiting for your injury to heal and doing some exercises. To succeed in your injury recovery program, there are many essential factors that you'll need to be aware of, and some things you should avoid as well. If this is your first time in self-management, it's really important that you take the time to read all the sections in this book, including the parts about professional advice, equipment selection, and mental focus.

Some chapters in this book contain general guidelines that apply throughout your recovery process. Other chapters contain instructions that apply to one specific recovery phase. Once you have read and understand all the principles in *The Running Injury Recovery Program*, you can start treating your injury using *The Running Injury Recovery Program Workbook*. The **Course Map** will guide you through all the steps you'll need to follow. As you perform your exercises, you'll record your results in your daily **Log Forms**, and the **Self-Assessments** will help you evaluate your condition and monitor your progress.

It's really important to move carefully and sequentially through each step in your recovery program. The Course Map for each phase includes certain **Clearance Checkpoints**, which are criteria for performance that you must complete before you can move on to the next step in your recovery program.

Clearance means that you have met those goals and you can safely progress to the next level. If you can't pass the test at a clearance checkpoint, you don't proceed. If at any time your injury gets worse, or you are reinjured, then you may have to re-assess and move back to an earlier phase in your recovery program.

The ultimate goal of these books is to return you to **functional running**. That means the *cause* of your dysfunction will be addressed, whether it is in your training habits, technique, or equipment. Throughout the four phases of recovery, you'll increase your strength, balance, and neuromuscular control. Your biomechanical skills will improve, and you will actually become a better runner. By the time you return to *post-recovery running*, you should feel strong and confident about your ability to handle any challenge you might encounter.

This running injury recovery program is not a quick-fix, but it is the most effective way I've found to approach running-injury management. It requires comprehension, commitment, and hard work on your part – but in my experience, these are all things at which lifelong runners excel!

* * *

Chapter 3
How Bad Is My Injury?

Running injuries can be complicated. When it comes down to actually managing your running injury, however, it's not the *type* of injury that's most important, it's the *severity*. I would rather manage an early-stage bone failure than a late-stage muscular running injury. The runner who has a less severe injury will progress through recovery faster, and return to running sooner, with fewer long-term effects than the runner who has a more severe injury – even if he gets professional care.

Remember, running injuries are caused by continuing to run with a dysfunctional running pattern, and the longer you run with that dysfunction, the more severe your injuries will become. In my practice as a physical therapist, I've seen many runners sidelined because they continued to run on a minor injury until it became so severe that it crippled them. An injury that cripples you can prevent you from running permanently – and that should be a wakeup call for all runners.

Here's an example: While running a marathon in Miami, I was running with an acquaintance (not a patient) who mentioned that her foot was bothering her. At the time, I didn't pay much attention. Later during the marathon, she said her foot was really hurting bad, and I started worrying. When I spoke to her the next morning, she was crippled with pain – she couldn't even walk.

What happened? I found out that she had been going to a sports medicine doctor, a podiatrist, who repeatedly injected her with cortisone and told her it was okay to keep on running. At the time, she thought her original injury wasn't severe enough to keep her from running, and getting the injections made her feel better and allowed her to compete. She got her last cortisone shot on a Thursday, ran the marathon the following Sunday, and severely ripped her plantar fascia. It took her four weeks to walk without crutches, six weeks before she could work or exercise, and she never ran again.

Why do runners keep running on an injury until it's so severe that it cripples them? They don't understand that taking medicine to feel better is not the same as actually getting better. This woman would not have continued running if she thought she was going to wake up one day and be unable to walk, unable to care for her children, or unable to fulfill her responsibilities. No one would do that. Using medication for pain and inflammation and continuing to run on an injury can only make your injury worse.

3.1 Staging Your Running Injury

Determining the *severity* of your running injury is the first step in your recovery program. The severity of your injury at the time you *begin* self-management helps determine which phase of recovery you will start in, and which type of recovery program you will follow. For example, if your injury is not too severe and you have no other complications, you may begin on a *self-paced plan* that will return you to post-recovery running quickly. On the other hand, if your injury is more severe, or if you have other complications to consider, you may have to slow down and follow a more cautious *two-week-interval plan*.

Over the years, I've developed a practical scale of **Running Injury Stages** (*Table 3-1*), that I use to evaluate the severity of a running injury, increasing from Injury Stage 1 to Injury Stage 5. Each of the five stages is associated with certain emerging symptoms, based on my long experience with running-injury patients. Along with the emerging symptoms used to determine stages 1 through 3, I've added a list of **Red Flags** which describe the more serious symptoms you might find in those stages. Just being in Stage 4 or Stage 5 is Red Flag. No matter which injury stage you are in, if you encounter any of the symptoms listed as Red Flags, you should stop running immediately and address the problem.

3.2 The Five Running Injury Stages

We can evaluate the severity of a running injury by two main criteria: The first depends on when your pain occurs, and how long it lasts. The second reflects how much that pain affects your normal **activities of daily living (ADLs)**. ADLs include things like walking, going up or down stairs, bending over, squatting, or standing up.

If you experience any of the warning signs described in these five Running Injury Stages, you should take immediate steps to correct the problem and make sure it doesn't get any worse. Those steps should include treating your injury (either through self-management or qualified professional care) and correcting the cause of your injury, which usually involves modifying your training habits, technique, or equipment.

Injury Stage 1 is an unfamiliar and disconcerting pain that appears while you are running. It might be a pain that comes after running 10 miles, or after only a few minutes. It continues as long as you are running, but stops when you stop running. This is the first warning sign of an injury. Find and address the cause of the problem before your injury becomes any more severe. In Stage 1, a Red Flag is pain that alters your stride, which is a more severe injury than just pain upon exertion. If pain alters your stride, you should begin self-management immediately.

Injury Stage 2 is pain at rest, after you stop running. A little bit of muscle soreness is normal when you're in training, but an unusual or prolonged pain is not. If the pain is still there after you stop running, you need to pay close attention. Find and address the cause of the problem before your injury becomes any more severe. In Stage 2, a Red Flag is pain that disturbs your rest. If pain disturbs your rest, you should begin self-management immediately.

Injury Stage 3 is pain that persists during your normal daily activities (ADLs), such as walking or going up or down steps. You might be getting up from your desk and have some ache or nagging pain that bothers you. In Stage 3, a Red Flag is pain that limits or makes you avoid normal ADLs. Find and address the cause of the problem, and start self-management immediately.

Injury Stage 4 is pain that you take medication for. This is a very important factor. Medication masks the severity of an injury, and allows it to get much worse if you keep on running. Taking *any* type of medication for pain or inflammation for a running injury (including over-the-counter anti-inflammatories, prescribed medications, or injectable treatments) is a big Red Flag. You must stop running immediately, wait until the medication is out of your system, and then re-assess your injury stage to see if you can self-manage. If you can't do without the medication, you should seek qualified professional treatment.

Of course, there are times when pain medication is appropriate – such as when pain disturbs your sleep. If you do need medication to manage your injury, you have to stop running; but that doesn't mean you have to sit around and do nothing. Your recovery program will include alternative exercises for you to do until your course of medication is over, and the medication is out of your system. In my office, that time frame is 24 hours after the last dose for most oral medications, and three weeks after administration of most types of injectable treatments.

Injury Stage 5 is pain that cripples you. It prevents you from walking normally, and significantly affects the performance of ADLs such as climbing stairs, squatting down, or getting out of a chair. Stage 5 is a huge Red Flag. Start self-management or seek qualified professional treatment immediately.

Determining the severity of an injury on this Running Injury Stage Scale is the first thing I do when I treat any type of running injury. For example, if a patient

Table 3-1

Running Injury Stage Scale

Injury Stage	Emerging Symptoms	Red Flags
Stage 1	Pain while running	*Pain that alters your stride*
Stage 2	Pain at rest (after running)	*Pain that disturbs your rest*
Stage 3	Pain during your normal daily activities	*Pain that interferes with or makes you avoid ADLs*
Stage 4	Running injury pain that you take medication for	*Being in Stage 4*
Stage 5	Pain that cripples you	*Being in Stage 5*

comes to my office and says, "Bruce, I'm training for a marathon and at ten miles my foot is killing me," I first ask if the pain continues after he stops running. If he says no, then I ask him if he's having pain that interferes with his daily activities. If he says no to that, then I ask if he's taking any medications for the pain. If he says no to that as well, then he's at Injury Stage 1.

3.3 Avoiding the Abyss

Note that, even if you are at Injury Stage 1, pain-wise, as soon as you take any medication for it – suddenly you're at Injury Stage 4, only one step away from crippling. It doesn't matter whether you're taking an over-the-counter anti-inflammatory, prescribed medications, or injections administered by a doctor. If you use *any* medication that masks the pain of a running injury and keep on running, you can end up crippled. Stage 5 is the abyss of crippling injury from which you may never return. You do not ever want to be at Stage 5.

Remember also that any *type* of running injury, I don't care what is, can increase in severity from Injury Stage 1 to Injury Stage 5. Sometimes runners think "Oh, it's just muscular shin splints; that's not so bad." Then they start taking Advil and keep running on it, or go to a doctor and get cortisone shots and keep running on it, and their injury goes to Stage 5 – which is crippling.

Over the years, I've treated too many patients who have come to me with crippling injuries that they developed because they took pain medication and continued to run. In my professional practice, if a patient insists on taking medication to keep on running, including any type of prescribed oral or injected medications, I can't help them. In my office, that's a deal breaker. I've had patients say, "Oh, it was prescribed; my doctor said it was okay." Well, if they're going to run on cortisone shots, I don't want anything to do with it. They're not going to Stage 5 on my watch. That's the way it is, and I won't budge, and I won't do the therapy session. This policy has served me well. No patient of mine who has followed this advice has escalated from a lower-stage injury to a crippling injury – ever.

Let's be clear: When a running injury gets to Stage 5, it can be life-altering. Pay attention to the increasing severity of the injury stages, start-self management early, and seek qualified professional evaluation if necessary. Address the cause of the problem. Above all, never run on an injury while on medication for pain and inflammation.

3.4 Injury Stages and Clearance through the Phases

The Running Injury Stage Scale is used as a self-assessment tool to determine where you will begin your recovery program, to help monitor your progress during your recovery program, and at each clearance checkpoint throughout the four phases of recovery.

You may begin your injury recovery program in Phase One with a running injury in any stage of severity from 1 to 5, and with Red Flags. The goal of Phase One is to self-manage your symptoms down to lower stages on the scale until you have no Red Flags. At that point, if you find that you have used your best efforts at self-management and still are not able to resolve your symptoms or meet the clearance requirements for Phase Two, then you should seek professional help.

You can progress to Phase Two in your recovery program when your symptoms have improved and you have no Red Flags. As you progress through each phase, and the difficulty of your exercises increases, your emerging Stage 1 and Stage 2 symptoms may reappear temporarily, but they should resolve themselves as you master the exercises in that phase. To clear any phase, you must resolve any Stage 1 or Stage 2 symptoms that arise during that phase, and have no Red Flags.

Do not proceed through any Red Flag or Stage 3 symptoms. If at any time your symptoms become worse than Stage 2, or if any Red Flag appears, you must stop what you are doing and go back to the previous phase and get clearance again.

Staging your symptoms on the Running Injury Stage Scale is more than just a useful tool: It's the central concept of a good running-injury management plan. It tells you where to begin; it gives you an objective way of measuring your progress through the phases. It also helps you determine when you are cleared to take the next step. Using this method opens a safe and manageable pathway to recovery from any type of running injury.

* * *

Chapter 4
What Type of Injury Do I Have?

When you are seeking help for a running injury from a healthcare professional, you don't want to go to someone who tells you to point to where it hurts, and then immediately gives you a diagnosis without so much as a simple physical examination. I call that the "point to it" diagnosis. Sadly, runners are too often quickly "diagnosed" this way, without a proper medical history or physical examination. That's an invitation to misdiagnosis.

The problem with diagnosing musculo-skeletal injuries is that the area where we perceive pain is not unique to a specific injury. The pain you feel might not even be in the same region as the injury, because pain can radiate to different parts of the body. In fact, the **pain pattern** you feel can be the same for different types of running injuries, or different for the same type of running injury, depending on your individual circumstances.

No one should diagnose you based solely on a description of your pain. For example, if you point to pain on the outside part of your knee, chances are good that you'll be diagnosed with **iliotibial band (ITB) syndrome**. Pain along the outside of the knee is common among runners, but ITB syndrome, calf strains, hamstring strains, and even some stress fractures can all cause pain that makes us point to the outside of our knee. The area of pain may be similar, but the basic problems and rehabilitation processes for each injury are quite different (*Table 4-1*).

Another common misconception in diagnosing running injuries is that **patellofemoral pain syndrome (PFPS)** is the most common running injury, and the cause of most running-related knee pain. Some healthcare professionals are quick to diagnose a runner with PFPS as soon as they hear he has knee pain. We know that PFPS is anterior knee pain due to a patellar (knee cap) tracking problem that causes dysfunctional contact between the patella and underlying bone. We also know that PFPS is the precursor to **chondromalacia**, which is a softening of the cartilage at this contact point, and that advanced chondromalacia is **osteoarthritis (OA)**.

Here's the problem. Numerous studies have shown that there is no increased knee arthritis in runners. So how can the number one running injury be the precursor to OA? It can't! In my experience, the number one anterior knee pain diagnosis in runners is actually **patellar tendinosis** (one type of runner's knee), not PFPS – and runner's knee has a different pattern of symptoms and dysfunctions than PFPS.

Misdiagnosis of running injuries is a common problem, so the real question is, how can we get a reliable diagnosis of a running injury? Healthcare professionals have no good databases or medical protocols to guide them in the diagnosis and treatment of running injuries, and that's probably the main reason why so many runners' injuries get misdiagnosed.

I confess that dealing with other healthcare professionals' misdiagnoses has been a career-long frustration for me. When I started out as a hospital physical therapist, learning how to manually identify a musculo-skeletal dysfunction, I often got to know the patients' injuries way better than their doctors knew them. It wasn't unusual for me to discover that one injury had been diagnosed as another. It was only when I manually worked with the patients and really pinpointed their dysfunctions that we found the real injury – which often made the treatment they had been prescribed irrelevant.

The point is, as runners, we should be aware that diagnosing a running injury is not an easy task, and it should never be a "point to it" diagnosis based on a pain pattern alone. Pain and dysfunctional running have to be linked to actual physical impairments so the true source of the problem can be fully understood and treated.

4.1 Injury Regions

Runners who come to my P.T. office are diagnosed with many different *types* of running injuries, including plantar fasciitis, shin splints, Achilles tendinitis, runner's knee, and iliotibial band syndrome. In the real world of running-injury management, however, running injuries don't translate into a particular diagnosis, but as body parts or **regions** that have been injured by dysfunctional running.

For example, symptoms of foot pain in the lower (**plantar**) surface of the heel and/or arch upon arising in the morning may lead to a diagnosis of plantar fasciitis in runners. However, this area of the foot is made up of many different structures, not just the plantar fascia. When it comes down to self-management, the diagnosis of plantar fasciitis isn't all that important because you're not going to treat just the plantar fascia. You have to address the dysfunctional effects of running on the entire arch region as a unit. For self-management of most running injuries, it won't be necessary for you to know the names of the specific anatomical structures involved, as long as you can correctly identify the injured region and progress in your recovery.

In this book we divide running injuries into ten major regions: the toe, arch, heel, shin, calf, band, knee, hamstring, hip, and buttock. Each is identified by specific symptoms and dysfunctions that we will pinpoint in Phases Two and Three. For now, let's concentrate on some other specific factors you'll need to consider before you can begin your injury recovery program.

4.2 Self-Assessment and Self-Management

In my P.T. office, I do much more than make a diagnosis before I prescribe treatment for a running injury; I do a complete **evaluation**. A professional evaluation of a running injury must be hands-on, and includes a wide range of factors that can contribute to running injuries. When I do an evaluation, I first determine the *severity* of the injury and take a full medical and running *history*. Then I make a complete and thorough musculo-skeletal examination, looking for the specific areas of *tenderness*, *stiffness*, and *weakness* that are characteristic of certain *types* of injuries. I examine the patient's running shoes for fit, wear and function; then I do a **gait analysis** on the treadmill, looking for a dysfunctional running stride that relates to that injury. Finally, I put all of these factors together into an individualized injury-management plan that I schedule, supervise, and continuously monitor in my office.

When you begin to prepare your own **self-management plan** at home, you'll have to consider all of these factors as well. Your *Self-Assessment* may take a little longer than a professional evaluation because you not only have to learn the steps and procedures, but you'll also need to understand the reasoning behind them. That's what this book is all about, teaching you what you need to know to assess your own injuries. The *Workbook* will then guide you, step-by-step, through your recovery program. Remember, self-assessment has one major advantage over professional evaluation – you can feel your own pain, stiffness, and weakness first-hand. No one knows your body better than you do, and that's an important key to success.

4.3 Simple Injuries versus Complex Injuries

Once you have determined the *severity* of your injury, the next step in your self-assessment is to determine what *type* of injury you have. Your basic running injury recovery program will vary depending on whether your injury is *simple* or *complex*.

A **simple running injury** is defined as one type of injury, in one region, in one leg – and the injury comes from dysfunctional running (a nontraumatic injury). A

complex running injury, on the other hand, involves more than one type of injury (including traumatic injuries or pre-existing medical conditions), or more than one body region.

A complex running injury typically results from ignoring a simple running injury, or from taking pain meds or injections that mask the pain, and then continuing to run on the injury until it gets worse and affects multiple regions. A complex running injury can also begin with a traumatic injury or other medical problem that causes a dysfunctional running pattern.

Here's an example: Say you have a traumatic ankle sprain, and you run on it before you've fully recovered your strength and range of motion in the injured ankle. You adjust your stride to **compensate** for the stiffness and weakness on that side, and your stride becomes altered and unbalanced – that's *dysfunctional running*. Running with an altered stride can cause a nontraumatic running injury in another region, higher or lower than the ankle, in addition to your traumatic ankle sprain.

Now you have a complex injury. It's not going to follow a simple assessment pattern because it's a *compensatory*, secondary running injury resulting from the sprain or other traumatic injury, not directly from the running. It will also require a different recovery plan than a simple running injury.

When you start developing your own recovery program, it's important to take into consideration every factor that affects the complexity of your running injury, including any pre-existing conditions that affect your running.

Box 4-1   Evaluating Symptoms

As you progress through the Phases, you will be using certain physical tests to help you identify your specific injury regions, and to evaluate your progress:

- In Phase Two *self-mobilizations* you will locate specific areas of *tenderness* that correlate with the pain you feel when you run on your injury.

- In Phase Two *stretches* you will discover areas of *stiffness* or inflexibility that correlate with the muscle tearing and scarring caused by your running injury.

- In Phase Three *closed-chain exercises*, you will find regions of *weakness* that correlate with loss of muscular strength and neuromuscular control associated with your running injury.

- In Phase Three *walk/glides*, and in Phase Four *plyometrics*, you will find the dysfunctional running pattern (**gait dysfunction**) that caused, or was caused by, your running injury.

In Phase Two and Phase Three, the purpose of many of your *Self-Assessments* will be to evaluate your specific areas of tenderness, stiffness, weakness, and gait dysfunction, and to measure any differences between your injured leg and your non-injured leg.

For example, *Table 4-1* outlines the results of some of the self-assessment tests we use to identify injuries that occur in and around the iliotibial band (ITB). Since so many running injuries that cause pain in the outside of the knee are misdiagnosed as ITB syndrome, it's important to distinguish among the types of injuries that cause pain in this region, including the hamstring, calf, and some stress fractures. These functional tests help me differentiate between different types of injuries.

Table 4-1: Evaluating Pain around the ITB

	BAND	HAMSTRING	CALF	STRESS FRACTURE
Tenderness	Found on the outside of the knee, often accompanied by visible swelling.	Found on the back of the thigh, anywhere from knee to buttocks.	Found in the calf muscle – the muscle in the back of the knee that goes to the ankle.	Found in any weight-bearing bone of the injury region.
Stiffness	Reduced range of motion from the hip and buttock down to the upper leg.	Reduced range of motion in the Straight Leg Raise test.	Difficulty flexing the foot upward (on the uphill incline board).	Reduced range of motion in the injury region.

(*Table 4-1* cont.)	BAND	HAMSTRING	CALF	STRESS FRACTURE
Weakness	Difficulty balancing on one leg OR difficulty kicking out to one side.	Asymmetrical weakness and inflexibility in the hamstring area during kickback.	Difficulty flexing the foot downward (to lift body weight).	Unable to hop on one leg after icing and resting for 3 weeks; OR difficulty balancing on the injured leg.
Altered Stride	Side-to-side wobble at the hip OR leaning to one side while running.	Pushing off from the inner side of the big toe; OR short, asymmetrical, OR twisting kickback.	Pushing off from the inner side of the big toe; OR short, asymmetrical, OR twisting kickback; OR outward rotation of leg; OR circular movement of the lower leg.	Pain in the injury region that alters stride.

4.4 Pre-existing Conditions: Osteoarthritis

If you have any *chronic* pre-existing condition that affects your ability to run – such as a previous traumatic injury (including surgeries), or a diagnosed medical condition (such as osteoarthritis) – you still have to meet the same standards and criteria for training and safety as other runners. Any pain that alters your stride, or pain that causes you to take medication in order to run with a running injury, is not acceptable for any runner.

Osteoarthritis (OA) by itself is not a running injury. As long it's properly cared for and medically supervised, a person can run with OA – but it is a pre-existing disease that complicates a running injury. Because OA is often managed with anti-inflammatory medications, any running injury combined with OA is automatically a Stage 4, complex running injury, and the runner must take the recovery pathway for a complex injury.

For example, one of my long-standing patients, "Jim," was a lifelong elite distance runner. One day, Jim came into my P.T. office limping with Stage 5 hip and buttock pain. Because of the severity and complexity of his symptoms, I gave him Phase One treatment to put out the fire, then sent him to his medical doctor for a diagnostic workup. When it came back, it showed that Jim had developed advanced OA in his hip. Jim began a supervised course of medication to control the symptoms of his OA, and we were able to work together to keep him running safely for another ten years – until his hip deteriorated to the point that he had to have hip replacement surgery.

It's important to understand that elite distance runners like Jim are the only group of runners who develop OA at a higher rate than the general population, and even then it only occurs in the hip. Many runners who don't have arthritis worry that running will wear out their knees, cause arthritis, and eventually leave them disabled and unable to run. These fears persist despite the many studies that show that running does not cause OA. In fact, studies show that most runners actually have less arthritis than non-runners. Unlike mechanical parts in machines, our knees have healing mechanisms. With increased normal use such as walking and running, our knees actually become stronger and build up a tolerance to loading, and that can protect against OA.

Things that actually *do* increase your risk of knee osteoarthritis include excessive loading of the knees due to obesity or heavy lifting (which may cause you to use abnormal movements when carrying heavy loads), and sports that require you to perform irregular twisting, turning, pivoting, and kicking movements that stress your knees. In runners, the risk of knee osteoarthritis increases when you run on an injury that affects the alignment and loading mechanism of the knee – and knee surgery will only increase that risk.

4.5 Treating a Complex Running Injury

When we treat a complex running injury involving a *pre-existing* trauma or medical condition, those factors have to be managed and brought under control first. You may have to get a medical clearance that says you are healthy enough to run, and be physically able to attempt the vigorous exercises needed to strengthen your body in preparation for running.

When we treat a complex running injury involving an *acute* trauma (including surgery), the traumatic injury is treated first – then we treat the running injury. If there are multiple injuries, we start with any traumatic injuries, followed by the most severe nontraumatic running injury (as defined by the Running Injury Stage Scale). When those have been managed down to lower stages, then we progress through the other injuries in order of severity. We continually re-evaluate all your injuries – both separately and collectively – until you've reached a full recovery.

Let's look at an example of a multi-region, complex running injury: "Carlos" was a 32-year-old Miami law enforcement officer who wanted to get on the SWAT team. To qualify, he had to increase his running. Early into his training he had pain in his right foot, which he self-diagnosed as plantar fasciitis. Assuming the problem was with his shoes, he visited a running store and bought a good pair of supportive training shoes, then returned to running and continued to progress.

Carlos later developed iliotibial band (ITB) symptoms in his right leg. He visited a physical therapist (not at my office) and the treatment he received consisted of Pilates and tape! That P.T. referred Carlos to a different running store where he was told that his new running shoes caused underpronation, and that he should run naturally in "barefoot technology" shoes. When he went for a run in his new "barefoot" shoes, his injuries immediately got worse, and he started having trouble doing his job.

The first time I met Carlos at my P.T. office, I found Stage 5 running injuries in both his arch and his band – that's two regions and therefore a complex running injury. I found his running dysfunction by observing his running pattern on the treadmill (*gait analysis*). He had an external rotation at the hip that made him run with his toes pointing out. Because he ran with his feet sticking out, and the right one sticking out more than the left, he would slap his foot and overpronate, and then he would waddle at the hip.

My evaluation of Carlos' history was that the first, stabilizing shoes he bought had helped his original problem, overpronation, but did *not* help the external rotation in his hip. Correcting the overpronation with more stable shoes had allowed Carlos to increase his mileage, which put more stress on his hips. This allowed his injury to move up the kinetic chain from simple plantar fasciitis to complex fasciitis with ITB. When Carlos tried to solve the problem by switching to "barefoot" shoes, the plantar fasciitis came back with a vengeance. Then the Pilates and tape "treatments" he received (which didn't treat anything) allowed his injury to get much worse.

When treating complex injuries such as Carlos', I always focus on the worst impairment first. Usually I can combine treatments for similar impairments in each region. In rehabilitation, I'm constantly jumping around between the injuries, constantly re-evaluating all the injuries separately and collectively, and changing priorities as each injury progresses through the recovery phases at its own rate.

The point of the story is, complex injuries require complex solutions. It's better to avoid complex injuries in the first place. If you follow the guidelines in this book, you'll learn to self-manage your running injuries at an early stage, before they become too severe or complex.

4.6 Pathways to Recovery

Whether your injury is simple or complex, there is always a pathway to recovery. Remember, it's not the *type* of injury that's most important, it's the *severity*. Using the techniques in Phase One, every runner should be able to manage their injuries downward on the Running Injury Stage Scale and get clearance to enter Phase Two, and then achieve sufficient mobility in Phase Two to enter Phase Three.

What will differ for each individual is the length and direction of your path. Simple injuries and complex injuries will take separate routes through Phases Two and Three, and have different requirements at the clearance checkpoints. By the time you reach Phase Four, any complex injuries will have been resolved, and the two recovery pathways will again converge.

Since your physical condition and functional abilities will constantly be changing over the course of your recovery, you'll be continuously re-assessing your status and adjusting your individualized recovery plan, guided by your Course Map and *Workbook*. It's an ongoing process throughout the phases of recovery. However, before you can start your recovery program you'll need to finish reading this book – that's the "education" part of Phase One.

When you start your *Workbook*, you'll fill out *Self-Assessment 1* (Parts A, B, C, and D), which will document your injury and the relevant parts of your medical and running history. The results of *Self-Assessment 1* will determine the level at which you will begin your recovery program. You won't really get into the physical examination parts of your recovery program (and determine whether your injury is simple or complex) until you reach Phase Two in your *Workbook* – and there are Clearance Checkpoints you will have to pass before you can enter Phase Two. Meanwhile, if you have any Red Flags, you will have work to do in Phase One, which begins in the next chapter with Self-Help.

* * *

Chapter 5
Entering Phase One: Self-Help

It's that moment when you first feel the pain and know you've been injured. You now have three choices: First, if it's a bad injury, you're going to seek a qualified professional evaluation. Second, you might decide to tough it out and ignore it; or even worse, take medications and keep running – well, if you're reading this book, that's not an option. Third, you can use the guidelines in this book (along with the *Running Injury Recovery Program Workbook*) to manage your injury yourself.

I am always surprised by the number of runners I meet who have severe injuries (injuries with Red Flags) but don't think this is a problem. For example, "Elliot," a new patient, came to my P.T. office for his first appointment with pain in his shin. "I'm sure it's only shin splints," he said, "It's no big deal." Elliot was a young runner who had only been running for two months, and was training for his first marathon. He was up to 10 miles on his long run, and feeling very proud of himself. When I took his history, he admitted to having pain that altered his stride, and that he was no longer able to run the same way he did before. Those are two big Red Flags.

When I examined Elliot, I could see and feel swelling along his shin, which he didn't even realize was there. When I pressed on the shin bone, it caused the same pain he felt while he was running. Then I asked him to do a square-hop exercise – one of the exercises we use for diagnosing running injuries. He did fine on the uninjured leg, but when it came time to hop on the injured leg, he just couldn't bring himself to do it. He was psychologically, physiologically, and neuromuscularly **inhibited**. When he finally did try it, the hopping reproduced his running pain – right at the same place I had found his bone pain, tenderness, and swelling.

Like many young people, Elliot was minimalizing his symptoms by thinking they were no big deal and he could keep on running. In fact, Elliot was probably one run, one fall, or one awkward movement away from opening up a hairline fracture of the tibia – an injury that could have been life-altering.

Acting "tough" by ignoring an injury and continuing to run on it is a bad idea. Remember, any type of running injury can go from Stage 1 to Stage 5 and cripple you – seriously. Pay attention, and start managing your running injuries as soon as possible.

5.1 Medication for Pain and Inflammation

No matter what type of injury you have, you've got tissue damage and your body responds with **inflammation** – swelling, heat, tenderness, and soreness at or near the injury site. It's the first step in your body's natural repair system for any injury. You might have tiny, microscopic tears that resolve themselves in a day or so, or you might have great, bruising tears that require lengthy rehabilitation. That's why we separate injuries by severity rather than type.

What you must *not* do when you are injured is to take medication for your pain and inflammation and keep on running. That will only make your injury worse. If you have inflammation, you should stop running and treat the injury, not just the pain. That means temporarily avoiding any triggering activity – including running and any other activities that trigger your pain. This is the only time during your recovery that you should *avoid* weight-bearing exercise – while the injury is new and "red hot." This period of **avoidance** will end as soon as your Red Flag pain is under control.

This is also the only time it's okay to take pain medications – while you're not running. Medication can be an important part of recovery if your sleep is disturbed and medication is necessary for rest, but there must be no running until the medication is out of your system. Any time you take medication for a running injury, you are at Injury Stage 4.

5.2 Recovery Phase One: Getting Started

Once you have read all the chapters and understand all of the concepts in this book, you will be ready to start the Self-Assessments in Phase One of your *Running Injury Recovery Program Workbook*. You'll document your injury, your running history, and your medical history (*Self-Assessment 1*), and you'll determine two important things: (1) that you do have a running injury, and (2) which stage of severity you are in, on the Running Injury Stage Scale.

In Phase One, you will fall into one of two recovery groups based on your Injury Stage. *Group 1* includes only those who have running injuries in Stages 1, 2, or 3, with no Red Flags. *Group 2* includes anyone with Red Flags in Stages 1, 2, or 3, and everyone in Stages 4 and 5 *(Table 3-1).*

The self-help system for running injuries is called **PRICE** – protect, recover, ice, compression, and elevation. In Phase One, both recovery groups will begin with PR – protection and recovery – a process that you will learn about throughout this book. Only *Group 2* will **ICE** – a combination of ice, compression, and elevation used to reduce the swelling caused by acute inflammation. *Group 1* will implement PR measures, then move on to Phase Two as soon as they can pass the Clearance Checkpoints on their Course Map.

Protection means identifying and modifying, as well as you can, the reason for your injury. The first thing to do is protect the injury and allow it to recover. That could mean a change in footwear, modifying your exercise program, or a temporary period of rest.

Recovery is about moving from higher stages on the Running Injury Stage Scale back to lower stages, and actively working to regain normal movement, strength, and function in the injured structure. It's not a passive process. Your recovery program will progress in difficulty as your injury recovers.

Ice means ice packs used with compression and elevation (**ICE**). Icing must be done properly [**Box 5-1**].

Table 5-1
Guidelines: Phase One

	Group 1	Group 2
Phase One Treatment Group *Self-Assessment 1D*	*No* Red Flag symptoms or visible swelling within the past 2 weeks.	*With* Red Flag symptoms or visible swelling within the past 2 weeks.
Phase One PT Time	Progress directly to Phase One Clearance.	Begin ICE for 20 minutes, 3 times per day until symptoms improve (**Log Form I**).
Phase One Clearance *(Self-Assessment 1E)*	1. Take steps for Protection and Recovery of you running injury. 2. The symptoms of you running injury have improved. 3. Complete *Self-Assessment 1E*.	

You should ice 360 degrees around the injured structure whenever possible.

Compression: Put pressure on the injured structure by compressing the ice pack over or around it, using Ace bandages or Velcro straps.

Elevation: While you are icing and compressing, elevate the injured structure above your heart level for 20 minutes. Ice, compression, and elevation are always combined. We don't go into ice baths because they don't allow the injured structure to be elevated above the heart.

5.3 Learning to ICE

The clinical indication for an ice pack is not that you're in therapy – the indication is that you need it right now! If you have any Red Flags or visible swelling, you will *ICE*.

In my P.T. practice, when you have something swollen, we teach you how to ICE the first time you come in, then we instruct you how to do it at home. We don't ice you again in my office because you shouldn't have to waste twenty minutes of therapy time on ice – we've got much better things to do with that time. If the patients in my office can learn to ICE at home, so can you. As a bonus, once you know how to ICE properly, you may never have to pay to get iced by a therapist again!

Everyone tells runners to ice an injury, but practically no one instructs them how to do it correctly. After thirty years of experience as a physical therapist, I know that if I just tell my patients to ice, they're not going to do it; or if they are doing it, they're not doing it right.

Side Tracks: What is Runner's Knee?

"Runner's knee" can be confusing. It's a catchall term that people have applied to every problem around the knee, ranging from knee trauma to knee-joint misalignment to softening of the knee cartilage (chondromalacia).

Another confusing thing is that, according to some writers, runner's knee isn't even unique to runners. They also apply the term to injuries caused by other athletic activities such as biking, and to traumatic activities such as jumping.

In this book, "runner's knee" means an adverse effect on the knee region which is caused by dysfunctional running. Sometimes pain around the knee is diagnosed as iliotibial band syndrome (ITB), sometimes it is diagnosed as patellofemoral syndrome (PFS), and sometimes it's diagnosed as patellar tendinitis or tendinosis. No matter which exact tissues are damaged, runner's knee can cause severe swelling because the knee has many interconnected pockets that can build up and hold fluid – and that can be very painful and alarming.

Many different intrinsic and extrinsic factors can contribute to runner's knee, including muscle imbalance, or problems with your running technique, stride, or footwear. As with any running injury, it's important that you address the *cause* of runner's knee in any injury management program.

If you're not icing properly, you're just putting cold compresses on your boo-boo! So, I don't just tell my patients to ice, I teach them how to *ICE*. I teach them what they need to do, how they need to do it, and when it should be done. That, to me, is a really good use of my time.

This was brought home to me (literally) when my daughter Tracy moved away to college. She was training for her first half marathon, and she called to tell me that her knee had swollen up. It was the first time she'd ever had a swollen knee and she was having trouble getting the swelling to go down. She told me she had read every running article and tip she could find, and they all said to ice, but no one described the right way to do it.

In fact, the proper way to ice a swollen knee – the way I teach my patients to do it – just isn't out there in the popular running literature, so my daughter never learned how to ice her knee correctly until we talked about it. Once she knew how to do it, Tracy got the swelling in her knee down, and was able to self-manage her runner's knee and move on in her training.

Proper icing **[Box 5-1]** includes three main elements: a good ice pack, compression of the ice pack 360 degrees around the injured structure when possible, and elevation of the iced body-part above the level of the heart **[Box 5-2]**.

Finding a good ice pack can be difficult. When I ice a patient in my office, I use professional ice packs that I order from a physical therapy catalog. You can find a variety of them on the Internet, and in some pharmacies. However, there is nothing magical about them, and – since you don't use ice packs every day – you can make your own ice packs from zip-top bags **[Box 5-1]**. They won't look fashionable or sexy, but they'll do the job just as well.

Remember, there's no need to ice through the entire course of your recovery. You only need to ice if you are in *Group 2*, and only while you're in Phases One and Two. That said, if you start running and get a little too aggressive, and your injury gets worse, then obviously you have to back down and start icing again. It's not unusual to have a few minor setbacks and need to *ICE* if you are working hard to progress through your recovery.

5.4 Clearing Phase One

Whether you start Phase One in Group 1 or in Group 2, you have work to do. Everyone who is considering self-management for a running injury should read through *all* the chapters in this book before starting the *Workbook*. As you complete the general requirements for Phase One, you can check them off on your Course Map.

Once you begin the *Running Injury Recovery Program Workbook*, you'll be following the specific guidelines for your recovery group in *Table 5-1* Guidelines: Phase One. You'll be ready to start Phase Two when you have completed the *Checkpoint to Enter Phase Two* on your Course Map.

* * *

| BOX 5-1 | The Proper Way to ICE |

To ice at home, you'll need one or more ice packs with enough surface area to completely cover and wrap around the injured structure, a pillowcase or thin toweling, small ice cubes or crushed ice, some water, some stretchy wrap such as an Ace bandage or Velcro wrap, clips or tape, and a place to lie down and elevate your injured body-part after you've iced it.

1. Prepare your ice packs:
- For convenience and no worries about leakage, I recommend professional, gel-filled ice packs that you can buy from your pharmacy or on the Internet and keep in your freezer.
- To make your own ice packs, you'll need several large, heavy-duty, zip-top bags (quart or gallon size). I recommend freezer bags with strong zippers to reduce the chance of leaking cold water all over yourself and your house. Use enough zip-top bags to completely cover and surround the injured region(s). Fill each zip-top bag about half full with a 50/50 mixture of ice and water. The water is important – don't reduce it. There should be enough ice and water to distribute evenly all the way around the injured structure. Get all the air out and seal the bag securely. Put some pressure on the bag to check for leaks, then put the first bag in a second bag as insurance against leakage.

(Box 5-1 cont.)

2. Use the cover that came with your gel ice pack, or put your zip-top bag(s) in the pillowcase or lightweight towel to keep the plastic off your skin.

3. Wrap the ice pack completely around the injured structure (360 degrees) so that the gel or ice is evenly distributed.

4. Wrap the stretchy bandage all the way around the ice pack to completely enclose and compress it against the injury. Secure the bandage with clips or tape.

5. Elevate and support the injured structure so the ice pack is higher than your heart. For a running injury, that means you'll be lying down **[Box 5-2]**.

6. Leave the ice pack on for 20 minutes with the structure elevated. It will be cold and you will feel a burning sensation for about 5 minutes; then it will start to feel numb. The water and pillowcase are there to keep it from getting too cold. While your leg is elevated, you can pump the muscles in the parts that aren't wrapped (for example, moving the foot or lower leg) to help bring the swelling down.

BOX 5-2   ICE Positions

ICE Position 5-1

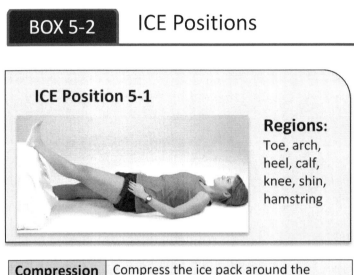

Regions:
Toe, arch, heel, calf, knee, shin, hamstring

Compression	Compress the ice pack around the injured region.
Elevation	Lie on your back and elevate the injured leg above heart level.

ICE Position 5-2

Region:
Band

Compression	Compress the ice pack around the injured region.
Elevation	2. Lie on your side with the lower knee bent and the upper knee straight. 3. Elevate the upper leg above heart level.

ICE Position 5-3

Region:
Hip

Compression	Place the ice pack next to the skin (inside your shorts), along the front side of the hip.
Elevation	Lie on your back with knees bent.

ICE Position 5-4

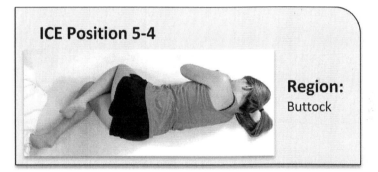

Region:
Buttock

Compression	Place the ice pack next to the skin (inside your shorts), against the back side of the hip.
Elevation	Lie on your side, injury side up, with knees bent and spine straight.

I picked up my guitar and play kinda
Just like yesterday
I get down on my knees and pray
That we don't get fooled again.
  – The Who

Chapter 6
The Right Recovery Plan:
When to Seek Professional Help

My own search for the right recovery plan for my running injuries has been a driving force throughout my life. I started running as a kid in New York, as an alternative to being the preferred target of my fellow P.E. students in dodgeball. I was fifteen and there were two things I thought were really cool: rock music and Jim Fixx's book *The Complete Book of Running*.

Running laps on my own every day, it wasn't long before I developed an awful running injury. I recall our family doctor saying he could give me an injection for the pain, or I could stop running, but nothing about actually finding or treating the problem. Since I was working part-time in a deli and had some money of my own, I went into a running specialty shop and told them my problem. They were the ones who actually treated the *cause* of my injury – they got me out of my Converse sneakers and into my first pair of proper running shoes – and that was my first education on shoes and running injuries.

In my teenage and college years, running became an important balancing force in my life. I was running three miles, three times a week, but when I tried to run any longer I started having trouble with injuries. I was "injury-prone" and still looking for some real help for my running injuries. What more could I do? I figured that studying physical therapy was the only way I was ever going to find the right way to take care of my running injuries – and that's why I became a physical therapist.

6.1 Lifting a Box: A Model Recovery Plan

In my physical therapy studies, one model we learned for treating back injuries was called "Lifting a Box," which was based on **functional outcome**. The idea was that if your job was to lift and carry boxes, and you were injured by lifting a box, then we should teach you correct lifting techniques and strengthen your lifting muscles so you wouldn't get injured again. So, if we had a patient who had crippling back pain, unable even to roll over in bed, we'd work diligently to return them to normal function. In other words, we didn't discharge them until they could lift and carry boxes *better* than they did before.

As a P.T. student, I learned all the approved medical techniques (**protocols**) for evaluating and treating back injuries, including medication, hands-on therapy, and special exercise programs for back patients. I also learned that, in order to reduce the risk of future back injuries, it was important to identify and correct the specific problem that led to that injury. What I did *not* learn was how to treat running injuries. I was constantly asking my professors and fellow therapists for information, including some who were runners, but no one seemed to know much about it. I discovered that, although there are plenty of scientific studies on back injuries, there are very few good studies on running injuries. And, without a good database of information, there are no medical models for running injuries that are equivalent to those for back care.

Since I'd always been an injury-prone runner, and had gone into physical therapy largely to get some real information on how to deal with running injuries, I was both surprised and disappointed. The upside was, I was in school learning manual therapy, and I was getting my running injuries worked on by good manual therapists. Though they didn't have specific protocols for my injuries, they knew how to treat nontraumatic injuries in general, and I was learning how to do that by being worked on. As it turned out, learning by experience was the best way to do it.

After graduation (and marrying my wife, Sherry, a nursing student), I continued learning manual therapy for running injuries by taking advanced manual therapy classes, getting advanced certifications, and having my running injuries worked on by the instructors and other P.T.s. As I started building my practice and getting to know other P.T.s, I was still learning by getting the best P.T.s to work on me.

By this time, Sherry and I had moved to Miami and I joined the Miami Runners Club, where I really started studying the biomechanics of running. All of those runners were a lot better than me. They were stronger than me and they were faster than me. I would watch them with fascination and wonder, how are they doing that? I started analyzing what they did and how they were doing it – a bit like anthropology class! By hanging out with them and treating their injuries, I started to understand the complex relationships between running injuries and running habits, techniques, and equipment – all the things I hadn't learned in P.T. school.

Finally, all the necessary factors were coming together and I was able to answer some of the questions I'd had since I was an injury-prone teenager in New York. Through the study of many different runners at the Miami Runners Club, a growing professional knowledge of orthopedic physical therapy and management of nontraumatic injuries, and learning with other physical therapists to treat my own running injuries, I was beginning to adapt and develop my own protocols. As a physical therapist, I could finally say I had a real recovery plan for treating running injuries.

6.2 Choosing Qualified Professional Help

In the treatment of running injuries, there are times when self-management just isn't enough, and qualified professional help can make all the difference between a quick and successful recovery, or a long and slow decline into crippling injury. For a runner, pain upon exertion is always there to some degree, so how bad does an injury have to be for you to seek professional help? My rule of thumb is, if you're concerned about any injury, you should see a qualified professional for evaluation immediately, even at the lowest injury stage [Box 6-1].

Box 6-1 — Choosing Professional Help

Seek qualified professional help if you answer *YES* to any of the following questions:

1. Are you unsure about your ability to plan and follow through with a self-management program?

2. Do you have any pre-existing medical condition (such as neuropathy), or regularly take any medication (including oral or injected anti-inflammatory medications or pain medications) that might affect your ability to assess your pain level?

3. Does your current injury involve a trauma, surgery, or illness that might affect your physical ability to follow a self-management program?

4. Are you taking any type of medication (prescribed, injected, or over-the-counter) for pain or inflammation for your running injury, and continuing to run?

5. Are you experiencing any Red Flag symptoms that are not getting better with PRICE, or that are worsening?

6. Are you worried or unsure about your injury?

7. Would you like to get a professional opinion before undertaking any self-help program?

8. Are you unsure about your answers to any of the above questions?

Qualified professional help means a healthcare professional who is knowledgeable about running injuries, and who takes the time to take a full medical history and make a thorough physical examination. Again, most doctors and physical therapists aren't trained in running injuries, so finding qualified professional help isn't always easy. If you go to a doctor who prescribes medication, or injects medication, and tells you it's okay to run, that's *not* professional help. In my world, that's just wrong. Medication can never treat the cause of a running injury. It only masks the injury and allows it to get worse. Even if you're only taking an over-the-counter anti-inflammatory medication such as Advil, it may mask the pain enough for your injury to get worse if you continue to run.

If you go to a doctor who recommends surgery for a running injury, you should always get a qualified second opinion. In most cases, running injuries are nontraumatic and can be treated by physical therapy rather than surgery.

I learned that lesson long ago, when Sherry and I first moved to Miami. My neighbor "Jean," who was a fine runner and a founding member of the Miami Runners Club, had bumped her knee and suddenly she was crippled. Her knee was so swollen that she couldn't walk, let alone run. Seeking professional help, she had gone to doctors who had recommended surgery – a diagnostic knee arthroscopy, since MRIs and CT scans were not available at the time.

Jean asked me for a second opinion. When I took a thorough history and examined her knee, I found the real problem: runner's knee, which is weakness and pain below and around the kneecap, with swelling that spreads. She had aggravated the underlying running injury when she bumped her knee. I made an ice pack and taught her how to ICE. Within a couple days her knee was no longer swollen and felt much better. Then we worked on an active knee-strengthening program and quickly got her back to running. Thirty years later, she is still running well, and she never did need surgery on that knee.

6.3 Runners with Pre-existing Medical Conditions

Runners who have a running injury that is complicated by any pre-existing medical condition (including traumatic injury, surgery, or disease) are advised to get medical clearance before choosing self-management. The recovery program in this book and the accompanying *Workbook* requires that complex cases must enter self-management in Group 2, which will follow a careful, steady path of rehabilitation designed to avoid aggravating any existing problems.

There is one group of runners in particular that can benefit from professional injury management – those who are on long-term oral anti-inflammatories such as **cortisone** (*e.g.* Prednisone) for a medical condition. For a healthy runner, getting cortisone injections is always a bad thing. For a runner who also has an inflammatory disease, cortisone may be a medical necessity, but it has the same negative effects on the runner.

Treating a runner who is taking cortisone can be very tricky. Cortisone is a powerful anti-inflammatory that not only masks the symptoms of a running injury, it blocks your ability to feel whether your training is making you stronger or breaking you down. If you are being treated with cortisone for a medical condition, it will be difficult for you to follow the directions for self-assessment because you can't trust your perception of pain. In other words, it would be a good idea to ask a professional to monitor you.

Here's a good example of how professional monitoring helped one of my patients: "Rhonda" was an experienced distance runner who also had inflammatory bowel disease that had to be managed on cortisone. Running was especially important to her because hunger and depression are common side effects of cortisone, and training helped her keep her weight down and her spirits up.

Rhonda was training for her sixth half-marathon when she developed worsening hamstring pain and came to my P.T. office for help. I knew she couldn't effectively self-assess her pain due to the cortisone, and that she needed me to objectively assess her progress during her injury management and training. Since I was both Rhonda's P.T. and her running coach, I was able to monitor her closely throughout her post-injury training. That allowed me to fast-track Rhonda through the recovery program for a "simple" running injury. If she had tried self-management following the guidelines in this book, she would have had to follow the recovery plan for a "complex" injury, which requires at least two weeks in each phase, and she would have missed her race. Because I provided Rhonda with constant, professional hands-on evaluation, she was able to quickly and happily reach her running goals.

Generally speaking, it's always a good idea to have any injury that is severe, or complicated by pre-existing illnesses or injuries, evaluated by your qualified healthcare professional. If your healthcare professional clears you to proceed, then you can follow the principles and guidelines for recovery in the *Running Injury Recovery Program*.

6.4 An Active Treatment Plan

Remember, the first step in any injury management plan is protection. As soon as you are injured, you should stop and protect the injured region, and begin self-help (PRICE) as needed.

If you do decide on professional help for your running injury, your healthcare professional should provide you with an individualized recovery plan that has two equally important parts: **active treatment** of your running injury, and education to help you run better with a lower risk of injury in the future **[Box 6-2]**. Passive treatments – such as cold packs and heating pads, or low-voltage stimulation and functional electric stimulation, or redundant exercise – are secondary methods used to promote greater comfort. They make you feel better, but they don't play a major role in the recuperative process.

Active treatment – including therapeutic exercises for flexibility, strength, and endurance – is the physical therapist's most effective method of treatment. Other parts of an active treatment plan may include postural training, modification of running habits and techniques, or education about the use of equipment (such as strength training equipment, reusable ice packs, stretching and self-mobilization devices, running shoes and inserts,

HOW TO:
Evaluate Professional Care

1. *Independent evaluation*: For your initial evaluation, your healthcare provider should take a complete medical and running history; give you a thorough physical examination, including your footwear and a gait analysis; then provide an appraisal of the dysfunction and a summary of the appropriate treatment which includes a plan for returning to running.

2. *Close supervision*: Your healthcare provider should personally oversee all aspects of your treatment program. A technician may oversee your performance of certain exercises, but the healthcare provider should decide *which* exercises you need, and show you how to do them correctly. The healthcare provider should observe and modify your running stride as needed.

3. *Goal-oriented treatments*: Any treatment you get should be specifically designed to enhance your strength, flexibility, or endurance. Your program should develop or reinforce proper training habits and techniques. Your healthcare provider should have a plan for footwear modification during and after recovery. The reasoning for each treatment or modification in technique or equipment should be explained to you.

(Box 6-2 cont.)

4. *Hands-on care*: Every visit should involve direct treatment and evaluation by a qualified healthcare provider. At no time should care by an aide or unlicensed assistant be a substitute for professional attention.

5. *Individualized program*: Since no two runners or injuries are exactly alike, your program should be customized to you as an individual. Your healthcare provider should consider your previous running experience, running goals, occupation, lifestyle, and personal tendencies when assigning your educational and treatment programs.

6. *Active involvement*: You should be provided with exercises and lifestyle-modification advice that extend your recovery process beyond office visits to your home, work, and running environment.

7. *Discharge planning*: Your healthcare provider's treatment program should have a specific goal for the conclusion of office visits. Your discharge program should include on-going running and lifestyle recommendations to minimize the possibility of a recurring problem.

and even sports bras). Home exercise is also an important part of an active treatment plan because it helps speed recovery between office visits and builds proper habits for long-term conditioning.

Running can be part of an active treatment plan, but it has to be done properly, following your healthcare professional's recovery program. It is *not* okay to run if you are *not* following your instructions, or if pain is disturbing your sleep, or if you are progressively having to modify or reduce daily activities, or if you are using medication for pain or inflammation. You should always be progressing (moving to lower stages on the Running Injury Stage Scale). During your recovery program, your healthcare professional should monitor your progress based on a return of physical function as measured by strength, flexibility and endurance.

These principles of an active treatment plan will apply whether you choose professional help or self-management. Either way, your best plan is always to address any problem as soon as you notice the first signs and symptoms. If you correct your problems early, you can usually avoid having to see me or any other professional to treat a severe or complex running injury.

* * *

"With all that voodoo physical therapy out there..., how can you tell if what you are getting is helping or useless?"
– James J. Irrgang, president of the Orthopaedic Section of the American Physical Therapy Association, 2010

Chapter 7
Things to Watch Out For:
Dope, Tricks, and Tips

When you really need expert advice about a running injury, it can be hard to find. What's easy to find is all kinds of drugs, tricks, and tips that can frustrate, confuse, and even sideline you. Runners get all kinds of "tips" about running injuries from other runners, from the Internet, and from running-industry media and marketing – but that's not the same as getting good expert advice. Unfortunately, the "dope" and tricks often come from our coaches and healthcare professionals – even when they have the best of intentions. One of my biggest frustrations as a physical therapist comes when healthcare professionals prescribe or administer drugs or "trick" treatments that block pain but don't address the runner's basic injury problem. At best, some of these tricks are a waste of time and money. At worst, some of them can make your injury worse, or even cripple you.

Here's an example: "Sue" was an experienced marathon runner who came to my P.T. clinic after seeing many doctors and having many tests. She'd been having crippling hip and hamstring pain for months, ever since her last marathon, and was still unable to run. I discovered the cause – she'd run the marathon in defective shoes – and I was able to fully rehabilitate her complex Stage 5 injuries. It was a happy ending; she returned to running and was able to run many more marathons.

Fast-forward several years. I saw Sue at an out-of-town marathon, but she wasn't running. She was sidelined again with severe pain in her big toe. I told her it sounded like runner's toe and suggested she come in for therapy. She told me that, on advice of her physician, she had already decided on surgery – but she would come to me for post-op therapy. Unfortunately, she had been tricked into thinking that surgery was a foolproof solution. The surgery not only failed, it crippled her. She had a second surgery to correct the first, but despite extensive therapy, her running was severely impaired for the rest of her life.

Runners often end up being treated with drugs, tricks, and tips instead of with expert advice because most healthcare professionals have no specific training or agreed upon professional guidelines (*protocols*) for diagnosing and treating running injuries. The problem is, there's no good database on running injuries because there are very few good scientific studies on treating injured runners. How can any healthcare professional be expected to provide you with an expert opinion about your running injury when they have no accepted guidelines and very little good data to work with?

For most healthcare professionals, treating running injuries is a trial-and-error process. As a result, I see other doctors' and P.T.s' running injury "failures" all the time – runners who have been to several healthcare professionals and (after being treated with drugs, tricks, and tips) are still frustrated, unable to run, and desperate for help to manage their running injuries. Sadly, they've often just been told they shouldn't run because their healthcare professional wasn't able to find the problem – and of course, when you can't find the problem you can't treat it effectively. When healthcare professionals are faced with a running injury they haven't been trained to handle, and they have no running-specific protocols to provide them with direction, what can they do? Basically, they're stuck. Some just tell their injured runners not to run until they feel better. Others go for the drugs, tricks, and tips because that's the best they've got to work with.

When I treat running injuries in my clinical practice, I use what scientific information is available; combine it with my thirty years of experience as a physical therapist, running coach, and runner; and adapt what I've learned to manage each injury on an individual basis. Good injury management has to be hands-on, active, and progressive. No dope, no tricks, no tips.

You may be able to avoid a lot of these problems by understanding the nature of running injuries and treating them yourself, before they become too severe. In the rest of this book, you'll find some good expert advice to help you get healthy and return to running. In this chapter, however, you'll find some examples of dope, tricks, and tips to watch out for when seeking help elsewhere!

* * *

7.1 Running on Dope

Pain medication. Anti-inflammatory medication. Cortisone shots. These are the basic runner's pharmacy. As runners, we expect some pain and inflammation – and naturally we want to get it over with as quickly as possible, so why not bring on the drugs?

In this case, my professional policy is clear: No running on medication for pain or inflammation for a running injury. You can have medication for pain or inflammation if you're *not* running – but if you *are* taking medication for pain or inflammation for a running injury I'm not letting you run. Why? First, the inflammation is there for a reason. Medication masks the problem, and it delays healing. Second, there are some serious health and safety issues. I've even had patients who went to podiatrists who injected alcohol into the nerves of their feet to reduce the perception of pain! That drives me crazy. All I can do is tell the patient to stop it immediately or I'm out of it. I don't ask them how they feel about it.

Of course, this "no-meds" policy has made me some enemies among doctors who prescribe these medications, and it's made me some enemies among runners who ask for them. Despite annoying many of the podiatrists in town, I stand by my convictions because I've learned the hard way, from experience with my own patients. Before I had this policy, I was treating runners for ten years and watching them fall apart, again and again – especially the ones who were injecting cortisone and having body parts rip and blow up. It wasn't good.

So, finally, I just said I'm not going to do this any more. If you take medication for a running injury to block the perception of pain or inflammation, I'm not going to help you run, because it's just not safe. If you're willing to stop running until the medication comes out of your system, I'm here to help you. It's that simple. Since I started this policy, not one of my patients has had an "explosive" running injury while under my care – and that has made me lots of friends with caring healthcare professionals and coaches, smart runners, and parents of young runners!

7.2 Chemical Interactions

Believe it or not, explosive running injuries are not the worst thing that can happen to you if you run while taking certain medications. Running for long distances alters your body chemistry, and when runners with altered body chemistry also take a drug, the combined effects can be unpredictable. There have been cases of low blood sodium (**hyponatremia**) in runners, resulting in heart arrhythmias and death. Also, common non-steroidal anti-inflammatory drugs (**NSAIDS**) act as blood thinners, and there have been cases of excessive bleeding associated with muscle tears.

There are always newer, stronger anti-inflammatory medications coming onto the market, but none of them are really designed for running injuries. They're certainly not designed to be used *while* running. For example, studies show that although runners have a decreased chance of a heart attack when *not* running, they have an increased chance of heart attack *while* running. What happens if you take a new drug that we later find out increases your chances of heart attack? If you're running and taking medications that haven't been tested in runners, who knows?

The truth is, long-distance runners are such a small percentage of the population that drug manufacturers don't have to test their drugs for safety in runners. By the time we find out a drug is triggering something like hyponatremia in runners, people are dying. That's a real good reason not to run while taking medication for a running injury.

7.3 Banned Substances

Sometimes it's difficult to be sure exactly what is going into your body, or what the effects of a substance might be. In today's world you can find an unending list of performance-enhancing substances ranging from traditional herbal medicines to designer energy drinks to advanced biotechnology. There are even healthcare professionals who will give you questionable experimental treatments and surgical procedures. Here's a good rule: Know what's going into your body, no matter how it's administered or who recommended it.

Most performance-enhancing substances and procedures are prohibited by competitive regulatory bodies such as U.S. Track and Field, U.S.A. Triathlon, and the International Olympic Committee. My rule is, if a substance is banned for performance, it's also banned for injury management.

* * *

7.4 Magic Tricks

In a *New York Times* article titled "Treat Me, but No Tricks Please," Joseph Feinberg, a doctor at the Hospital for Special Surgery in New York, is quoted as saying, "Very often, I think the hot packs, cold packs, ultrasound and electrostimulation are unnecessary. For sure, in many cases these modalities are a waste of time." I agree. The following are a few specific tricks that healthcare professionals use to make injured runners *think* something helpful is happening. (My profession, physical therapy, has some *great* tricks!)

1. *Electrical stimulation*: This is one of the favorite tricks of my profession. When we stimulate your sensory nerves (called A and B fibers) with an electrical device, it blocks the C fibers, which are the pain fibers. In other words, sensory stimulation blocks the *perception* of pain. It's like when you have a running injury and you rub it, it feels better. You put burning liniment on it, it feels better. You put tingly electric stimulation on it, it feels better. It's called the **gate control theory**. We stimulate the sensory nerve to block the perception of pain, but it doesn't fix anything. In fact, pain management for a simple running injury shouldn't be such a big deal. If you don't run on it for a few days, it feels better! (And if it doesn't, it might not be a running injury, and you should see your doctor for further evaluation.)

2. *Randomly changing weight bearing*: Random changes include the plastic inserts someone gave you to put in your shoes, or the innersoles you bought over-the-counter at the drugstore, or any type of "magic cushions" you put in your shoes. I take all of those out. I'm not

talking about inserts fitted specially for you by a qualified professional to address a known underlying problem. I do occasionally use shoe inserts when medically necessary as part of Phase Three recovery – but that's not a random change. If a shoe insert is the *only* injury treatment you're getting, that's just a trick.

3. *Redundant nonspecific exercise:* This is used to buy time while the runner is healing. It's a trick. Runners are often told to do some sort of general exercise for a month, but nonspecific exercise does nothing for your injury. It's redundant. What you *should* be doing is exercising to a purpose – to regain the strength and mobility you need to get back to running.

4. *Placebo medicine:* Placebo medicine actually works very well for self-limiting problems, but it never works for an ongoing problem such as a running injury. A running injury is caused by a dysfunction in your running, and becomes chronic because you keep on running with the dysfunction. Proper medical treatment must address the *cause* of the running injury (usually your running equipment, habits, or techniques). If not, as soon as you start running again you'll find the problem is still there – or it will manifest itself in another way. Anything you do that doesn't change the dysfunction in your running (such as rubs, bracelets, and moist heat) can really be considered a placebo.

5. *Needless surgery:* Occasionally I treat runners who've had needless surgery because a physician made a diagnosis based solely on imaging studies. The problem is, many running injuries don't image on x-ray, CT scan, or MRI. Say you have a pain caused by a running injury *around* a joint, and you also have a pre-existing problem *in*

that joint. That pre-existing problem is going to image, and that's what they're going to operate on. And then, six weeks later in post-operative therapy, I'll find your untreated running injury. Before having surgery for any running injury, runners should always be evaluated by a qualified, independent running specialist. Again, that means someone who is familiar with running injuries, and who takes the time to talk with you, take a complete history, and do a really thorough physical examination – not just imaging.

6. *The feeling of support that doesn't support:* Runners use things like tape, bands, compression sleeves, or Ace wraps because they like to feel secure, but that's just an illusion. All those flexible, rubbery things may give you the feeling of support, but they will never actually support your leg while running. Taping and wrapping are part of one of the biggest problems in running-injury management – the quick fix. People want a fast cure with little or no work, and trick themselves with all kinds of magical supports! There is no quick fix. There is no secret cure. There is no magical support. It's all just stretchy stuff on your skin, and it will never manage a running injury. The only way to properly manage a running injury is to address the injured structure itself and fix the components of running that are distressed.

7.5 Problems with Taping

Over the past few years I've seen runners covered with tape in every color of the rainbow and taped in every possible direction – but when they start running and sweating here in our tropical Miami climate, the tape usually peels off and they're left with a decorative streamer trailing behind them.

What were they hoping to accomplish? I've heard claims that tape promotes healing by pulling the skin away from muscles and allowing more circulation and blood flow. Then I've heard that special tape supports muscles, realigns structures, and redistributes biomechanical forces! So it's both freeing the muscle from the skin *and* controlling the muscle? No, it's a trick! No matter what the color, size, or "special materials," it's still just tape on the skin, and it will never control muscles during an activity as powerful and dynamic as running.

So, how did taping get started? Specialized taping such as McConnell taping and Kinesio taping is used by physical therapists, along with other therapies, for treating various conditions. Often taping is used to enhance body-awareness training, maintain proper posture, and achieve optimal joint biomechanics during low impact, low velocity activities. The tape doesn't *make* you exercise the right way, it *reminds* you to exercise the right way. That said, practicing conscious awareness of your body can achieve the same result without the sticky mess.

Unfortunately, the widespread misuse of therapeutic tapes has led to the wrong idea that tape is somehow a cure for running injuries. Not only will tape *not* cure your running injury, it can allow your injury to get worse. Tape provides a false sense of security and stability, and by running with tape you are more likely to cause damage to an existing injury. Using tape does not make it okay to run when you have an injury.

* * *

7.6 Problems with Bands and Compression Sleeves

Please don't put any tight tape, band, strap, or compression sleeve around your leg and go for a run. I've seen runners wrap tape or other compression devices so tightly around their leg that they create a tourniquet in order to run through pain. An even worse idea is to leave a compression device on *after* you run. Anything that forms a tight circle around your leg interferes with your blood circulation and can cause serious problems.

This is what happens: When we're deep into a long run, our calves act as a second heart. The veins in our legs become enlarged (**vasodilation**), and the muscles of our calves are pumping blood back up to the heart through the veins. With vasodilation, there is so much blood in the veins of our legs that, if we suddenly stop moving, the blood pools and we can pass out – especially after a marathon. In the past, it wasn't uncommon for marathon runners to stop moving at the finish line, pass out, and end up in the emergency first-aid tents. Runners didn't always understand why this happens; it's something we've learned about fairly recently through sharing information with the medical profession.

Now that we understand the problem, we've addressed it by extending the finish lines at races to keep people walking longer, to keep their calf muscles pumping and their blood circulating until their bodies readjust. The answer to preventing a sudden collapse is to keep walking, *not* to put a tourniquet around your leg – that's just scary! Nevertheless, watch any long-distance race and you'll still see many runners doing just that with knee support bands or compression sleeves.

Why do runners do it? Some marketers of compression sleeves actually recommend them for use in recovery. One brand of compression sleeves even promised to "increase oxygen blood flow to the lower legs, pin-point compression to shin and calf muscles, and reduce recovery time keeping your legs fresh." I have to disagree. Compression sleeves have elastic bands that circle your legs at the top and bottom, and they can't increase anything other than pressure.

There's another and even more serious reason why I won't use or sell knee bands or compression sleeves to runners. There is growing evidence of increased risk in runners of **deep vein thrombosis (DVT)**, a blood clot that forms in a vein in the leg, then breaks loose and causes a heart attack or stroke. This risk increases when runners leave compression devices around their legs *after* running and at rest. In my practice I have made the diagnosis of DVT in runners – not calf pain – and I have a real concern about anything that restricts circulation in runners' legs during recovery.

Simply stated, compression can't improve the way you run, or aid in blood flow while running, or aid in post-race recovery – but it *can* cause severe health problems at rest after running. Don't be tricked by advertising that tries to convince you otherwise.

7.7 Avoidance Tricks

Avoidance can also be a trick. If you have a running injury and you avoid running long enough, then when you *do* return to running your training essentially has to start over from scratch. Not only are you not an injured runner, you're no longer a runner at all! Generally, if you avoid running for six months, the running injury is gone, but so is your runner's body.

I've also noticed that, when runners return to running after a prolonged absence, they often make random changes in their running style, training technique, or equipment. Whatever that change is, it becomes their new magic trick. For example, I've heard my patients say things like, "Look, I was injured, but I took off my running shoes and now I'm able to run injury free because I'm barefoot." My response to that was, no, dude, you didn't take off your running shoes and immediately run twenty-five miles a week barefoot. You couldn't run for a long time. Then you started running very gradually, and you built up your mileage by running *very* carefully and slowly, barefoot. It wasn't taking off your shoes that helped you recover, it was the avoidance. You started over from scratch. I'd much rather teach you to run "barefoot" in your running shoes – and protect you from puncture wounds!

The same idea applies to any trick treatment that keeps you occupied while you avoid running. Any treatment "works" as long as you don't run, because running injuries are caused by running, and if you don't run they'll get better by themselves. On the other hand, if the trick treatment doesn't work, it's because your problem isn't the injury, it's a dysfunction in your running.

In the end, avoidance makes things worse because it weakens the injured structure. When you have an injury, the worst thing you can do is to not load the injured structure properly during recovery. But here's the problem, the structure was injured by running, so to strengthen the injured structure you have to move slowly and carefully (**submaximally**) through the phases of recovery – increasing the load at the right time, in the right amount, with the right technique, and using the right equipment. I'm talking about progressive, weight-bearing loading. At the same time, you'll be doing neuromuscular re-education, and learning better running techniques to help you run smoother. That's not avoidance – it's hard work. It takes proper attention, proper frequency, proper intensity, and proper equipment. Everything has to be right. We'll be talking a lot more about how to do that in later chapters.

7.8 Breaking the Injury-Avoidance Cycle

Studies show that most running injuries occur during the first three years of running, and that runners who train continuously through those first three years not only have fewer injuries, but their injuries are less severe. However, if you are injured and avoid running for six months, you not only have to start training your body again from scratch – you may have to start over with that three-year period of "beginners" injuries as well.

A big problem is that many runners return to running after an injury without ever addressing the factor that caused their injury in the first place, whether it was equipment choices, training strategies, or technique. When this happens, more injuries soon occur, and complex injuries can pile up. Nothing really heals. You start over again, you pick up another injury, and you drop out. You never really get through those important first three years of progressive, base-building toughening. It becomes a vicious cycle of injury and avoidance. Without a clear way out, you can end up discouraged and labeled as "injury-prone."

There is a solution. You don't have to choose between complete avoidance or running on an injury and making it worse. You can break the injury-avoidance cycle by taking active steps to get over your injuries *and* to correct the underlying problem at the same time. You have to do both, or you can find yourself repeating that cycle.

In other words, even with a running injury, you don't have to stop running entirely. If you catch an injury early, and address the problem with the right injury-management program, you won't have to go through the avoidance, and you won't have to start over from scratch. Following the guidelines in this book can help you work through the recovery period and break the cycle of injury and avoidance.

7.9 Shoe Tricks

Magic Shoes: This trick is related to avoidance. It's when you haven't run for a while because you were injured, but now you're better. You have a new pair of shoes, and you're starting your training over from scratch. You might associate feeling better with the new shoes, and suddenly they become your "magic" shoes. You're mentally locked into them, and you never want to change them – or at least you never want to try any other style of shoe.

Here's the problem with magic shoes: manufacturers change the models every year. The style name stays the same, but changes are made in design and manufacturing. Even if you try to get around the yearly model changes by stocking up on your favorite shoe, there's another problem. The foam in the shoe has a two-year shelf life. Sitting in the box, it dries out and doesn't provide the same protection as a fresh shoe – so you won't be in your magic shoes very long!

Don't get locked into the *idea* of a shoe instead of the reality. Go to a good running specialty store and get some expert advice on the new models. If your body can't adapt to changing shoes, then it's not adapting when you run – and that's another thing that can *cause* injuries. When someone tells me, "There's only one type of shoe I can run in," I think, those must be magic shoes!

Unstable Trainers: What about those specially-engineered shoes that promise to build your muscles or simulate barefoot running? As a physical therapist and owner of a running-specialty store, I'm often asked my opinion about certain lines of shoes that are supposed to give you a better workout or achieve other positive physical effects. In a perfect world, these wonder shoes would help solve knee and back problems, relieve tension, ease joint pains, turn you into a more efficient runner, and even tone and firm your buttocks and thighs.

Personally, I would love to find a shoe that could build muscles for me, prevent injuries, and make me a better runner! As a physical therapist, however, my concern about these shoes is that – while most athletic shoes are designed for stability, support, and cushioning – shoes that are marketed to "rock" you, "bounce" you, or

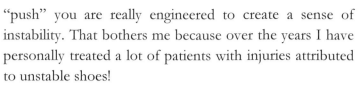
"push" you are really engineered to create a sense of instability. That bothers me because over the years I have personally treated a lot of patients with injuries attributed to unstable shoes!

I believe a running shoe that is properly designed, manufactured, and fitted is an important part of training and exercise, not the solution to a running problem. My professional opinion is that if you're having issues with a body part, the solution is to correct the biomechanical dysfunction at the root of the problem, not to buy a trick shoe.

Bottom line: Some manufacturers have made claims about the health benefits of certain kinds of shoes, and several of them have paid substantial fines for false advertising. If I believed the claims for these shoes, I'd endorse them and sell them in my running specialty store, but so far that's not happening.

7.10 Money Tricks

There's one last trick I have to mention: *Referral for profit.* This is a biggie that has grown up in the past few years to cause friction between independent physical therapists and big, corporate medical institutions. I have to point out that this isn't just my personal opinion. The entire physical therapy industry is up in arms. The American Physical Therapy Association (APTA) has published a fine position paper on the subject which you can find online if you are interested.

The point is, many HMOs, hospital systems, and physicians groups have discovered that they can boost their income by having their own physical therapy clinics.

When they can't find a problem to operate on, or to treat with medication, they can still make money by giving you a diagnosis and sending you to physical therapy.

Of course, I believe qualified physical therapy is a very good thing, so what's the problem? It's a question of conflict of interest. When a therapist is hired and paid by a doctor, do you think he or she ever wants to disagree with their boss' diagnosis? I think not. I've been there and done that. I started out working as a physical therapist in hospitals, and I had constant, ongoing disagreements with some doctors over their diagnoses and prescribed treatments – when I knew I was right and they were wrong. That's one of the reasons why I started my own physical therapy clinic.

Let's be clear. I'm definitely not saying that physical therapists are always right, or that we know more than doctors. What I *am* saying is, sometimes it takes an independent, ongoing examination of the patient to get a complete picture of the situation. The patient and the physical therapist can work together over a longer term to accomplish that. Basically, the APTA's position on the subject is that referral for profit is a common occurrence, and that it sometimes gets in the way of good injury management.

7.11 Running Injury "Tips"

What are "tips" for running injuries? They're all the odd suggestions and ideas that we get from other runners, books, magazines, and running-industry ads because we can't find good, knowledgeable medical advice. Have you ever looked on the internet for "tips" on running injury management? I have, and some of them are awful.

As a physical therapist who specializes in treating running injuries, I even get running-injury tips from my own professional association. Do you really want "tips" from your healthcare professionals? No, you want expert advice! Again, that means advice from a qualified professional who is knowledgeable about running injuries, who takes your full history, and who does a complete physical examination.

Tips aren't based on facts – they're based on anecdotes, fads, and marketing. As such, they're ever-changing and never-ending. Here I'll give just two examples of "tips" that I've seen recently about "core" strengthening, and "injury prevention."

"Tips" to Strengthen Your Core: Here's an important running tip I found in a running magazine: "Do Pilates to Strengthen Your Core." This is a reoccurring theme I hear from patients who come to me after other treatments have failed – that their treatment was "Pilates-based." Of course I ask the patient exactly what they were doing in this therapy. The most common answer: "Well... I was strengthening my core." When I ask what they did to specifically help their running injury, they have no real answer.

Joseph Pilates himself never made any claims about his exercises and running injuries. However, since the Pilates name was never trademarked, the name later evolved to mean many different things. As a result, we have no clear standards for what Pilates actually is, and there is a wide variation in the exercises and techniques that are being taught. The same is true for Pilates terms such as "core" and "powerhouse," which have no actual medical definition, so any practitioner is free to define them in any way he likes. When I get a patient who tells me that their previous physical therapy was "Pilates-based," I think the other therapist probably missed the actual diagnosis and never addressed the disorder at the root of the running injury.

To be clear, there's nothing wrong with doing Pilates or any other type of exercise. In fact, it's perfectly appropriate to do any exercise you like in addition to running. I'm only saying that "Pilates" as we know it today is not a specific treatment for running injuries. We need to treat the weakness and stiffness specific to the running injury through proper running-based exercises.

"Tips" to Prevent Running Injuries: Like most runners, I buy all the popular running books and magazines and I have a great collection of books, written by wonderful runners and coaches, that have words like "eliminate injuries" or "injury-free running" on the cover. That's great marketing!

The sad truth is, we don't know how to eliminate running injuries. The greatest runners with the greatest coaches in the world have running injuries. I'm always talking with other P.T.s and healthcare workers who are also runners about our shared injuries! Sometimes we can look back and see one particular thing we did wrong that caused the injury, sometimes we can't.

The problem with saying that any one piece of advice is going to eliminate or prevent running injuries is that most running injuries have an interacting group of causes (**multifactorial causes**) that include both internal (*intrinsic*) and external (*extrinsic*) factors. We can never pin down every one of these factors and measure their relative contributions. There is no simple answer. We just have to move forward from where we are.

Of course we can control some external factors through our habits, technique, and equipment; and we can modify some internal factors (such as muscle development and control). However, some intrinsic factors – our basic, individual body structure – we can't change. As a result, there are some lucky runners with great intrinsic factors who are injured less, and there are others (like me) with less-than-perfect intrinsic factors, who are injured more.

My feeling is, if a coach doesn't admit that you can get injured using his training techniques, there's a real problem. I'm a certified running coach, and I admit it – I've had people injured while I was coaching them. I've learned from my mistakes, and I've learned from their mistakes – but injuries still happen. As a coach, if I really help people to run great, with great equipment and great technique, they'll advance to doing harder and harder things until they run into the limits of their intrinsic and extrinsic factors, and eventually they'll have a running injury. We fix it, we learn from it, and we move on to bigger and better things! The only sure way I know to prevent a running injury is, don't run.

So, although the guys who write popular books like the *Pose Method* ("eliminate injuries") and *CHI Running* ("injury-free running") are great runners and coaches, and can give you a lot of good tips, they haven't eliminated running injuries. I see as many running injuries in my practice today as I ever have.

Bottom line: It's interesting to read a magazine or Internet article about how one particular runner made a mistake and ended up with one particular injury, and I enjoy reading books by great runners and coaches who have found a method that works for them. However, if the advice isn't specifically designed for you and your running injury, it's still just a "tip."

7.12 The Real Secret: A Good Injury Recovery Plan

What it comes down to is this – there are some runners who can get away with tricks. They don't get hurt easily, and they don't have to train as hard because they were born with great running mechanics and their bodies are just more efficient than most. In my opinion, that's due to good luck and genetics. The rest of us have to work harder, and we get running injuries!

Here's *my* tip to runners: If something sounds too good to be true, it usually is. There is no magical drug, machine, shoe, tape, or "tip" that will fix your running injury. I've seen every trick there is, and they're all pulling a rabbit out of a hat. Passive care may feel good, but it takes active treatment to get you back in the race.

This is the essence of what I teach my injured runners: Running injuries are caused by a dysfunction in your running – something goes wrong in your equipment, your habits, or your techniques. When this happens, you need to find the dysfunction that caused your injury and correct it with a well-designed injury recovery program that addresses your specific dysfunction. It's all about moving forward through the phases of recovery and getting you back to running safely.

Chapter 8
Running Shoes
and Running Injuries

Problems with running shoes are an avoidable cause of running injuries. Running in the wrong shoe may cause a serious injury, or it may be one of many factors that contribute to an injury. Even when you get the right shoe there's a chance that it might be defective, and that may also cause an injury.

It happened to me back in the '90s. I was at the peak of my triathlon career, well-trained and running at my best when, unknowingly, I got a pair of running shoes that were defective, and I wore them while racing a half Ironman in Clermont. The next morning I woke up in pain, with Stage 5 plantar fasciitis, and it took me almost a year to get over it.

In a way, that was a revelation. As a physical therapist, I was able to associate a very specific injury with a very specific source, and a very specific pattern of shoe defect. It motivated me to do a lot of research, and I started publishing articles on running injuries and defective athletic shoes. I documented my injury for an article in the *Journal of Orthopaedic & Sports Physical Therapy* (*JOSPT*). This was actually the first publication in the medical industry that defined defective shoes and their role in injuries – a problem that is still going on today. That article led to many more publications, lectures, and a number of news stories that appeared on national TV.

Researching that story also got me to really understand the shoe market. In fact, I learned so much about the running-shoe industry that I decided to open my own running specialty shop where runners could come in and get expert advice and find the shoe that is right for them. Basically, running led me to my career in physical therapy; physical therapy led me to running triathlons; and running a triathlon in a defective shoe led me to studying running shoes and opening a running-shoe shop in Miami called *The Runner's High*.

8.1 Documenting Defective Shoes

After my injury, I started documenting a worsening pattern in the manufacture of running shoes. By the late '90s essentially all athletic shoe manufacturing had been relocated to Asia, and both the quality and design were deteriorating.

During my research, I found that there were no universal standards for what a running shoe should be. The U.S. Bureau of Standards had some guidelines on the coefficient of friction (to keep athletic shoes from being too slippery) but that was about it. So, that's where I started. I developed and published some basic standards for running shoes, such as a shoe shouldn't rock or come apart. That might sound really obvious, but those were the very first published standards.

Perhaps I shouldn't have been surprised, but at the time, no one in the shoe industry wanted to hear about my research. The advertisers for shoe companies didn't want to know about it; the shoe companies didn't want to know about it; and the medical sector really didn't want to get involved with examining people's running shoes. My work on running shoes was basically blocked by the running industry. This was before the Internet was widely available, and the only way to get the word out was through TV, magazines, newsletters and lecturing. However, the American Medical Athletic Association and the American Running Association did support me, along with the Miami Runners Club and South Florida Triathletes, and the word gradually spread.

When I was finally ready to open my running specialty shop, I was determined that the shoe vendors had to meet my standards for an acceptable shoe. I made the decision that, if I couldn't get the vendors to agree on what they would take back as defective, I wasn't going to open the store. Fortunately, when I presented my research to the shoe vendors, they agreed that if any of their shoes had the defects I specified, they would take them back, no questions asked. I'm proud to say that for more than twelve years now, all of my shoe vendors have lived up to that promise – at least in my store. We check the shoes as they come in, and when we find pattern imperfections (**defects**), the manufacturers have always addressed my specific questions and made corrections to the products.

Of course, that doesn't mean manufacturers can't sell defective shoes in other stores. The industry admits to a three percent defect rate overall. That means that three out of every 100 people who buy a new pair of shoes get a manufacturer's defect. It also means that three out of every 100 people who are shopping for a new pair of shoes after an injury (when they are most vulnerable) are getting defective shoes. Studies show that once you've been injured, you're more likely to be injured again within the next year, so this already-vulnerable population faces the real possibility of buying new shoes that can make their injury worse.

Depending upon the vendor and the line, there are some shoe models that I consider as having a 100-percent defective rate because they were manufactured in a way that I define as a defective shoe. That includes shoe models that are designed to wobble when they're brand new. I can go into any of the big sporting-goods stores today and buy as many defective shoes as I did in the late '90s. In that respect, nothing has changed.

8.2 Hitting Your Stride

Different shoes are designed for different running strides. In your recovery program, you'll be using three types of strides: a **fullfoot stride** with a heel-to-toe motion for fitness walking; a **flatfoot stride** for gliding; and a **forefoot stride** for plyometrics. All three are used for accelerations. For post-injury running you need a shoe that will allow you to run in all three of these strides while protecting yourself from the inevitable missteps that occur as you're learning to do them correctly.

It's important to recognize that individual runners have different natural strides. If you look at elite distance runners, you'll see some running with a fullfoot stride and running very fast. You'll also see elite runners with a flatfoot stride. You'll even see some elite runners with a very efficient forefoot stride who run entire marathons on their forefoot. The interesting thing is, you can find all three types in the same marathon, running together at the same pace, all in the same pack.

When it comes to running injuries, I find it's generally not the *type* of stride that's the problem, it's a sudden, unintended *change* in stride. For example, a shoe failure (something collapsing or coming apart in your shoe) can change your stride and cause an injury.

Sometimes a shoe-induced change in stride can combine with other factors and, over time, cause an injury. That was clearly the case with one of my patients, "Anna," who was a great group coach and team leader with the Miami Runners Club. She had come back to marathoning after a long break, raising a family, and she had developed shin splints that turned into a stress fracture.

What pushed Anna over the edge was a model change in her usual shoe, in which a stable shoe became unstable. It wasn't the only cause of her injury; it was just one of several contributing factors. Anna came to my P.T. office for therapy, got fitted with more stable shoes, and went on to run many more marathons.

I also learned an important lesson from running with Anna: *Intentionally* varying your stride (in a proper, controlled manner) while training can improve your fitness. Since the biomechanics of each type of stride is different, training with different strides or at different paces can help reduce stress and avoid nontraumatic injuries. Anna incorporated walk breaks into her distance runs. Other runners at the Miami Runners Club ran throughout training, but would occasionally run a bit slower or faster. All of us are capable of running with different strides at different times, and exercising our ability to change and adapt helps make us stronger and reduces our risk of injury. It's good to purposely mix up your training – as long as it's done in a safe, gradual, and controlled manner.

In this book, the concept of mixing up your training is built into your injury recovery program. During your recovery, you'll use different exercises with different strides to strengthen different muscles. It's important to remember that, during your recovery program, you won't be running the same way you ran before your injury. You'll purposely progress through a controlled series of strides – from fitness walking and gliding to accelerating and plyometric strengthening exercises – each using your foot in a very specific way. After you've completed your recovery and return to regular training, you may decide to run a different way, but in post-injury running, your stride is going to be very carefully controlled.

8.3 Hitting the Wall

While we're discussing strides and running injuries, let's talk about "the wall." In a marathon, the wall is glycogen depletion. We store enough carbohydrates (in the form of glycogen) in our muscles and liver to run about 18 to 20 miles, and then we hit the wall of glycogen depletion. Our muscles run out of fuel, and it really hurts. It slows us down and alters our stride, and that's a critical stage when injuries can occur.

Hitting the wall is also hard on our running shoes. I've observed that, regardless of mileage, shoes worn in a marathon wear out much sooner than shoes worn only in training. We select our shoes to function with our normal running stride, but when our stride changes radically due to pain and fatigue, our shoes aren't supporting that stride. Our shoes affect our stride, and our stride affects our shoes.

Once we get past the wall, maybe the hurt doesn't entirely go away, but at least it usually gets better. When runners get through the wall, fat burning kicks in, we feel better, and our stride improves. I've heard many ultra-marathoners cheer with joy when they get past the wall in their "first" marathon.

8.4 Why Shoes?

As this book was being written, the barefoot running fad was sweeping the nation. Runners all over the country were taking off their shoes and hitting the roads, pavement, dirt, grass, and sand. But barefoot running wasn't invented in 2009 when Christopher McDougall's best-selling book, *Born to Run*, was released. Coaches have always worked with their athletes barefoot on the grass or track in drills that promote mindful running.

As a triathlete, I'm particularly interested in barefoot running because I run barefoot in the transition from swim to bike – and that can be a half mile or longer on asphalt. Since I was never a great athlete, I practice my barefoot transition because it's a place where I can make up some time. So I'm not against barefoot running, as long as it's done safely and not overhyped as one of those "magic tricks" that are going to solve all of your running problems.

For example, many barefoot proponents claim that running barefoot corrects your form and keeps you from landing on the outside of your heel. I don't buy that. In reality, the strike zone for running depends on your pace and intention. I can intentionally run in any type of stride, both shod and unshod. And, while running barefoot does promote a softer strike, it doesn't magically correct your technique. Whether wearing shoes or barefoot, you always want to be conscious of your body's balance, be light on your feet, and listen to your running for sounds of problems such as overstriking and foot slapping.

Another claim I've heard is that wearing running shoes weakens the intrinsic muscles of the foot, and therefore causes running injuries. Some barefoot enthusiasts even advise injured runners to run barefoot. Medically speaking, that's bad advice. First, there's simply no scientific support for the idea that running in shoes makes the intrinsic muscles of the foot weak. Second, the injured runners I treat in my P.T. practice are often unfit for running, and it would be malpractice for me to have them run barefoot. When you are injured, you need a shoe for protection. Third, studies show that the incidence of running injuries is higher during the first year after a running injury, and also during the one-year period of transition from a training shoe to barefoot running or a "barefoot technology" shoe. Changing to barefoot running within a year after an injury is just asking for trouble by combining two high-risk factors.

Because I work in health care, my biggest concern with barefoot running is not actually biomechanical, it's about some major health and safety issues. Unfortunately, as the barefoot craze began to grow, many barefoot activists took a militant stand against any type of shoe. Some completely ignored important safety concerns, and put runners at great risk by making claims based on no medical expertise or evidence.

If you're going to run barefoot, you have to be prepared for injuries from cuts or puncture wounds. For example, you should have a first-aid kit nearby and keep your tetanus shots up to date. Think about the complications related to HIV, diabetes, and other medical conditions. Here in South Florida, we also have to worry about parasitic infections. Barefoot running may be less risky in deserts and remote, sparsely-populated areas – but I'm in Miami, and *I've* cut my foot while running barefoot on the beach! No matter how long you run barefoot, there's no way your skin is going to toughen up enough to ward off a rusty nail or sharp glass.

Nevertheless, throughout the history of running, coaches have always had occasions to train runners barefoot. As a coach, I've trained runners barefoot. Running barefoot can be fine with proper precautions, training and technique, and for runners with optimum running fitness and strength, but it's not for runners who are unfit or injured. It's simple – when you're unfit or injured, always begin training in a protective shoe. Then, when you're fit, you can progress to less supportive and lighter shoes for performance!

The bottom line is, taking off your shoes doesn't magically make you run better, and properly-fitted shoes are not the cause of running injuries. A bad shoe can definitely contribute to a running injury, but the real cause of most running injuries is a dysfunction in the way you run.

8.5 "Barefoot" Technology Running Shoes

With all the hype surrounding barefoot running, you'd think that shoe vendors would be worried. On the contrary, many vendors embraced the barefoot fad and saw it as a marketing opportunity. I select all the running footwear sold at my running store, so I see all the new shoes and hear all the pitches. For example, one sales representative originally introduced a particular well-known product at my store as a water sandal. Then, after *Born to Run* became a best seller, the rep returned and introduced the same product as a running shoe, claiming that it mimics barefoot running. How does a water sandal suddenly become a running shoe? It doesn't. Only the marketing strategy changes. (In my vocabulary, a "shoe" has laces, a "sandal" has straps, and a "sock" just slips on.)

If we actually look at the weight-bearing surface of a racing flat or track spike and compare it to the weight-bearing surface of a water sandal (or water sock), they're about the same. Of the three, the racing flat feels best when you run in it; the track spike is designed to be the fastest; and the water sandal sort of runs and feels the way you'd expect it to – it really wasn't designed for running. It *is* true that some elite ultra-marathoners have historically raced in water socks, but that's simply because these athletes are generally larger than other runners and racing flats are just too small for them. It not that they don't like racing flats, it's just that the shoes don't fit them.

"Shoeing down" with racing flats or track spikes for performance is a long-standing running tradition that works well specifically for top-notch runners who are fit, healthy, and have the biomechanical ability to run with less external control and protection. Unfortunately, this concept can't be universally applied to all runners. Many of us don't run safely or efficiently in very light footwear.

So, when my sales rep tried to market a water sandal to me as a way to reduce running injuries, it immediately raised a red flag. As I've said before, injured runners don't need less protection and stability, they need more! Once people started running in those water sandals, users from all over the nation started reporting a variety of running injuries, some of which were crippling. As a result, the vendor added a disclaimer to their website, essentially advising runners to consult a physician before running in these shoes.

Similar problems apply to running in any type of minimalist shoe, and many other shoe manufacturers are now posting warnings about running in their minimalist shoes. Unfortunately, many barefoot enthusiasts are still promoting these products. In the current edition of his book *Barefoot Running*, author Michael Sandler highly recommends not only that particular brand of water sandals, but moccasins, beach socks, dancing shoes, and various other forms of minimalist shoes as an adjunct to barefoot running. At the same time, he warns that "This can result in a whole host of overuse injuries…" and recommends going barefoot first. Paradoxically, while Sandler says that, when it comes to the risk of injury while running barefoot, "The greater risk is getting injured in a shoe," he also devotes an entire chapter in his book to injuries caused by barefoot running.

I want to state clearly that barefoot running and "barefoot" technology shoes should *never* be used to manage a running injury. During this period of post-injury running, you need more protection, not less! If your shoe contributed to your injury, the answer is to get properly fitted with the right shoe, not to go without.

8.6 What is "Natural" Running?

Another popular fad is "natural" running. The term "natural" has been used to describe everything from running in bare feet to "natural" variations of different running styles. Some advocates even call for people to run in their bare feet to find out how they run "naturally."

However, there seems to be no general agreement about what constitutes "natural" running in humans. If we're referring to "natural" as it occurs in *nature*, we can look at animals. Many behaviors come to animals instinctively, developed over time by the environmental influences of natural selection. But humans don't always act instinctively, and we tend to modify our environment to suit ourselves rather than waiting for natural selection to fit us to our environment. Evolutionarily speaking, once we invented weapons, agriculture, and cars, walking and running were no longer essential for our survival.

The truth is, most modern humans don't have an instinctive, naturally-efficient running gait. For our running to appear "natural," a coach or trainer has to carefully observe our activity and guide us to improve our endurance and maximal running potential while inflicting the least amount of harm on our bodies. There are certainly some individuals who have more innate talent for running than others, but those who become professional athletes actually receive even more coaching and training to build upon their skill.

On the other hand, if we interpret "natural" to mean *primitive*, we'd have to look back at man as he functioned long ago without footwear. All we really know about prehistoric man is that he was typically shorter than modern man, faced different obstacles than those we face today, and probably had a shorter lifespan. Unfortunately, we have little evidence of how he ran or what type of stride he might have used. I'd assume that, if he were gathering food or firewood, he walked home. Maybe if he found something exciting, he'd have more of a distance stride. If he were out hunting, and suddenly found a bigger animal hunting *him*, he'd probably be sprinting! You'd think there would be this purposeful difference – the same as we see in runners today.

In our post-industrial times, we shouldn't be so concerned about being a "natural" runner. It's more about being able to run efficiently with your own individual stride. If your shoes hurt you, or make your feet slap or clunk, or are unstable – that's just badly-fitted shoes. Take responsibility for your shoe choice. Follow the guidelines in this book, and you should be able to find a shoe that suits your needs.

8.7 "Natural" Technology Running Shoes

Don't be confused by shoes that are advertised as "natural" running shoe technology – that's just another fad in marketing, similar to the "barefoot" technology marketing plan. "Running naturally in barefoot technology" became popular along with books like the *Pose Method*, which promotes running "naturally" on your forefoot. At that time, a new running shoe vendor came out with a shoe that had a wedge under the forefoot, and the idea that it made you run on your forefoot was part of their marketing campaign.

Of course, I don't have a problem with people who *normally* run on their forefoot, but I do have a problem with the idea of *making* you run on your forefoot. Very few runners can maintain a forefoot-striking stride for any significant amount of time. I've observed runners reaching fatigue while wearing this vendor's shoes, and it definitely changed their running mechanics. In my opinion, when that happens, such a shoe can become unsafe due to the absence of any real support behind the forefoot.

Interestingly enough, a couple of years later, when the *Chi Running* book came out promoting the "midfoot strike," this same vendor marketed their product as the *Chi* running shoe, despite the fact that author Danny Dreyer says it is "mandatory to have very flexible, thin-soled shoes," and that he runs "almost entirely in racing flats" with no elevated heel. At that time, the vendor claimed that their shoe was designed to make you land on your "midfoot" – even though their shoe design hadn't

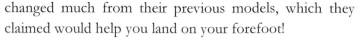

changed much from their previous models, which they claimed would help you land on your forefoot!

I agree with Dryer's idea that "the primary cause of injury is poor running form and poor biomechanics," although I would add poor running habits to that list. What it comes down to is this: As long as you are healthy and running well, any shoe that protects your feet from hazards and allows you to maintain your proper form is fine with me. But, when you are unfit or injured, you need a protective and supportive shoe for your recovery program.

8.8 Running Barefoot In Your Shoes

There are some runners who can run well in any shoe. I've met many gifted athletes who have tried everything on the market and can run safely in all of them without ever suffering a running injury. I'm not one of those gifted few, and it doesn't take very much to throw me off my stride. I've suffered some very severe injuries both from defective shoes and as a result of too aggressively wear-testing some questionable products.

Your goal should not be to run with a particular style or in a particular shoe, but to run with proper balance. Where you land is not as important to your balance as where you push off. When you're running, you always want to push off through your big toe, whether you're wearing shoes or barefoot. As a running coach, I always train people to "run barefoot inside their shoes." It's important to feel that balance. In your recovery program, you'll be doing balance exercises both barefoot and in shoes, but you will not be running barefoot.

A final thought on barefoot training: The purpose of running is not to toughen our feet, and people who can't run well in shoes don't magically run better barefoot. The important factors are still training, instruction, and mindfulness. Sticking your foot in a shoe doesn't change the way your brain communicates with your muscles and your balance receptors. You're either purposely controlling your feet or you're not. In later chapters, we'll discuss mental strategies to help you focus on your feet, especially when you're recovering from a running injury.

Runners today have the potential to enjoy their sport for many years, so it's important to promote anything that keeps you healthy and active over the long term. That includes both proper footwear and knowledgeable injury management .

* * *

Chapter 9
Choosing the Right Shoe

Everybody knows that I'm a "shoe geek," so people are always asking me what running shoe they should buy. I can't answer that question for you specifically, because every individual has a different combination of biomechanics, running techniques, and foot shape. What I can do is teach you *how* to find the right shoe, which is a really important factor for **post-injury training**.

The easiest way to make sure you get the right shoe is to go to a really good running specialty shop that has knowledgeable salespeople and a wide range of reliable running shoes that you can try on and test out. Not all shoe stores are the same. Some owners and staff are super knowledgeable. Others only care about making the sale. The latter will just sell you whatever's hot, and they sell by fad.

For post-injury training, it's important to find a shoe that fits *and* supports your foot properly. You want the weight-bearing surfaces of your foot to be balanced and stable. You want the shoe to cushion and protect your foot, but not be too soft and unsteady. You want it to be supportive, but not brick hard.

During the recovery period, it's better to have too much shoe than not enough shoe. My long-term experience is, if I put somebody in *too* supportive a shoe, their feet might get sore or they might not perform great, but I don't see an awful reoccurrence of their injury. They don't blow up when they're in too much shoe. On the other hand, I have seen runners blow up in too little shoe – a shoe that's not supportive enough. I've also seen it happen when patients have suddenly switched to minimalist shoes or barefoot running. So, while you're in post-injury training, it's really essential to choose a shoe that will protect and support you until you have fully recovered.

9.1 Function, Fit, and Feel

Proper support means different shoes for different people. Post-injury, we're looking for a shoe with just the right combination of *function, fit*, and *feel* [**Box 9-1**]. At my running store, we carry a broad spectrum of different shapes and styles to choose from, but when it comes down to the shape of your foot and the specific type of support you need, it inevitably gets down to just a few choices.

When we're helping you choose a shoe, the first thing we do is get you on the treadmill to find out how much *functional support* you need, which varies by individual and the type of running you're doing. Each person has a unique combination of biomechanical factors that have to be correctly matched with the right training shoe.

Next, we narrow down the choices to the shoe that *fits* the shape of your foot perfectly. We look at the shape of the shoe and the shape of your foot. A properly-fitting shoe is the correct length and width that will hold your foot securely on the platform and prevent excessive movement when properly laced. We want to see the bottom of the foot sitting evenly on the bottom of the shoe. The shoe should fit like a glove, particularly in the heel and midfoot, and leave a little wiggle room for your toes.

Finally, we get you back on the treadmill and see how your shoes *feel* – nobody else can feel them for you. A post-injury running shoe should feel like it's holding and hugging your foot. You should feel your bones sitting evenly on the platform – nothing rubbing or digging in during running. The shoe should feel firm to your heel-strike while walking, and firm on initial strike while running. Depending on whether your foot is naturally supple or stiff, the correct amount of support should control or allow movement in a way that lets you transition smoothly from strike to pushoff, and you should feel minimum resistance with the pushoff. New shoes should always feel great!

Once you have selected your shoes, remember to check them regularly for signs of wear and deterioration. You should redo your shoe tests approximately every 50 miles of wear, and replace your shoes *before* they can cause a critical failure.

HOW TO:
Choose a Post-Injury Shoe

Choose your shoe by function, fit, and feel:

1. Function means support. The particular type of support you need depends on your dysfunction (as determined by gait analysis). We have two tests for function: the **Break Test (*Figure 9-1*)** and the **Twist Test (*Figure 9-2*).**

- For post-injury training, choose a shoe that breaks easily at the forefoot, under the metatarsal heads.
- Select a shoe model that provides the right type of support for your dysfunction. If your foot is excessively loose, look for a firmer shoe to correct that. If your foot is excessively stiff, look for a supple shoe that doesn't restrict motion. You'll check for the right amount of twist by the feel and sound of the shoe when you run on the treadmill.

2. Fit: Among the shoes you have selected by function, choose the model that best fits your foot:

- *Size and width:* No matter what the size says on the shoe box, or what the shoes look like, turn them over and look at the bottoms. Two pairs of shoes that look the same size from the top can have radically different lengths and widths in the platform.
- *Shape:* Look at your foot, and look at the shoe. How well does the shape of the shoe match the shape of your foot?
- *Support:* Put the shoes on. All the bones of your foot must rest comfortably and evenly on the bed (platform) of the shoe.

(Box 9-1 cont.)

- *Fit:* Standing with your weight in the shoe, feel all around your foot with your hands to see how well the shoe fits the shape of your foot. There should be at least a centimeter (almost half an inch) of room between your longest toe and the front of the shoe.
- *Lacing:* When the shoe is properly laced, the upper part of the shoe should strap your foot snugly to the platform. The shoe should not be too tight, and it should not be too loose.
- *Socks:* Select a sock that has padding in the right places to complement the fit of the shoe.

3. Feel: If you are buying shoes in a running specialty store, they should have a treadmill that you can run on to test the feel and function of the shoe:
- Is the shoe comfortable when you run in it? The shoe should work well with the entire foot, with no rubbing or digging anywhere.
- Listen to the sound of your running on the treadmill. It should sound light and even, with no slapping or clunking.
- Focus on how the shoe feels on the strike, the transition to the forefoot, and on the pushoff. It should feel stable, supportive, and centered (balanced); there should be no wobble or excessive twisting at any point in your stride.

Figure 9-1: The Break Test

Break is where the shoe bends fore-to-aft.

- Hold the shoe with both hands, front and back, and bend the toe upward.
- The shoe should break at the forefoot (the metatarsal heads), which is the widest part of the shoe (the toe box).

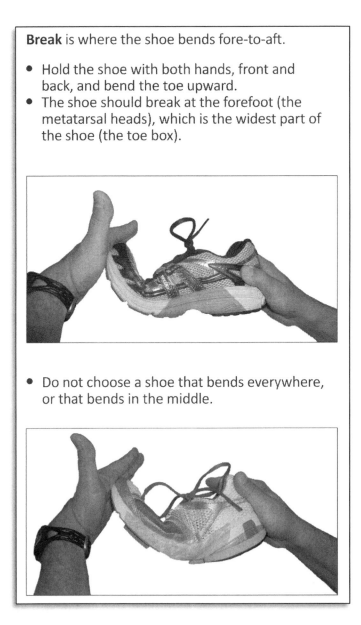

- Do not choose a shoe that bends everywhere, or that bends in the middle.

Figure 9-2: The Twist Test

Twist is the rotation along the long axis of the shoe, which determines how much inward roll (pronation) there is.

- Simultaneously twist the heel of the shoe outward and the toe of the shoe inward.
- There should be some twist, but not so much that the shoe becomes unstable.
- Choose a stable shoe that has just the right amount of give in the middle, as determined by your individual function analysis.

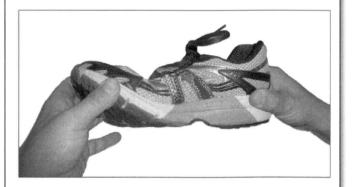

- Do not choose an unstable shoe that twists excessively in the middle.

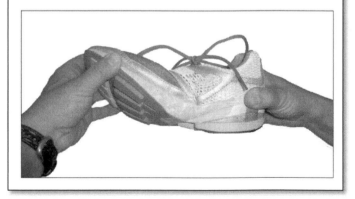

9.2 Heel Height

Heel gradient means the height difference between the heel and forefoot of a shoe. Most shoes have some degree of heel gradient, ranging from almost-flat to ultra-high fashion heels. Wearing elevated heels may have started as a fashion statement, or for some other reason, but the important thing is that different heel gradients change the way your body feels and functions.

Many shoe manufacturers put a heel gradient into their athletic shoes to help lessen the impact of weight-bearing activities. When you wear a shoe with a heel gradient, your body responds by shortening certain muscles and tendons, particularly the Achilles tendon. Once this happens, changing from a shoe with a higher heel gradient into a shoe with a lower heel gradient – or to a shoe with no heel, or to running barefoot – puts a tremendous amount of stress on your Achilles tendon and up the entire kinetic chain of movement toward your spine. Conversely, changing from a flat or low heel gradient to a slightly higher heel gradient gives your Achilles tendon a little bit of slack and decreases stress up the kinetic chain. The extra slack feels better on your body as it lessens the amount of tension in your leg. In fact, studies show that as little as 10 millimeters (less than a half-inch) of heel gradient lessens the strain in your ankle, knee, and hip joints.

When a running injury occurs, your body tissues rip and tear on both the visible (**macroscopic**) level and cellular (**microscopic**) level, and you need to reduce the stress on the damaged tissue so it will heal properly. The worst thing you can do when you're injured is to change from a supportive shoe to a flat, unstable shoe – or to go barefoot. For post-injury management, I advise my patients to wear a supportive shoe with a 6- to 12-millimeter heel gradient to reduce stress on the tendons and muscles that surround the joints.

When you've recovered from your injury and return to **post-recovery running**, it's important to reintroduce any kind of stress on the body slowly and gradually, including returning to a lower heel gradient. If stress is introduced too quickly, it will increase your chance of reinjury.

9.3 Types of Shoes

The function of some types of running shoes is obvious. For example, you can see that *racing shoes* such as track spikes, spikes for cross country, and racing flats for asphalt are ultra-light and have little support – they're designed for performance.

Among different types of *training shoes*, however, the distinctions aren't always so obvious. For example, a lightweight trainer is in-between a racing flat and a protective training shoe. I define a racing flat as a shoe that bends in the middle, which is used for forefoot activities. I define a lightweight trainer as a shoe that bends at the forefoot (the **metatarsal heads**), which is used more for flatfooted activities.

A training shoe is basically a molded, cushioned platform on which your foot rests, with an "upper" that laces up and holds your foot in place on the platform. The platform has a cushioning layer that may be uniform, or it may be thicker at either the toe or the heel. There's also a variable amount of plastic that stabilizes the shoe and determines its flexibility. Inflexible shoes can cause calf muscles to overwork and can contribute to certain injuries. Shoes that are too flexible will not support and protect your foot properly.

Because you're going to be doing a wide variety of activities during *post-injury training* (including hopping, stepping, walking, gliding, and accelerations), we're looking for a proper, supportive training shoe that breaks in the right place and doesn't twist excessively in the middle. For hopping and stepping, you need a shoe with good stability. For fitness walking, you want a shoe that heel-strikes well. For gliding, you want a shoe that strikes well on the whole outside edge, and that supports the entire foot well during the transition. You also want a shoe that pushes off well, and is well padded, because you'll be doing accelerations and plyometrics on your forefoot. The goal is to find all these things in one training shoe.

Within the general category of training shoes, individual models can be further classified by their amount and distribution of cushioning (cushion-toed shoes, cushion-heels, or cushioning heel-to-toe) and by their stability (neutral, mild stability, stability, and motion control). A **neutral shoe** is balanced between support and cushioning. A **stability shoe** has less cushioning and more stabilizing structures. A **motion control shoe** has the most stabilizing structures.

Among all the brands and models of shoes available, you'll find a continuum of all these factors, so it's usually possible to find a shoe that exactly matches your needs. Understand that running-shoe manufacturers don't make corrective shoes or shoes specially designed for injured runners – they make shoes to run in. That means you won't find these classifications written on any shoe box. I've found that vendors generally don't like the idea of pre-classifying shoes because they don't want to limit people's selection when they're buying shoes.

Nevertheless, I do use different models of shoes to correct specific running dysfunctions by selecting certain shoes from the broad range available, and I personally categorize all the shoes I sell into functional classes for this purpose. To find out which specific corrections you need, you may want to do a gait analysis with your healthcare provider or running specialty store. Once you know what to look for, you can choose the best shoe for yourself.

9.4 About Laces and Socks

Triathletes and lots of other people love elastic laces. I don't use elastic laces for post-injury running. For post–injury running I want the shoe laced properly all the way through from the bottom up, and I want a sock that complements the fit of the shoe. In a well-fitted post-injury shoe, the foot is strapped snugly (not squeezingly tight) to an even, smooth supportive surface, and the whole unit works as one.

9.5 Gait Analysis

Choosing the right running shoe is all about your individual biomechanics and running technique. I've worked with many runners over the years, and it doesn't take me long to recognize an individual's stride – to me, it's as individual as their face. I've recognized runners I've worked with, from behind, in a marathon field of 25,000 people, without even knowing that they were there!

Gait analysis simply means analyzing your individual stride, and observing the effects of different running shoes on your stride. At my P.T. office, and at my running store, I can make a video recording of a runner's stride as he's running on a treadmill in different shoes, and go around 360 degrees using mirrors. Then I play it back in slow motion to analyze the data.

The treadmill is an excellent tool for this. I've observed the same runners, both on the track and on the treadmill, and their strides remain consistent whether they're running in light, less-supportive racing shoes, or in more-supportive training shoes. A properly fitted shoe doesn't radically change your natural biomechanics, and neither does the treadmill.

However, your stride does change when you're injured or wearing the wrong shoes. On the treadmill, an ill-fitting shoe is immediately obvious. I can hear the sound of a shoe that's too firm or too soft from the next room! If the shoe is too hard, it's too supportive – you don't get a smooth transition and you hear a clunk. If the shoe is too soft, it's not supportive enough, and your foot slaps. On the video recording, you can hear it and you can see it. In post-injury training, if I see different motions on the left and right foot, I'll work on correcting the most injured side first.

For video gait analysis, I start the runner out in a minimalist shoe or racing flat so I can observe his basic biomechanical *function* without the influence of a training shoe. (I never let runners run barefoot on the treadmill because it's just not safe.) While he's running on the treadmill, I'm looking for feet that roll in or roll out (**overpronation** or **supination**), resulting in an unstable stride, and I'm looking for "non-neutral" gait patterns that result in imbalance. These may include:

- *Excessive pronation or supination:* For runners who have excessive pronation (inward foot rotation), we look for a shoe in the stability category. The shoe should be stable and supportive with relatively little twist. Limiting the amount of movement in the rearfoot gives the runner maximum support upon foot strike. A runner who supinates (rolls the foot outward) will benefit from a less stable, more cushioned shoe with more impact-resistant materials such as gel or air.

- *The forefoot runner:* Forefoot runners normally need shoes with plenty of padding under the metatarsal heads, and that are very bendy to help them stay on their toes. However, in post-injury training, you're going to be doing a lot of heel-to-toe motions, so you need a shoe that is stable throughout and doesn't bend in the middle, but is well padded and flexible at the forefoot.

- *The excessive heel striker:* If you look at the bottom of your shoes and see that the back edge of the heel is worn down – that's excessive heel striking. All that heel smashing can result from forced decelerations, or from loss of balance when you're fatigued. Nothing good comes from of that kind of weight-bearing. Even when you're trying to do these exercises properly, missteps are bound to happen; so if you have a tendency to end up on your heel, you should protect yourself with a shoe that has plenty of support at your heel strike-zone.

Once I've seen what kind of functional support a runner needs, I can determine which category of shoe he needs to correct that particular dysfunction. Again, I'm not trying to radically alter his natural stride, I'm just trying to support and stabilize his stride so he can run safely.

When we've narrowed down the shoe selection to a certain category of shoes, we take a break from the treadmill to select the shoe model with the right *fit*. We can use socks with padding in different areas to fine-tune the fit until it's just right. If we find several models that fit, we'll do a gait analysis with each shoe to see which model works the best.

I don't ask the runner how the shoe *feels* until I'm satisfied with the fit and function. Then I tell him what he should be feeling for in the shoe. Once we have the right shoe with the right fit, and we have them laced up properly, we go back to the treadmill for more gait analysis. Then the runner tells me how the shoe feels, and I observe his gait to see how well the shoe is functioning.

9.6 Defective Shoes

Parts of all running shoes are made by hand and are subject to imperfections. According to the manufacturers themselves, about three percent of all new running shoes are defective. I've had a few pairs of defective shoes myself, and nothing is more frustrating than being injured by a poorly-made shoe.

Box 9-2 *HOW TO:* Detect Defective Running Shoes

1. Construction:
- The upper, midsole, and outer sole should be attached firmly and evenly.
- The shoe should be glued together correctly and continuously at all locations.
- The upper (mesh portion) should be glued straight into the sole.

2. Symmetry and Stability:
- Place the shoes on a flat, level surface. The sole of the shoe should be level with the surface on which it is resting.
- Place the left and right shoe side by side and check that both shoes have the same symmetry.
- Look at the backs of both shoes and check that the center line of each is vertical.
- Press down and rock each shoe from side to side. If the shoe rocks side to side, it may not adequately prevent your foot from rolling excessively.

3. Support:
- When using a shoe with air pockets or gel pockets, check to see if they are still inflated. Sometimes these pockets deflate, leaving the shoe with no support.

4. Deterioration:
- Some materials within the shoe (such as foams, gels, and rubbers) have a limited shelf life. Be sure that the shoe selection at your running shoe store is current.

If you want to recover and prevent further injury, you have to check new shoes for any type of defect that makes them unstable, unbalanced, or otherwise affects the way they function [**Box 9-2**]. A shoe with an uneven lining can unbalance you and cause a running injury. A shoe that isn't level, or has air or gel pockets that have collapsed, can cause a running injury. A shoe that falls apart because it hasn't been glued together properly can cause a running injury.

Shoes that rock, intentionally or unintentionally, also cause injuries. A shoe that rocks side-to side is defective. Some shoes are designed to rock front-to-back. I personally consider any shoe that rocks to be unstable and therefore defective.

Don't be one of the three percent of injured runners who buy defective running shoes. Remember to check for manufacturers' defects every time you buy a new pair of shoes.

9.7 Other Things to Watch Out For

Old Shoes: I don't want people to wear old shoes during post-injury training. Old running shoes have the wear pattern of the dysfunctional gait, so it's better to have new shoes. Even if you love the shoe, it's still an injury shoe and you should get new ones. Another reason to get new shoes is deterioration. The foam in these shoes dries out in two years and loses its structural support, even if they've been sitting on the shelf and never been worn – so you don't want to wear old models that have been sitting around. Go with a fresh, new-model shoe that meets your post-injury shoe guidelines.

Aftermarket Insoles: The platform of a training shoe is designed to cushion and support your foot, and the sock liner on top complements the fit. When you stick extra stuff on top of that, you're ruining the fit of the shoe – guaranteed. It raises your foot up and creates another instability, and that makes your shoes wear out faster. I don't use aftermarket innersoles, and if my patients are using them, I tell them to get rid of them.

Model changes: A lot of people think that if they stick with the same type of shoe, no matter what, they won't get injured. The truth is just the opposite. Surveys show that runners who will only buy a particular make or model of shoe have more injuries than runners who are willing to change. That's because shoe manufacturers can radically alter the fit and function of a model without changing the model name. You have no way of knowing when that happens unless you're paying close attention to your shoe selection when buying running shoes. A model change can negatively impact what the shoe does to your foot and delay your recovery.

When you choose your post-injury training shoe, you don't want to automatically buy the same shoe you've always had. However, you don't want to start randomly experimenting with new shoes either. Always examine the shoes you're buying for defects, and make an informed decision on based on function, fit, and feel.

* * *

Gestalt: a structure, arrangement, or pattern of physical, biological, or psychological phenomena so integrated as to constitute a functional unit with properties not derivable by summation of its parts.
– Merriam-Webster's Medical Dictionary

Chapter 10
Entering Phase Two:
Manual Therapy and Self-Mobilization

Manual therapy can be defined as a group of skilled, hands-on therapeutic techniques used by healthcare professionals in the diagnosis and treatment of various musculo-skeletal conditions. At my P.T. office, manual therapy is our entryway to evaluation and treatment, and it's how we monitor the patient's progress. I use manual therapy at the beginning of each session with a patient to see how they're progressing, to loosen them up, and to get them fired up before we go into the gym and exercise.

I also teach my patients manual-therapy techniques that they can use on themselves at home, which we call **self-mobilization**. Learning self-mobilization is a useful skill for any athlete, and it's especially important for runners who always have tight, knotty muscles. Sometimes these hands-on techniques can be the one element that makes the difference between getting better and not getting better.

For example, one of my patients was a college cross-country track athlete who was having trouble with her shin. "Debbie" came to me for help during her school break, but she had only one week before she had to go back to college, so I knew I had a challenge. Taking her detailed history, I found she was at Injury Stage 4 and taking prescribed anti-inflammatories to get through practice. Her team trainers had been treating her with ice and electrical stimulation, but she wasn't improving. She had a negative MRI, and her physician was recommending injectional therapy.

Fortunately, I was able to use manual therapy to pinpoint her problem and release the restrictions in her shin. After she got off the meds, she improved so quickly that we were able to get her through all four phases of recovery in one week – focusing on her shin and also on a list of other contributing factors that we discovered while taking her history. By the end of that week, I had taught her self-mobilizations to maintain her progress, and she returned to college with the skills and knowledge to self-manage her injury. From then on, her college running experience was great!

10.1 Muscle Imbalance and Body Awareness

I use manual therapy techniques to diagnose a condition by locating the very specific areas of tenderness, tightness, and weakness that are characteristic of different running injuries. I also use manual therapy as a part of rehabilitation to decrease pain and swelling in a joint or soft tissue, to increase freedom of movement around the joints, to improve muscle mobility and contractility (muscle relaxation and contraction), and to improve sensory feedback from tissues to the neurological system.

Using manual therapy as a treatment for pain works a lot like electrical stimulation and other pain-relieving techniques. It stimulates sensory nerves and temporarily blocks the perception of pain. However, just blocking the feeling of pain doesn't do anything to help your underlying problem. Unless you also address your dysfunction, the pain will come back when you return to the activities or conditions that triggered your running injury.

The longer-lasting benefits of manual therapy are all about regaining function. Any injury causes tissue damage which results in scarring and tightness (loss of mobility). Manual therapy loosens you up by pulling the muscle apart and **releasing** the scarring and tightness – letting the muscle relax **(muscle relaxation)**. An injury also causes weakness and loss of muscle control (loss of neuromuscular function). Manual therapy **activates** muscles and makes them contract **(muscle contraction)** to help you regain muscle control and strengthen the weakness.

The stiffness, scarring and weakness caused by a running injury can affect your running long after the injury has healed. For example, if a muscle is weak and shortened, or if the joint is stiff, it can pull you out of alignment and you can develop an abnormal running movement to compensate for that weakness. We call that **muscle imbalance**. Muscle imbalance is related to two changes in muscle function: (1) a tightening of a major muscle group (**mobilizing muscle**); and (2) a weakening of a smaller muscle that controls movement or joint position (**stabilizing muscle**).

Injuries also affect the communication pathways between your nervous system and your musculo-skeletal system, which reduces your strength and muscle control. We call that a loss of **body awareness**. These neuromuscular problems affect the way you control your posture and other biomechanical factors, including any muscle imbalance.

10.2 The Gestalt of Manual Therapy

Manual therapy is a really hard skill for physical therapists to learn. The ability to find the weakness and stiffness in another person and understand the biomechanical details of it by touch alone is a psychomotor skill that really does take 10,000 hours of practice with ongoing instruction to master. That's 40 hours of hands-on work every week for five years, just to become competent at these skills.

A therapist who has truly mastered manual therapy skills achieves something I call the "**Gestalt**" of physical therapy. It's the whole relationship – the therapist and patient in a groove, almost instinctively understanding the problem together. That's what our hands are on – the Gestalt – and P.T.s who don't use manual therapy don't have that. It's an immeasurable quality.

Not every therapist can master manual therapy to that level. I've trained a lot of young therapists in my career, and their skill levels do vary. However, in my office, manual therapy is a skill that absolutely must be mastered. When I evaluate a new therapist, I have them work on my running injuries (because, as a patient, I can feel when it's done right), and I have fired some of them because I thought their skill level was not growing.

As a runner, you should know when manual therapy is being done right. You can feel when your therapist finds that tenderness and stiffness, and gets in there and activates it and releases it. Recognizing that feeling is the key to success when you do your own self-mobilizations. You are the best person to find that area of tenderness and work on it because you are the one who feels it directly. You control the muscle contraction (activation) and relaxation (release). If you can master self-mobilizations, you won't have to rely so much on finding the right therapist and developing that Gestalt – you can do it for yourself!

In this book, I describe what you should feel for in term of tenderness, muscle contraction, and muscle relaxation while you are doing your self-mobilization and stretching exercises. However, the best way for you to really understand good manual therapy skills is to receive good manual therapy. If you go to a manual therapist, pay attention while he or she works on you, and try to figure out how they get into the right spot with their hands, or with a mobilization tool. If you can feel them finding and working on the problem spot, try to do the same thing for yourself at home to help develop your own self-mobilization skills. Even if you go to a therapist who knows the manual therapy techniques but doesn't specifically know the running injuries, you can still learn some good self-management techniques from them.

10.3 Variations on a Theme

Physical therapists, chiropractors, osteopaths (DOs), and massage therapists – we're all manual therapists. We all use skilled, hands-on therapeutic techniques. I've spent a great deal of time working with many manual therapists around the country, and I've learned many different approaches (or "schools") to manual therapy. I find that the newer schools do basically the same stuff as the older schools – they just use different names for it. Occasionally, I've even thought that I invented a really great new technique, only to find it in an old osteopathy book from the 1930s!

Techniques do vary a bit from therapist to therapist simply because *our* anatomy is different. I've learned some really great techniques from master manual therapists that I could never do because their hands and bodies were so much different than mine. However, when it comes to hands-on therapy, there's really nothing new out there. It's still skilled hands working on bodies in need.

In studying with all these master therapists, my main goal was to discover some specific manual techniques for managing running injuries. However, none of the schools, and none of the masters I studied with, ever identified how a manual therapist would approach a running injury differently than they would an injury in a nonrunner. Since no school taught that, I came to the conclusion that no school was any better or worse than any other when it came to dealing with running injuries.

Nevertheless, I knew that a runner's injuries *are* different. The diagnosis is different, the treatment is different, and how I approach those injuries manually is different. So I learned general manual skills from the masters, and I learned manual therapy for runners by treating many different runners. Over the years, I pulled together all that information from many sources and developed my own system of manual therapy for treating running injuries.

10.4 Direct, Dynamic, and Progressive

In my P.T. office, we use our own set of methods and techniques (*protocols*) designed specifically for injured runners. When it comes to running injury management, we use techniques that are **direct**, **dynamic**, and **progressive**.

Generally speaking, manual therapy can be done directly or indirectly, and it can be done aggressively or lightly. When pain wakes you up at night or limits your daily activities (Injury Stage 2 or higher), I begin with more gentle manual therapy. While there is swelling, I'm more indirect – I use my hands to find the swelling and drain it. Once you're out of that pulsing severity stage, I get into manual therapy more aggressively. I go *directly* into the injury to activate the muscles and release the restrictions. I work on it hard, and the patient works with me (remember the Gestalt!). With runners, I'm dealing largely with young, healthy patients, so I can be quite aggressive and quite direct. I don't dance around anything in manual therapy.

Manual therapy can also be active or passive. In other words, you can lie there while we work on you, or you can do things (like moving or resisting) while we work on you. In my office, we go *dynamic,* which means we work with the patient using lots of active/passive resistance.

Manual therapy should always be *progressive.* We progressively work our way through all of the tissues affected by the injury. We go progressively deeper and wider over time, not just on the spot that hurts, but finding other associated areas of stiffness, tightness, and weakness. We work progressively to free up the restrictions from many different angles.

Progressive therapy is particularly important when we're treating complex running injuries involving more than one region or structure. For complex injuries, we determine the severity of injuries at different regions, then we start first with the area that's most impaired and proceed through the phases of recovery.

10.5 Manual Therapy and Pain

When applying manual therapy to a patient, I often work at a high pain threshold. In other words, it hurts. As a highly-trained and experienced physical therapist, if I find the right spot and it needs to be worked on, I'm going to go in there and work it, free it up, and get that muscle to activate just in the right spot. The point is not to cause my patients pain; the point is to mobilize the scarred and knotted tissues.

For a physical therapist, purposely working above the patient's pain threshold takes a very high level of skill and experience. On a pain scale of 1 to 10, with 1 being minimal pain and 10 being the worst pain you can imagine, I sometimes have to work at pain level 10 with

Side Tracks: Chronic Pain

Chronic pain is a real issue in this country. Many people have conditions that hurt them continually and severely. Some have medical causes, some are caused by trauma, and some are caused by other kinds of damage – but they all have one thing in common. It's really not an option whether they hurt or not. Things have happened to them, and their pain is chronic.

Early in my career I worked as a P.T. in a hospital chronic-pain treatment center; and when I started independent practice, I shared office space with a psychiatrist who specialized in chronic pain. That was an important experience for me because pain is a theme throughout any type of injury management, and there are many different philosophies of pain management. Some of the lessons I learned there have been invaluable in my coaching career, such as teaching runners not to let pain upon exertion alter their stride.

Most running-injury pain is not chronic pain. When you run long distances, it's going to hurt some, and you can get some painful injuries; but, if you address them promptly and correctly, they don't have to become chronic. However, running injury pain *can* become chronic if you continue running on the injury, especially if you take pain meds to continue running. That's Injury Stage 5 – pain that is crippling. How and when you deal with a running injury is important to help prevent chronic pain.

runners in advanced injury stages. A therapist should never attempt to work that deep and hard unless he or she has had many years of experience and lots of training. I don't want my younger therapists working that deep and hard, and when you start doing manual therapy on yourself, I don't want you working that deep and hard either.

When you're using mobilization techniques on yourself, it's important not to confuse pain with results. Pain is not beneficial; it's just a side-effect of the mobilization. You should never be overwhelming your pain threshold. Never go over a 5 or 6 out of 10 on the pain scale. Anything higher than that is not self-mobilization, and you just shouldn't be doing it.

That said, because you are working on yourself and experiencing what's going on in your body first-hand, you're not likely to make a mistake that causes excessive pain. When you're doing self-mobilization, there is actually more room for error in your technique than you have when a therapist works on you. That's another advantage of becoming your own manual therapist!

10.6 Flexibility through the Phases

In Phase One of your recovery program, you treat your acute injury, protect it, and let it recover until it is no longer severe (PRICE). In Phase Two, you'll take the first steps toward actually fixing your muscle imbalance, and start working on body awareness. You'll continue in the recovery group you started in during Phase One, based upon the *severity* of your injury on the Running Injury Stage Scale.

Group 1 includes only those who have *no* Red Flag running injuries. This group has less severe injuries, and does not need to ICE in Phase Two. The goal for *Group 1* is to find and correct their problem and get to post-recovery training as quickly as possible.

Group 2 includes all those who have Red Flag injuries. Runners in *Group 2* will have more work to do in the early phases of recovery because they have more difficult problems to deal with, and we don't want to risk reinjury to any tissues that had signs and symptoms of inflammation in Phase One.

If you fall into *Group 2*, you shouldn't be discouraged. Instead, think of it as a positive step forward. It means you have identified one or more significant problems that affect your running, and you're setting out on a pathway that can actively address those problems and safely return you to running. It's important for you to stick with your program and put in the extra time and effort required, rather than moving into Phase Three too quickly and having your Red Flag symptoms reappear.

Phase Two has two main goals: The first goal is *self-assessment*, in which you will use self-mobilization and stretching exercises to identify and pinpoint the location of your injury. The second goal is to regain *mobility* using self-mobilization to free up the tightness and scarring, and stretching exercises to improve your flexibility and range of motion.

Using self-mobilization and stretching exercises to locate the tenderness and tightness associated with your injury is an important diagnostic tool. It improves your *body awareness* of the dysfunction and helps you focus both mentally and physically on the target that you'll need to hit throughout your recovery.

You'll continue to use self-mobilization and stretching exercises in combination throughout the phases of your recovery program. Your stretching exercises will help you locate specific regions that you'll need to work on with self-mobilizations, and the self-mobilizations will help you achieve symmetry and range of motion in your stretches.

As you loosen up and move into Phase Three, you'll start using closed-chain exercises to help locate even more weakness, tenderness, and stiffness, and you'll continue with your self-mobilization and stretching exercises to maintain the flexibility you achieved in Phase Two.

In fact, you'll be constantly re-examining yourself and re-evaluating your areas of tenderness, stiffness, and weakness throughout the phases of recovery. As you do each flexibility exercise, always try to analyze and make a note of where it feels stiff. As you work on strengthening, always try to analyze where you feel weak. As you move from phase to phase, you should encounter no severe worsening of tenderness, stiffness, or weakness.

You should also incorporate self-mobilizations and stretches into your normal, *post-recovery* routine. This is what works for me: I go for a run. I go for a quick swim to cool off. I do self-mobilization and stretching. Then I do closed-chain exercises. That's kind of my weekday "there's always something to work on" routine.

You'll learn more about the stretching exercises in the next chapter. In this chapter, you'll learn how to do specific self-mobilization exercises to help you identify and free up your particular injury region or regions.

10.7 Goals of Self-Mobilization

Self-mobilization means using manual therapy techniques on yourself. Your main goals in self-mobilization are (1) to identify the tenderness and stiffness in the region affected by your running injury, and (2) to loosen up the tissues and increase your mobility. For clearance in Phase Two, you'll have to achieve **symmetry** in your mobility. That means you must work on the tight spots until you have an equal degree of flexibility and range of motion on both sides of your body.

Finding the tenderness gives you a target to focus on. When doing self-mobilization, you've got to think about what you're trying to accomplish. You're not just randomly rubbing stuff; you're trying to identify a very specific tenderness that is associated with a specific restriction of movement. You're trying to find something in your body's biomechanics that has tightened, weakened, or is out of alignment.

Once you've found the tight spots, you'll use friction and deep pressure to try to pull the scarring and constriction apart, and free up the tissues. You can try all sorts of combinations, coming at the problem from different directions. You should feel free to be a little bit creative when looking for the problem spot – it might not be exactly where you think it is.

I've selected one, two, or three good self-mobilization exercises for each of our ten running-injury regions, which will help you identify and loosen up restrictions. No matter which region is affected by your particular injury, you should try all of the self-mobilizations and stretches and locate any other areas of tenderness, tightness, and weakness you might have.

It's important to understand that finding stiffness and tenderness in a non-affected region, or in the same region in the uninjured leg, does not make a simple injury complex. Stiffness or tenderness that doesn't correlate to your running pain is not part of your running injury. However, it does mean that you've found a few more areas you can work on in Phase Two, and we want to take advantage of this opportunity to really loosen everything up!

The good news is, you don't have to spend a lot of time doing this. Self-mobilization should be done a little at a time, spread out over the entire healing process. It's just a few minutes incorporated into all the other aspects of your recovery program, but it's very important.

10.8 Tools for Self-Mobilization

Each self-mobilization exercise is specific to a region, and each uses a specific type of mobilization tool *(Table 10-1)*. Tools can pinpoint an area precisely and don't require a lot of hand strength. I use tools to work on my own tender spots when I do my self-mobilizations, and I'm often surprised by how much more easily I can feel the tenderness when I use tools rather than my own hands.

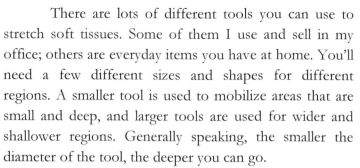

There are lots of different tools you can use to stretch soft tissues. Some of them I use and sell in my office; others are everyday items you have at home. You'll need a few different sizes and shapes for different regions. A smaller tool is used to mobilize areas that are small and deep, and larger tools are used for wider and shallower regions. Generally speaking, the smaller the diameter of the tool, the deeper you can go.

At my office, I use an assortment of massage sticks with rounded rubber tips for manual therapy when my hands get tired. These are great for running injuries because runners' legs are so muscular and can get very tight. I use smaller tips for deeper regions, and wider tips for shallower regions.

Another specialized tool I use for running injuries is a rolling massage stick that has a series of knobby rollers in the middle and a hand-grip on each end. Using two hands allows you to press the rollers harder into large muscles such as the calf, band, or glutes. You don't just roll or "glide" the massage stick over the area, you have to work the stick at an angle to press the edges of the knobs into the sore spots.

At home, what works best for me is a golf ball, a tennis ball, and the lower edge of a vitamin bottle or shampoo bottle. What these all have in common is the right degree of firmness, and edges that are smooth, curved or rounded. You don't want to cut or bruise yourself with a sharp edge. A variety of tools with different sizes and shapes will give you options for working smaller or larger areas, and deeper or shallower regions.

Table 10-1
Tools for Self-Mobilization

Professional Mobilization Tools	Home Mobilization Tools
Small massage ball	Golf ball
Medium massage ball	Tennis ball wrapped in athletic tape
Rubber-tipped massage stick	Plastic vitamin bottle
Roller massage stick	Roller massage stick

10.9 Techniques for Self-Mobilization

To find the tenderness associated with your running injury, you'll use your mobilization tools to **roll** and **strum** over and around each region that you think is affected. In physical therapy, **rolling** means pressing down on the tender soft tissue (muscle or tendon) with the mobilization tool and rolling it along the structure with a downward, twisting pressure. **Strumming** means moving the tool side-to-side, at right angles to the muscle fibers, like strumming a guitar. You can also alternate rolling and strumming by moving the tool in circles and by pressing down into the tissue from different angles. The idea is to find a motion and angle that reproduces the pain you felt while you were running, and that can reach and release the tightness in the muscle or tendon.

Once you have located a tender spot, you'll roll and strum with the mobilization tool while simultaneously *contracting and relaxing* the muscle in a specific pattern. To contract and relax the muscle effectively, you'll also have to do each self-mobilization in a specific position that allows you to really work the region.

You'll be doing each self-mobilization exercise for 30 seconds. Contract and squeeze the muscles in the region you are working on for a count of 3, then relax for a count of 7, then repeat. Do three 10-second sets, alternating contraction and relaxation. Learning to do this while rolling and strumming at the same time may take some practice, but you'll be able to feel when you're doing it right.

Make sure to use enough pressure to evoke a low level of pain, and search for tender points that evoke slightly more pain than other areas. Look for tender spots that correlate to regional stiffness in your stretches. Work with it. Don't bruise yourself, but don't be afraid of changing things a little bit. Find the approach that works best for you.

10.10 Guidelines for Self-Mobilization

When you're doing self-mobilizations, what is normal for you to feel, and how can you know if you're doing it correctly? Here are some general guidelines:

1. More is not better: It's about the quality of effort, not the quantity. Don't spend all day on it or apply all your might to it. Think about what you're doing. Try to pinpoint the tenderness and reproduce the pain you felt while running. What are you trying to free up? Can you feel a tight, sore spot in the injured region? Are you hitting the target tissue? You have to focus precisely on what you're doing.

2. *Don't hurt yourself:* The goal of feeling for tenderness is to locate the restriction. When you locate it, you'll feel some pain due to the tightness and stiffness. Once you find the restriction, you shouldn't push your pain level to more than 5 or 6 out of 10 (where 0 is no pain and 10 is the worst pain you can imagine).

3. *Don't force movement:* You're just trying to relax the tightness. Ease into it slowly as your body allows. Combine self-mobilization with stretches through the affected region. Your goal is to achieve *symmetry*, which means that you should have the same mobility in the affected leg as in the unaffected leg.

4. *Check your results:* When you're done, recheck the tissue. Don't just rub it. You have to move it and feel it. Do your stretching exercises again. Can you feel a difference from where you started? Can you feel the region loosening up? Do you have a better range of motion?

5. *Take notes:* Complete the Mobility Self-Assessment (*Self-Assessment 2A* in the *Workbook*). Mastering self-mobilizations and stretches are an important part of your clearance to move forward through the phases.

* * *

Box 10-2

HOW TO:
Self-Mobilizations

General Instructions:

1. Collect your mobilization tools **[*Table 10-1*]**.

2. Using the mobilization tool, locate one point of tenderness in the affected region. Try different angles to pinpoint the area of restriction.

3. Press deeply into the tender spot with the mobilization tool, and release the restrictions using rolling and strumming movements.

4. While you are rolling and strumming, alternately contract the muscle for 3 seconds and relax it for 7 seconds. Repeat 3 times for a total of 30 seconds for each exercise.

5. Work at a pain threshold of about 5 or 6 out of 10. You want to press hard enough to release the tightness and restriction, but not hard enough to bruise.

6. Start with the tenderest spot in the affected region, then move on to other tender spots in the same region. Do not repeat self-mobilization on the same spot during the same P.T. session.

Region 1: Toe Mobilizations

Self-Mob 10-1: Toe 1

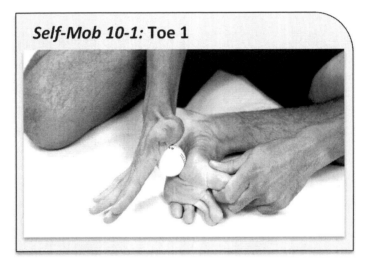

Mobilization Tool	Golf ball
Starting Position	Sitting, pull the big toe back until the tendon is exposed.
Action	1. Press the ball into the tender area of the bottom of the toe while extending the big toe up and out. Roll and strum. 2. Contract and relax the muscle by flexing the toe against your hand.

Self-Mob 10-2: Toe 2

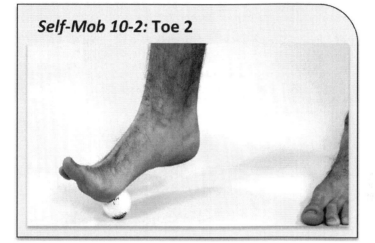

Mobilization Tool	Golf ball
Starting Position	Standing, flex the big toe up until the tendon is exposed.
Action	1. Press your foot into the golf ball and roll the ball under the tender spot on the bottom of the big toe while extending the toes. Roll and strum. 2. Contract and relax the muscle by alternately pointing and flexing the toes.

Region 2: Arch Mobilizations

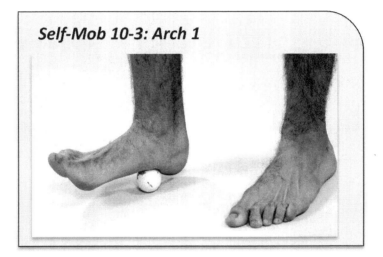

Self-Mob 10-3: Arch 1

Mobilization Tool	Golf ball
Starting Position	Standing, flex toes up and press the arch of your foot into the golf ball.
Action	1. Keeping the foot flexed, press and roll the ball under the tender spot in the arch of the foot. 2. Contract and relax the muscle by alternately pointing and flexing the foot.

Self-Mob 10-4: Arch 2

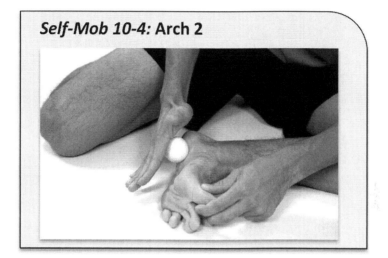

Mobilization Tool	Golf ball
Starting Position	Sitting, flex the foot and pull back on the big toe.
Action	1. Keeping the foot and toe stretched, press and roll the golf ball in circular movements over the tender spot in the arch. 2. Contract and relax the muscle by alternately pointing and flexing the toe.

Region 3: Heel Mobilization

Self-Mob 10-5: Heel 1

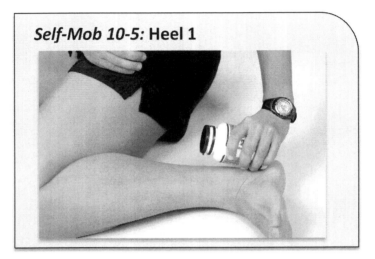

Mobilization Tool	Vitamin bottle
Starting Position	Sitting, press the bottom edge of a vitamin bottle into the Achilles tendon.
Action	1. Try different angles and positions to locate the tender part of the heel. 2. Contract and relax the muscle by alternately flexing and extending the foot.

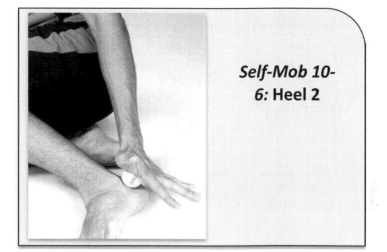

*Self-Mob 10-
6:* **Heel 2**

Mobilization Tool	Golf ball
Starting Position	Sitting, press the ball into the Achilles tendon.
Action	1. Roll the ball along the outer border of the heel and Achilles tendon. 2. Contract and relax the muscle by alternately flexing and extending the foot.

Region 4: Shin Mobilization

Self-Mob 10-7: Shin 1

Mobilization Tool	Golf ball
Starting Position	Sitting with legs crossed, press the ball into the muscle along the outer side of the shin.
Action	1. Pressing in, roll the ball up and down alongside the outer shin. 2. Contract and relax the muscle by flexing and extending your foot.

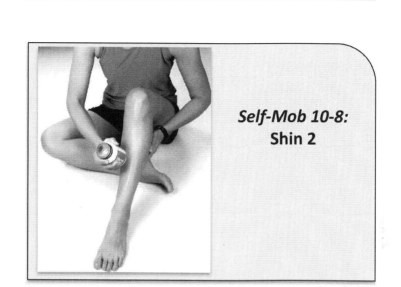

Self-Mob 10-8:
Shin 2

Mobilization Tool	Vitamin bottle
Starting Position	Sitting with legs crossed, press the bottom edge of a vitamin bottle along the muscle along the inner side of the shin.
Action	1. Try different points along the inner side of the shin to find the soreness. 2. Contract and relax the muscle by flexing and extending your foot.

Region 5: Calf Mobilization

Self-Mob 10-9: Calf 1

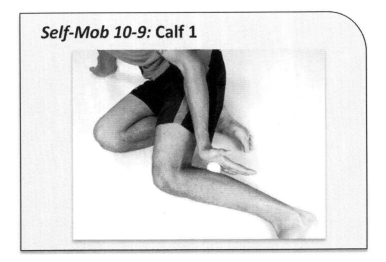

Mobilization Tool	Golf ball
Starting Position	Sitting, flex the foot and press the ball into the calf.
Action	1. Press the ball into the tender spots in the calf muscle. Roll and strum. 2. Contract and relax the muscle by flexing and extending the foot.

Self-Mob 10-10:
Calf 2

Mobilization Tool	Roller massage stick
Starting Position	1. Kneeling on one knee, press the roller stick into the calf. 2. Place weight on the forward leg and move the knee slightly forward to stretch the calf.
Action	1. Press the knobby edges of the rollers into the tender spots of the calf. Try different angles to find the soreness. Roll and strum. 2. Contract and relax the muscle by alternately flexing and extending the foot.

Region 6: Knee Mobilization

Self-Mob 10-11: Knee 1

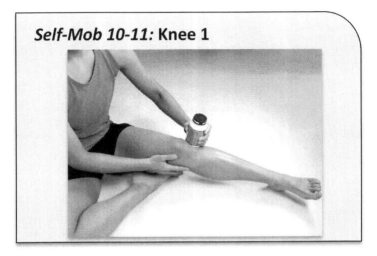

Mobilization Tool	Vitamin bottle
Starting Position	Sitting with your leg extended, press the bottom edge of a vitamin bottle into the tendon on the outer side of the knee and around the kneecap.
Action	1. Try different positions and angles to find the tightness and soreness. 2. Contract and relax the muscle by tightening the knee to straighten it and squeeze the knee tight.

Region 7: Band Mobilization

Self-Mob 10-12: Band 1

Mobilization Tool	Roller massage stick
Starting Position	Lying on your back, pull one leg up and across your body, keeping the knee straight.
Action	1. Press the knobby edges of the rollers into the tender spots along the outer thigh from hip to knee. Roll and strum. 2. Contract and relax the muscle by squeezing the buttock, and by straightening the knee and squeezing it tight.

Self-Mob 10-13: Band 2

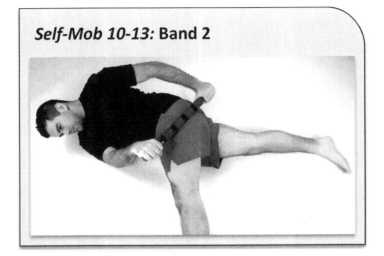

Mobilization Tool	Roller massage stick
Starting Position	Lying on your back, pull one leg up and across your body, keeping the knee straight.
Action	1. Press the knobby edges of the rollers into the tender spots in the gluteal region. Roll and strum. 2. Contract and relax the muscle by squeezing the buttock while bending and straightening the knee in a small range of motion.

Self-Mob 10-14: Band 3

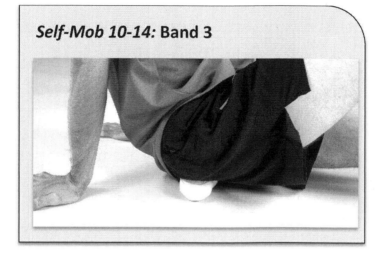

Mobilization Tool	Tennis ball
Starting Position	Sitting, position the tennis ball under one buttock with your knee bent and the opposite leg straight.
Action	1. Sit on the tennis ball to press it into the areas of soreness in the hip/gluteal region. Roll and strum. 2. Contract and relax the muscle by squeezing the buttock tightly.

Region 8: Hamstring Mobilization

Self-Mob 10-15:
Hamstring 1

Mobilization Tool	Roller massage stick
Starting Position	Sitting, position one foot flat on the floor in front of you and bend the knee until you feel a stretch in the hamstrings.
Action	1. Press the knobby edges of the rollers into the tender spots of the hamstring muscles. Roll and strum. 2. Contract and relax the muscle by alternately flexing and extending the knee with the heel against floor.

Self-Mob 10-16: Hamstring 2

Mobilization Tool	Roller massage stick
Starting Position	Lying on your back, bend one knee up toward your chest until you feel a stretch in the hamstrings.
Action	1. Press the knobby edges of the rollers into the tender spots of the hamstring muscles. Roll and strum. 2. Contract and relax the muscle by alternately bending and straightening the knee.

Region 9: Hip Mobilization

Self-Mob 10-17: Hip

Mobilization Tool	Tennis ball
Starting Position	Lying on your back with one leg straight and the opposite knee bent, place the tennis ball in the crease of the hip.
Action	1. Continue pulling your knee up toward your chest to compress the tennis ball into the hip. Move the tennis ball around a little to find the sore point. 2. Contract and relax the muscle by using hip muscles to squeeze the ball into the pelvis.

Region 10: Buttock Mobilization

Self-Mob 10-18: Butt 1

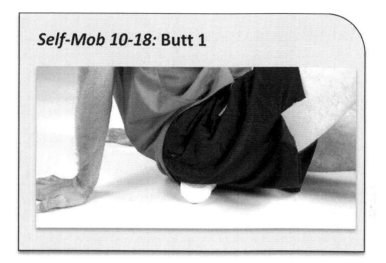

Mobilization Tool	Tennis ball
Starting Position	Sitting, position the tennis ball under one buttock with your knee bent and the opposite leg straight.
Action	1. Sit on the tennis ball to press it into the area of soreness in the hip/gluteal region.
	2. Contract and relax the muscle by squeezing the buttock tightly.

Self-Mob 10-19: Butt 2

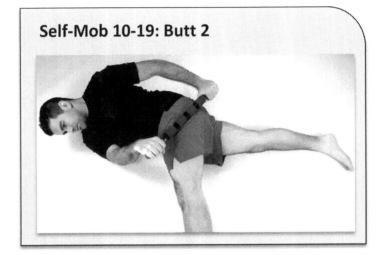

Mobilization Tool	Roller massage stick
Starting Position	Lying on your back, pull one leg up and across your body, keeping the knee straight.
Action	1. Press the knobby edges of the rollers into the tender spots in the gluteal region. Roll and strum. 2. Contract and relax by simultaneously squeezing the buttock tightly and bending and straightening your knee in a small range of motion.

Chapter 11
Keep It Moving:
Stretching and Flexibility

In the early 1990s, P.T. practices were changing with the advent of referral for profit. Doctors began setting up their own P.T. clinics (known as physician-owned physical therapy services or POPTS) in order to increase their financial profits. My office got busy, and still is busy today, with patients who went to POPTS and got very little treatment other than electrical stimulation, heat, ice, and redundant exercise. It's an easy kind of therapy to do, cheap to implement, and provides a minimal service based on the doctors' orders. Usually, the outcomes at POPTS are fine. As long as the patient has an easy problem, they'll get better no matter what the therapist does. The trouble is, if it's a complex problem, those passive treatments aren't going to take care of it. Doctors know that, and P.T.s know that.

Around that time, I was seeing so many new patients whose problems had not been properly addressed by POPTS that I was working 50 hours a week at my clinic. I liked my work, but the politics involved (and, frankly, the impression that some of the medical

167

community were placing financial gain above patient welfare) was getting me down. I needed something to cheer me up. I needed a new challenge – and that's how I got into triathlon.

Starting triathlon at a time when there was no Internet and few books on training for newcomers, I had the good fortune to meet "Jose" – a member of the Miami Runners Club and a great athlete. He came to me as a patient with chronic hamstring tears that limited his running, along with chronically disabling low back pain. He had multiple old rips in his back and leg muscles, and his legs were as stiff as could be. He couldn't reach, and he couldn't bend. I loosened Jose up and taught him how to take care of his back – how to keep it moving with stretching and flexibility exercises – and Jose taught me how to do triathlon. It turned out to be a great discovery for both of us.

Triathlon, of course, combines distance events in running, biking, and swimming. My running was okay (when I wasn't injured), and Jose helped me start working my way up from shorter to longer distances. I already loved biking, and triathlon really taught me the importance of correctly fitting a bike to a person's unique body mechanics. My main problem was, I could hardly swim. Jose introduced me to some great triathlon coaches and athletes who taught me how to swim, and I taught them how to do self-mobilizations and improve their flexibility.

You can see a trend here. Learning triathlon became another opportunity for me to work with athletes and teach them self-help skills. With Jose's encouragement, I created a class called *Myofascial*

Reorganization which combined self-mobilization and stretching exercises with body awareness and positive affirmation for improved performance. That class became very popular, and not just with triathletes. I taught it at races, I taught it to pros, and I taught it to cycling clubs and other athletic organizations. It was a great experience. My life got busier, and I learned some very valuable lessons that helped me grow professionally as I became more involved in triathlon races.

In this chapter, you'll learn some of the elements I teach in my Myofascial Reorganization class, focused on how they are used in running-injury management. Specifically, you'll learn how to use stretching exercises combined with self-mobilization to zero in on the location of your running injury, to treat the injury by releasing the tightness and stiffness, and to evaluate your progress throughout your recovery program.

11.1 Stretching and Running Injuries

Runners are always talking about the best time to stretch. Is it when you're warmed up or cooled down? My advice has always been, the best time to stretch is now, and the worst time to stretch is later. You should always find some time to work on your flexibility.

The recovery period is a perfect time to locate your areas of stiffness and work them out. When you have a running injury, stretching has to be part of your recovery plan because there's always tissue scarring and a loss of flexibility (tightness and stiffness) associated with an injury. You need to work out the post-injury scarring, but it's also a great time to work out any old stiffness you've developed through habitual movement patterns. The truth is, repeating the same thing over and over again doesn't make you a better runner; it makes you less aware and more stiff and awkward. In Phase Two of your recovery program, you'll have the opportunity to loosen up that tightness.

During your recovery period we'll also be making certain intentional changes in your customary movement patterns – and that requires good flexibility. Even though these changes are temporary, they're an important part of your recovery program and you won't be able to perform them correctly if you're all stiff. In fact, any time you make a change in your movement patterns – whether it's a change in technique or a change in shoes – habitual stiffness can become a new source of stress. Improving your flexibility can reduce that problem.

So, while you're in recovery I want you to do all of the flexibility exercises in this book, even the ones that don't relate to your injury. Stretching gives you more freedom of movement, and that freedom of movement is going to allow you to improve your running form – which will in turn help you recovery from your injury.

11.2 Stretching and Running-Injury Prevention

We often hear that stretching is important to prevent running injuries, but here's the deal: stretching does not prevent running injuries. It never did. Why? Running is what we call a mid-range activity. You don't need to stretch beyond your normal range of motion to run. You need to stretch to do gymnastics, or to kick a soccer ball, or to reach for a ball that's thrown or hit; but a mid-range movement such as walking or running does not require stretching. Therefore, stretching *per se* does not prevent running injuries.

In fact, an interesting sports-medicine statistic that's never been satisfactorily explained seems to indicate that runners who stretch have more injuries than runners who don't stretch. However, that doesn't imply cause and effect. I suspect the explanation is that runners who get injured go to healthcare professionals who teach them to do stretching exercises and, therefore, an injured runner would be more likely to stretch. In that survey, runners were asked "Do you stretch?" and "Have you been injured?" It didn't ask, "Did somebody teach you stretching exercises *because* you were injured?" The point is, when it comes to the *cause* of a running injury, whether or not you stretched beforehand is more or less irrelevant.

However, life requires stretching, so being really stiff actually does increase your risk for injuries in general. There is an important flexibility test that all healthcare professionals use, called the **straight-leg raise (SLR)**. You lie on your back, and your healthcare professional flexes your foot with the knee straight and sees how high up he can raise your leg. This simple maneuver involves the calves, hamstrings, hips, lower back, and all the other structures that limit straight-leg movement. The agreed upon standard is a straight-leg raise to 90 degrees. Whether you go to the orthopedist, the P.T., the athletic trainer, or the family doctor – we all do straight-leg raising, then we all say the same thing: "Oh, you're really stiff!"

* * *

Side Tracks: Yoga and Running Injuries (Why Swamis Didn't Run)

Patients often ask me if they should start doing yoga to help manage their running injury. I myself loved exploring yoga during my youth (in the '70s) and I incorporate aspects of yoga into my own training habits.

Traditional yoga was developed in India before the British colonization, as part of the physical, mental and spiritual rites of passage of adolescent, higher-caste male Hindus — not as therapy for runners. Today, yoga comes in many forms and variations, but none of them are specific to running injuries. In fact, the flexibility requirements, balance points and mental focus challenges for running injury recovery are very different from those in traditional yoga.

So, I say yoga is great, but it is of little benefit in helping you recover from your running injury because it is non-specific to your injury. Focus first on the skills and habits you need to recover from your running injury, and then take up yoga.

So, I teach all my patients certain exercises and stretches that will bring them up to a straight-leg raise at 90 degrees. Doing these exercises might not prevent running injuries, but it absolutely helps with other injuries that can affect your running, such as low back injuries and reaching injuries. If you're all stiff and have trouble reaching, and you reach and hurt your back, then you'll have back pain when you run. It's not really a running injury, but it can definitely contribute to a running injury.

11.3 Diagnosing Running Injuries

The medical definitions of traumatic strains and sprains have always been a puzzle to me. In physics, a strain is a force that a structure is receiving, and the damage to a structure resulting from excessive strain is called a failure. When the same thing happens to a muscle, however, we call the failure or injury of a structure due to excessive force a strain. In my earliest training, I remember P.T.s wanting so badly to define the force (such as running) as the strain, and call the effect on the region (the injury) the sprain. Of course we couldn't do it because that would mean changing the entire industry, so we use the term **sprain** for a failure of the ligaments (the fibrous, noncontractile tissues that hold the joints together), and the term **strain** for a failure of the muscle (contractile tissues). That's just the way it is. Either way, what it comes down to is a failure in the tissues.

In injury management, our main concern is not whether it's a muscle or a ligament that's been ripped; it's how severe the rip is. Microscopic tearing presents a different clinical picture than larger scale (**macroscopic**) ripping into the tissue structure – whether the rip is partial or complete. If the tissue is ripped completely, it kind of doesn't matter whether you've ripped your hamstring or another associated tissue – it's a really bad injury! Compared to that, a microscopic injury isn't so bad.

Diagnoses of running injuries are generally based on clinical exams because running injuries are not big, traumatic injuries; they're microscopic, nontraumatic injuries that tend not to image very well in diagnostic tests. Sometimes we can reconfirm them with MRI, but identifying a microscopic injury usually requires a careful, hands-on examination.

When self-assessing your own running injury, you'll use specific exercises to identify the damage and dysfunction caused by your particular injury. In the previous chapter, you learned how to use self-mobilization techniques to pinpoint areas of tenderness. In this chapter, you'll learn how to use stretching exercises to locate specific regions of stiffness. In later chapters, you'll learn how to use closed-chain exercises to find areas of weakness. As you progress through the phases of recovery, you'll learn to understand your injury and monitor your recovery process by re-assessing these areas of tenderness, stiffness, and weakness.

11.4 Introduction to P.T. Time

In your individualized self-management program, **P.T. Time** is the time you'll spend at home doing some of the things you might normally pay a physical therapist to do, such as icing, self-mobilizations, and stretching. When you choose to manage your running injury on your own, that means you've made a commitment to learn the techniques required to become your own physical therapist. Yes, it is a lot of work, but it's well worth the effort. To help motivate yourself, just imagine how much time and money you can save by not having to visit a physical therapist's office every day!

In Phase Two of your recovery program, you'll need to make a regular appointment with yourself every day for one hour of P.T. Time, consisting of self-mobilizations and stretches (and icing if needed). Your individual program will differ depending upon which of the two recovery groups you are in *(Table 11-1)*. Your recovery group is based upon the severity of your original injury, which you will determine during your initial self-assessment (*Self-Assessment 1* in the *Workbook*).

Group 1 (those with no Red Flags) will do stretching and self-mobilization daily, for 60 minutes a day, focusing on their affected region or regions. *Group 2* (those with Red Flags) will do 40 minutes of stretching and self-mobilization a day, followed by 20 minutes of icing for a total of 60 minutes P.T. Time. Group 2 must continue to ice daily for a minimum of two weeks before starting Phase Three closed-chain exercises, to make sure that all traces of inflammation are completely gone. Even if you don't see any obvious signs of inflammation, I don't want you to start weight-bearing exercises while the tissues are still irritable. That's a common mistake that runners make. They try to do too much too soon, and they end up swelling up and have to start all over again.

Table 11-1
Guidelines: Phase Two

	Group 1	Group 2
Phase Two Groups *(Self-Assessment 2B)*	Group 1 in Phase One **AND** *No Red Flags or visible swelling*	Group 2 in Phase One **AND** *No Red Flags or visible swelling*
PT Time	*Stretch/Mobilization Cycles* for affected and unaffected regions, 60 minutes per day (**Log Form C**).	1. *Stretch/Mobilization Cycles* for affected and unaffected regions, 40 minutes per day (**Log Form C**). 2. Continue ICE 20 minutes per day for a total of 2 weeks in Phase Two (**Log Form I**).
Phase Two Clearance *(Self-Assessment 2C)*	Cleared self-mobilizations and stretches as required for simple or complex injuries [*Table 11-2*].	1. All inflammation is cleared. 2. Completed 2 weeks of ICE in Phase Two. 3. Cleared all self-mobilizations and stretches as required for simple or complex injuries [*Table 11-2*].

Within each group, your goals for reaching *clearance* in Phase Two will also differ depending on whether your injury is simple or complex *(Table 11-2)*, which you will determine in your *Mobility Self-Assessment* (*Self-Assessment 2B* in the *Workbook*), using the principles introduced in this chapter.

If you are in Group 1 and have a *simple* running injury, you may be able to clear Phase Two with only one or two sessions of P.T. Time. This subgroup is not icing, and only has to improve flexibility in one affected region to achieve clearance.

If you are in Group 1 and have a *complex* injury (involving two or more regions, or other pre-existing medical conditions), you won't be icing, but you will have extra work to do. All complex injuries require more recovery time because they involve more complex tissue-mobility problems. An injury or disease in one region tends to play off another, and can affect areas outside of the primary injury region in ways that are unique to you as an individual.

If you are in Group 2 and have a *simple* injury, you will have to ice for at least two weeks before clearing Phase Two, but you will only have to improve your flexibility in one affected region.

If you are in Group 2 and have a *complex* injury, you must ice for two weeks, and you must meet all of the clearance requirements for complex injuries. Generally, those with complex injuries (whether in Group 1 or Group 2) require two weeks of daily P.T. Time to completely *master* each of the thirteen stretching exercises (achieve symmetry and a full range of motion on both sides) in order to clear Phase Two.

Table 11-2 A
Guidelines for Simple Injuries

Phase Two Recovery Subgroup *(Self-Assessment 2B)*	One nontraumatic running injury, in one region. **AND** No pre-existing injury or medical condition that affects your running.
Focus	Identify one region to focus on.
Goal	Limber up the affected leg and achieve *symmetrical* range of motion with the unaffected leg.
Guidelines	1. Go directly to the tenderest spots in the affected region that correlate with the greatest restriction and loss of movement. 2. As you clear the greatest restriction, progress to other tender spots in the affected region that correlate with other loss of movement. 3. Explore all stretches, but focus on one injury region.

Table 11-2 B

Guidelines for Complex Injuries

Phase Two Treatment Subgroup *(Self-Assessment 2B)*	Injuries in 2 or more regions **OR** Pre-existing injuries **OR** Pre-existing medical condition that affects your running.
Focus	Explore all regions to find multiple areas of restriction.
Goal	Achieve *full* range of motion on both sides of the body, in all regions.
Guidelines	1. Go directly to the region that is the most tender and restricted. 2. Start with the area of greatest tenderness and tightest restriction in that region, then progress to other affected regions. 3. Progress from the most severe to the least severe tenderness in each affected region and stretch all restrictions in all regions. 4. Must be able to master all stretches and clear all regions.

11.5 Techniques and Goals for P.T. Time

In my P.T. clinic, there are thirteen different **stretching exercises** that I routinely use to treat running injuries. Each exercise focuses on one or more of our ten basic running-injury *regions* (toe, arch, heel, shin, calf, band, knee, hamstring, hip, and buttock). As in self-mobilizations, some stretching exercises will require some simple equipment (such as a rope, stick, or incline board) that you can buy or make at home *(Table 11-4)*. You'll also need an area next to a doorway where you can lie down.

Table 11-4
Equipment for Stretches

Professional Equipment	Home Alternatives
Incline board	21.5" x 17" x 0.75" plywood propped on a half cinder block
Stretching rope	Belt
Massage stick	Heavy coat-hanger

In Phase Two, stretching and self-mobilization exercises will be used in combination for two related tasks: we use them to evaluate the regions and complexity of your injury, and as a method of treating the stiffness and loss of mobility caused by your injury.

First, you'll use stretching exercises to identify and pinpoint your injury regions (**affected regions**) *(Table 11-3)*, and to identify any other areas of stiffness or muscle imbalance (**unaffected regions**) that you'll focus on during your recovery program. In your *Mobility Self-Assessment (Self-Assessment 2A* in the *Workbook)*, you'll perform each of the thirteen stretching exercise for 30 seconds, and note particular areas of pain, stiffness, and asymmetry on your *Mobility Self-Assessment Worksheet*. Remember, there is always some stiffness involved in an injury or dysfunction, so look for the stiffnesses that are significant to your injury. Compare your left and right sides for symmetry in flexibility and range of motion. These areas will correspond with regions of tenderness you'll work on later in your regional self-mobilizations.

Your main goal in Phase Two is to treat the scarring and stiffness and restore a normal range of motion to the injured area. You'll be doing dynamic, progressive flexibility training – pulling muscles, tendons and ligaments apart. If you are in Group 1 (no Red Flags) you'll begin by stretching quite aggressively to free up the tightness and restrictions.

You should always do your stretching and self-mobilization exercises in the order of severity of your symptoms. The order in which you do your stretches may change as different regions improve at different paces.

Table 11-3: Injury Regions and Stretches

STRETCHES		REGIONS									
		1 Toe	2 Arch	3 Heel	4 Shin	5 Calf	6 Knee	7 Band	8 Hams	9 Hip	10 Butt
11-1	Wall/Toe Stretch with Rope	X									
11-2	Wall Calf Stretch with Rope			X	X	X					
11-3	Wall Hamstring Stretch								X		
11-4	Ankle-Knee Wall Stretch				X	X	X		X	X	X
11-5	Toes to Nose Stretch	X	X	X	X	X			X		
11-6	Toes to Nose, Belt Stretch			X	X	X			X		

(Table 11-3 cont.)

STRETCHES		REGIONS									
		1 Toe	2 Arch	3 Heel	4 Shin	5 Calf	6 Knee	7 Band	8 Hams	9 Hip	10 Butt
11-7	Straight-Leg Raise, Belt Stretch			X	X	X		X	X		
11-8	Straight-Leg Raise, Belt Stretch to Side							X			X
11-9	Cross-Leg Side Bend							X			X
11-10	Side Quadriceps Stretch						X			X	
11-11	Ankle-Knee Diagonal Stretch									X	X
11-12	Pelvic Stretch									X	
11-13	Back Incline Stretch		X	X	X	X					

If you are in Group 2 (with Red Flags), you'll be icing for 20 minutes at the end of your P.T. Time, for at least the first two weeks. In some cases, you may be able to combine your icing with some of your stretches. Since you'll be keeping the affected leg in an ICE position for a prolonged period of time, you might as well stretch the muscles while you're doing it. Don't start stretching aggressively until Stage 5 symptoms pass, and/or any Stage 4 medication is out of your system. When you are at Stage 3 or lower, you can start stretching more aggressively.

For both groups, your P.T. Time in Phase Two will consist of performing all thirteen stretching exercises (in the order determined in *Self-Assessment 2*) alternating with self-mobilizations in a very specific **Stretch/ Mobilization Cycle [Box 11-1]**, which will be different for affected and unaffected regions. You'll do one *Stretch/Mobilization Cycle* for each of the thirteen stretching exercises on your list.

Each *Stretch/Mobilization Cycle* for an exercise in an *affected region* consists of five 1-minute stretches, alternating with four 30-second self-mobilizations, for a total of 7 minutes. If you find that five repeats are not enough to loosen up a particularly tight area, you can build up to ten repeats. The goal is not for you to do more exercises, it's to get rid of the stiffness and to achieve symmetry and range of motion.

You'll also be doing stretches for areas that are not involved in your injury, to help correct any habitual stiffness or asymmetry. Each *Stretch/Mobilization Cycle* for an exercise in an *unaffected region* will consist of a 30-second stretch and 30 seconds of self-mobilization.

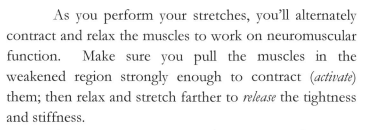
As you perform your stretches, you'll alternately contract and relax the muscles to work on neuromuscular function. Make sure you pull the muscles in the weakened region strongly enough to contract (*activate*) them; then relax and stretch farther to *release* the tightness and stiffness.

As you do each *Stretch/Mobilization Cycle*, you should always be re-evaluating the stiffness and tenderness in your injured region and comparing it with the same region on the other side of your body (*i.e.* compare the left leg with the right leg) and record your progress on your log form for Phase Two *Stretch/Mobilization Cycles (Log Form C* in the *Workbook*). If you have a simple injury, you can progress to Phase Three when you've achieved symmetry of mobility in the affected region, with equal range of motion on both sides of your body. If your injury is complex, you can progress to Phase Three when you've mastered all the stretches and have achieved symmetry and full range of motion in *all* regions (*Self-Assessment 2C* in the *Workbook*).

Once you have achieved the flexibility required for your group in Phase Two, your job is to maintain that flexibility as you progress through the phases, using a somewhat shorter and easier program. In Phases Three and Four, you'll continue with P.T. Time only two times per week, and record your results on a simpler *Log Form M: Maintaining Mobility* (in the *Workbook*). You can also start following the simpler instructions for *Stretch Mobilization Cycles for Unaffected Regions* [**Box 11-1B**] for all regions.

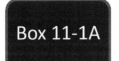

Box 11-1A Stretch/Mobilization Cycles for *Affected Regions*

1. Stretch
- Begin with the first stretch on your list of *affected regions*, following the instructions for that exercise.
- Perform the stretch for 10 seconds:
  -*Contract* the muscle for 3 seconds.
  -*Relax* the muscle and move deeper into the stretch.
  -*Hold* the stretch for 7 seconds.
- Repeat the *same* stretch (*contract, relax, hold*) 6 times for a total of 1 minute. Move deeper into the stretch each time you relax.

2. Self-Mobilization
- Choose a self-mobilization for your injury region.
- Use the mobilization tool to find the *tenderest* spot in the *affected region*.
- Following the instructions, use your mobilization tool to roll and strum the tender spot.
- While rolling and strumming, *contract* the muscle for 3 seconds, and *relax* the muscle for 7 seconds.
- Repeat 3 times for a total of 30 seconds.

3. Repeat
- Repeat *Part 1*, doing the *same* stretch.
- Repeat *Part 2*, but do self-mobilization on a *different* tender spot in the same region.
- Repeat the *same* stretch (*Part 1*) for a total of five times, alternating with four self-mobilizations (begin and end the cycle with the stretch).

4. Start the cycle over with the next stretch on your list of exercises for *affected regions*.

| Box 11-1B | Stretch/Mobilization Cycles for *Unaffected Regions* |

1. Stretch
- Begin with the first stretch on your *unaffected regions* list, following the instructions for that exercise.
- Perform the stretch for 10 seconds:
  -*Contract* the muscle for 3 seconds.
  -*Relax* the muscle and move deeper into the stretch.
  -*Hold* the stretch for 7 seconds.
- Repeat the *same* stretch (*contract, relax, hold*) 3 times for a total of 30 seconds. Move deeper into the stretch each time you relax.

2. Self-Mobilization
- Do self-mobilizations on any stretch that you find particularly difficult, or where you find tenderness that corresponds to stiffness.
- Stretch, do 30 seconds of self-mobilizations, then repeat the stretch to see if it has loosened up.

3. Repeat steps 1 and 2 with a *different* stretch. Cycle through the remaining stretches on your *unaffected regions* list until you have completed your P.T. Time.

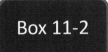

HOW TO:
Box 11-2 | Stretching Exercises

General Instructions:

1. For each session of *P.T. Time*, do all thirteen stretching exercises in the order determined by your *Mobility Self-Assessment* (in the *Running Injury Recovery Program Workbook*).

2. Combine each stretch with regional self-mobilizations, following the Stretch/Mobilization Cycles for your particular affected and unaffected regions.

3. Follow the instructions for each exercise carefully.

4. For symmetry, repeat each stretching exercise (except incline stretch) with both legs or on both sides.

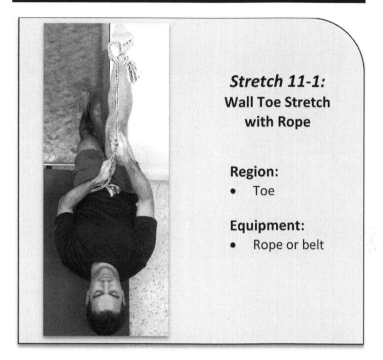

Stretch 11-1:
Wall Toe Stretch
with Rope

Region:
- Toe

Equipment:
- Rope or belt

Starting Position	1. Lie on your back in an open doorway, one leg raised straight against the wall, the other leg flat. 2. Tie a loop in the rope and slip it over your big toe.
Action	1. Pull the big toe back with the foot flexed, while slightly bending and straightening your knee. 2. Contract by pointing the toe into the belt. 3. Relax by using the belt to flex the toe and move the leg closer to the wall. Hold the deeper stretch position.

189

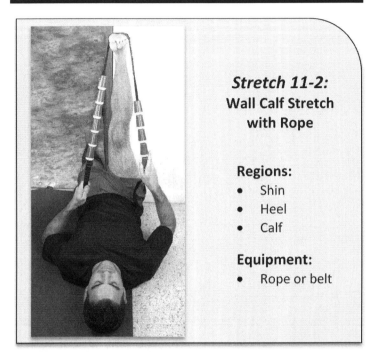

Stretch 11-2:
Wall Calf Stretch
with Rope

Regions:
- Shin
- Heel
- Calf

Equipment:
- Rope or belt

Starting Position	1. Lie on your back in an open doorway, one leg raised straight against the wall, the other leg flat. 2. Loop the belt around the ball of the raised foot.
Action	1. Flex the toes while straightening your knee against wall. 2. Contract by pushing your foot into the belt and straightening the knee. 3. Relax and pull the ankle deeper into the flex and your leg closer to the wall. Hold the deeper stretch position.

Stretch 11-3:
Wall Hamstring Stretch

Region:
- Hamstring

Equipment:
- None

Starting Position	Lie on your back in an open doorway, one leg raised straight against the wall, the other leg flat.
Action	1. Keeping the leg straight up against the wall, flex your foot (toes toward nose). 2. Contract by pushing your foot against the door frame. 3. Relax and move the leg closer to the wall. Hold the deeper stretch position.

Stretch 11-4: Ankle-Knee Wall Stretch

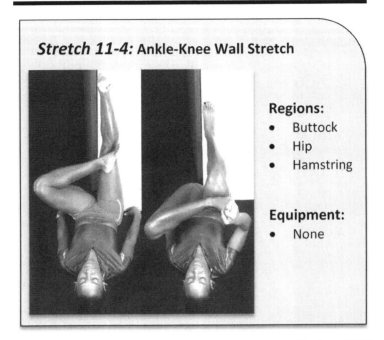

Regions:
- Buttock
- Hip
- Hamstring

Equipment:
- None

Starting Position	1. Lie on your back with your hips close to the wall. 2. Raise one leg straight up against the wall. 3. Cross the opposite ankle over the straight knee.
Action	1. Slowly bend the straight leg so the raised foot slides straight down the wall. Let both knees move toward the chest until you feel a stretch in the opposite hip. 2. Contract using the hip muscles to push the knee against the ankle. 3. Relax, slide the foot down the wall, and hold the deeper stretch position.

Stretch 11-5: Toes to Nose Stretch

Regions:
- Toe, arch, heel, shin, calf, knee, hamstring

Equipment:
- None

Starting Position	1. Lie on your back with both legs straight. Bend the knees slightly, with feet relaxed. 2. Grab behind one knee with both hands and raise that leg to a comfortable position, with the foot above your midline, keeping the knee slightly bent.
Action	1. With both hands behind the raised knee, flex the foot and toes toward your nose. 2. Straighten the knee, keeping the foot above your midline, maintaining the flex in your foot and toes. 3. Contract by straightening the knee and flexing the ankle (toes to nose). 4. Relax by bending the knee and relaxing the ankle. Hold the deeper stretch position.

Stretch 11-6: Toes to Nose, Belt Stretch

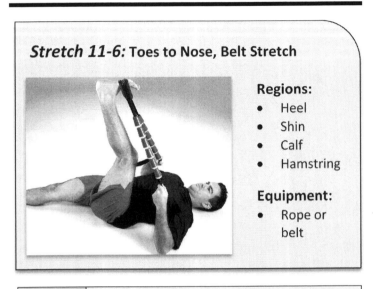

Regions:
- Heel
- Shin
- Calf
- Hamstring

Equipment:
- Rope or belt

Starting Position	1. Lie on your back with both legs straight. Bend the knees slightly, with feet relaxed. 2. Loop the belt around the ball of one foot and raise that leg to a comfortable position with the foot above your midline, keeping the knee slightly bent.
Action	1. Flex your toes to increase the stretch down the back of the leg. 2. Using the belt to maintain the flex in your foot, straighten the knee, keeping the foot above your midline. 3. Contract by pushing your foot into the belt and straightening your knee. 4. Relax by bending the knee. Hold the deeper stretch position.

Stretch 11-7: Straight-Leg Raise, Belt Stretch

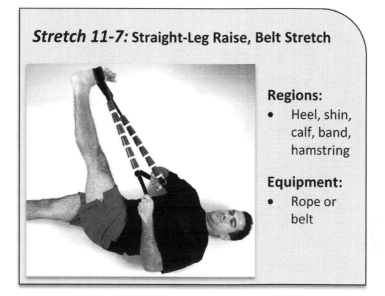

Regions:
- Heel, shin, calf, band, hamstring

Equipment:
- Rope or belt

Starting Position	1. Lie on your back with both legs straight.
	2. Loop the belt around one foot and pull the leg up, keeping the knee straight and the ankle flexed.
Action	1. Slightly rotate your hip so your toes point inward to increase the stretch along the side of your leg.
	2. Contract by straightening the knee and pushing the foot against the belt.
	3. Relax by bending the knee slightly. Hold the deeper stretch position.

Stretch 11-8: Straight-Leg Raise, Belt Stretch to Side

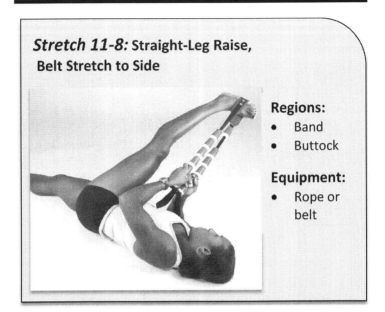

Regions:
- Band
- Buttock

Equipment:
- Rope or belt

Starting Position	1. Lie on your back with both legs straight. 2. Loop the belt around one foot and pull the leg up and across your body, keeping the knee straight and the ankle flexed.
Action	1. Turn your toes down towards the floor with your foot fully flexed. 2. Contract by using your hips to push your foot up into belt. 3. Relax and move the leg farther across your body. Hold the deeper stretch position.

Stretch 11-9:
Cross-Leg
Side Bend

Regions:
- Band
- Buttock

Equipment:
- None

Starting Position	1. Standing, cross one leg to the opposite side, keeping the back leg straight. 2. On the same side as the back leg, raise the arm overhead, keeping the body straight.
Action	1. Stretch to the side while pushing the hip outward. 2. Contract by pushing into the ground with the back leg and tightening the hip muscles. 3. Relax and bend farther sideways. Hold the deeper stretch position.

Stretch 11-10: Side Quadriceps Stretch

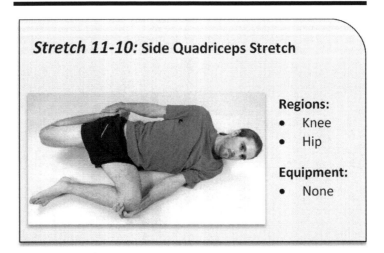

Regions:
- Knee
- Hip

Equipment:
- None

Starting Position	1. Lying on your side, use your lower hand to pull the lower knee forward, toward your chest. 2. Grasp the ankle of the upper leg with the other hand, flex the foot, and pull the upper leg backwards, toward your butt. 3. Keep your hips in line with your spine, and avoid twisting at the waist.
Action	1. Pull the back leg up toward your butt to stretch the front of the hip and knees. 2. Contract by tightening the knee and pushing the foot against your hand. 3. Relax the knee and pull the back leg farther toward the butt to stretch. Hold the deeper stretch position.

Stretch 11-11: Ankle-Knee Diagonal Stretch

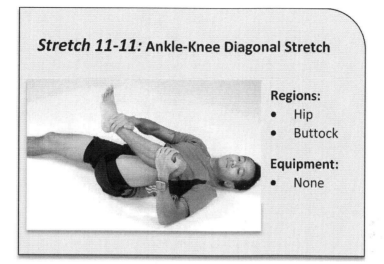

Regions:
- Hip
- Buttock

Equipment:
- None

Starting Position	1. Lie on your back with one leg straight. 2. Hold the bent knee up to your chest with one hand. 3. Grasp the outside of the ankle with the opposite hand.
Action	1. Pull the ankle and knees diagonally across your body, toward the opposite hip, until you feel a stretch in your buttock. 2. While holding the stretch, contract by pushing the ankle and knee against your hands. 3. Relax the leg and bring it up higher. Hold the deeper stretch position.

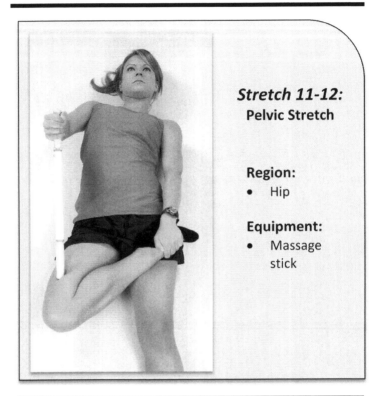

Stretch 11-12:
Pelvic Stretch

Region:
- Hip

Equipment:
- Massage stick

Starting Position	Lying down with one leg straight, pull the ankle of the other leg up to the opposite hip, forming a figure "4."
Action	1. Use the massage stick to push the bent knee down toward the floor to stretch the front of your hip. 2. Contract by lifting the knee upward to push into the massage stick. 3. Relax and use the massage stick to push the leg farther down. Hold the deeper stretch position.

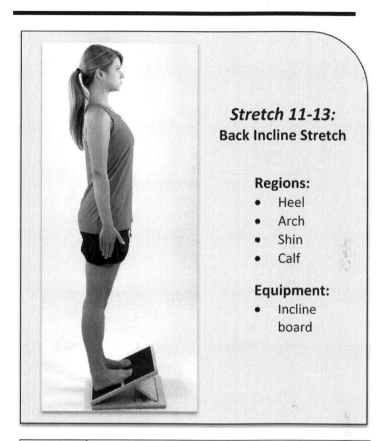

Stretch 11-13:
Back Incline Stretch

Regions:
- Heel
- Arch
- Shin
- Calf

Equipment:
- Incline board

Starting Position	Stand on an incline board, facing uphill, with feet and body straight.
Action	1. Balance your body evenly over both feet. 2. Contract and relax by pushing your feet into the incline board.

"The accumulated effect of psychological stressors (in and outside the athletic world) may cloud the mental functioning of the athlete and override physical conditioning enough to precipitate injury or prolong it."

– MJ Kelley, Jr., Journal of Sports Medicine and Physical Fitness

Chapter 12
The Psychology of Running Injuries

Sports psychologists believe that high levels of stress in any part of your life can reduce your ability to pay attention and focus on the task at hand. This in turn increases your risk of injury or reinjury during training, and can actually slow down your recovery time. In other words, anything that affects your brain affects how you train – and that includes all kinds of psychological influences.

Throughout post-injury training, you'll be focusing on locating and correcting the weakness and imbalance that caused (or was caused by) your injury. For example, during closed-chain exercises and glides you'll learn to control the weakness by balancing and progressively placing weight on your injury. You'll use neuromuscular re-education to improve the connections between your brain and your musculoskeletal system – to develop the mind-body connection. You have to feel it and consciously focus on it.

Any psychological factor that reduces your mental focus also reduces the effectiveness of your running injury recovery program. Throughout your recovery program, I want you to take the mental-focus factor very seriously. It takes an incredible amount of mental focus to maintain correct posture, balance, and control while simultaneously performing complex strengthening exercises and concentrating on your injury. It also takes a strong mental focus to conscientiously follow through with all the phases of your running injury recovery program. Consider it as a higher level of challenge!

12.1 The Psychodynamics of Group Running

Running can be a solitary sport, yet most runners run in some kind of group at least part of the time. It might be a group led by a professional coach – such as a school group, running club, or professional competitive organization – or it might be just a few friends running together.

Running with any group has lots of benefits. It provides a support system, encourages healthy competition, and it can be a great social activity. The downside is, if you normally run as part of a group, or with a coach, and suddenly you can't run due to a running injury, you'll also experience some psychological stress from being away from your group or mentor.

Nevertheless, while you're in this period of post-injury training, I don't want you in group training, and I don't want you being coached. I want you to concentrate fully on your running injury recovery program, and on overcoming your running injury.

If the thought of being away from your group or coach really bothers you – that's exactly what I'm talking about. Let's take a moment to understand why, psychologically, it's so hard to stay away and focus on your recovery.

First, people in running groups become really close friends, and that's a good thing – it pulls the group together. The *bad* thing is, when you're injured, you really miss your friends and want to be with them, which can lead to denial. You're tempted to ignore your injury, or take meds for the pain, in order to stay with your group, and that only makes your injury worse.

Second, the physical pain and stress of running causes your body to respond by releasing "happy" chemicals that promote feelings of excitement, euphoria, and emotional bonding – much like the psychological changes that soldiers go through during prolonged combat deployments. Specifically, we're talking about three **neurotransmitters** – chemicals that send messages through your nervous system and affect your brain.

The first neurotransmitter, adrenaline, is the hormone that revs you up for "fight or flight." Your heart beats faster, your senses get sharper, and you're primed to go. Adrenaline kicks in early, even before you start your run, in anticipation of a physical stress.

Second are the endorphins, which work as natural pain relievers. They make us a little goofy and silly as they help us deal with the pain and exertion of running. Endorphins are released during long, continuous workouts.

Our third neurotransmitter, oxytocin, is also released during long runs. Oxytocin has been called the "love hormone." It promotes intimate feelings of social contentment such as the emotional bonding between mother and child; or pair bonding with your mate; and yes, even orgasm.

It's no wonder that people in long-distance running groups become so close. Your adrenalin gets you excited about running; endorphins give you the "runner's high;" and then the oxytocin kicks in. In other words, long-distance runners get excited, then they get high, then they fall in love! It's true! I've been coaching running groups for twenty-five years, and I've seen it happen many times.

That brings us to the subject of why you shouldn't be training with your coach while you are in this period of injury recovery. In my P.T. office I have a therapeutic relationship with my patients – similar to that of a psychotherapist, but much more hands-on. My patients trust me, not only for good professional advice, but also to help heal their bodies with competent manual skills. Like a psychotherapist, a good P.T. has to deal with transference, counter-transference, and all the other psychodynamics of therapeutic relationships.

Running coaches have the same kind of relationship with their runners. No matter what coaching style or method your coach uses, it's still a relationship where the coach holds the psychological position of authority and trust. However, your coach and your P.T. have different goals. The coach's job is to train you for maximum performance, while the P.T.'s job is to rehabilitate your injury. Receiving conflicting advice and training instructions from multiple sources can only increase your stress and slow your recovery progress.

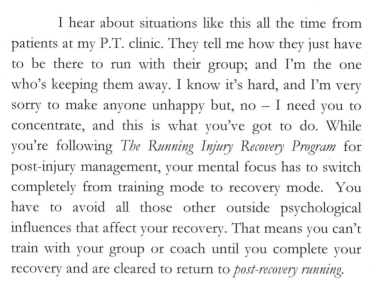

I hear about situations like this all the time from patients at my P.T. clinic. They tell me how they just have to be there to run with their group; and I'm the one who's keeping them away. I know it's hard, and I'm very sorry to make anyone unhappy but, no – I need you to concentrate, and this is what you've got to do. While you're following *The Running Injury Recovery Program* for post-injury management, your mental focus has to switch completely from training mode to recovery mode. You have to avoid all those other outside psychological influences that affect your recovery. That means you can't train with your group or coach until you complete your recovery and are cleared to return to *post-recovery running.*

12.2 The Fear Factor

Don't let the fear factor prevent you from getting prompt and effective treatment for your running injury. While everyone has some general fear of illness or serious injury, runners have the "double" fear that illness or injury might permanently prevent them from running. So much of a runner's life and self-identity revolves around running that a running injury can be psychologically devastating for any dedicated runner.

The danger is that the fear of "not running" can cloud your judgment and lead you to improperly manage an injury. This is especially true for any runner who has been injured and unable to run for a prolonged period of time. When a runner has spent a significant amount of time undergoing numerous diagnostic tests, and has endured a variety of different treatments from reputable doctors and P.T.s, and still ends up months later with no perceptible improvement, a despair can set in that leads to acts of desperation. Desperation to fix a running injury can drive runners to try any number of radical, experimental, or fringe-science treatments that range from the ineffective to the dangerous.

Don't allow the fear of long-term injury to escalate to despair and desperation. Most failed treatments stem from a lack of good running-management protocols among the healthcare community. I deal with other P.T.s' and medical doctors' "hopeless" cases all the time – and the problem is often just a case of misdiagnosis or lack of a good understanding of how to treat complex running injuries. The truth is, most running injuries can be successfully treated by a qualified professional without injections, surgery, or other extreme measures.

Another major fear factor that can result in improper injury management is denial. When a runner is injured, they may initially go into denial – an ineffective and potentially dangerous means of coping with the fear of permanent injury. Denial can cause you to ignore a simple injury, or to use medication to train through pain, which in turn can cause your injury to become worse.

Recognizing and accepting that every runner has the potential for injury is essential if you're going to approach these injuries responsibly. Part of this acceptance should include self-monitoring and prevention measures, along with a well-rounded training program. You need to learn the difference between the normal discomfort of training and the warning signs of an injury. It's important to address these warning signs as soon as possible, and not to ignore them. Denial of an injury feeds the runner's double fear. On the other hand, confronting your fear head-on is a healthy habit that promotes healing and an earlier return to running.

Here are three suggestions I can recommend to help alleviate the runner's double fear: One is having knowledgeable training partners and/or coaches who can help you avoid unnecessary injuries in the first place. Second is to have a back-up plan prepared for what to do in case of injury. That might include other exercise activities that you enjoy, such as spinning or swimming. Third is to keep a proper perspective on running. Maintaining healthy relationships with others outside of your running group can keep you from feeling psychologically isolated when you can't run with your group or coach.

As a runner, I've always shared the runner's double fear. As a young P.T. who specialized in running injuries, however, I developed an additional fear – the "triple fear" that my traditional sports-medicine education hadn't prepared me to effectively and specifically treat running injuries. I made it my professional goal to make sure that every injured runner who came to me got the best possible treatment and was given an opportunity to return to the sport we love.

Fortunately for me, my triple fear turned out to be a great inspiration for clinical research, teaching, and publication. Thirty years later, I can say that I *have* learned how to treat the injured runner quite specifically and effectively. By talking with and closely relating to each patient, one-on-one, I make sure that each person's individual needs are recognized. A thorough history and physical exam ensures that their injury is properly evaluated. For each individual, I develop a well-rounded treatment plan, organized into phases, that addresses the multiple components of their particular injury. In this way, I can help my patients overcome their fears and approach their injuries with optimism and the potential to become stronger, healthier, and safer runners. That's really what this book is all about.

12.3 Exercising Like a Meditation

What you are thinking about while you are running or exercising really does make a difference in your outcome. We call it **mental focus**, and it can encompass many things: While you're running, you can either focus on your running or on something else. You can have wide focus or a narrow focus. You can have an internal focus or an external focus.

An example of not focusing on your running would be listening to music while running, and purposely concentrating on the music to distract you from any pain. An example of external focus would be listening to your foot sounds while running. An example of internal focus would be paying attention to your balance. An example of a wide focus would be paying attention to your breathing, rhythm, pace, effort, and foot turnover. An example of narrow focus would be paying attention only to your strike pattern while running.

Throughout phases three and four of your recovery program, you will be doing exercises while using a **mental focus statement** that will help you concentrate on your goals, and actually make your workouts more effective. To help you find a focus that works for you during Phase Three, I have included a *general mental focus statement* in the instructions for each closed-chain exercise, fitness walking and glides. In Phase Four, your regional impairments will determine a *specific mental focus statement* which you will use during accelerations, hills, and plyometrics. (You'll prepare your specific mental focus statement in *Self-Assessment 31* in your *Workbook*.).

While doing each exercise, you should repeat the appropriate mental focus statement like a meditation mantra to help you create the ability to focus and to concentrate on doing the exercises correctly. You can expect to lose your concentration occasionally while exercising, and returning to your mental focus statement will help you regain your focus when you get distracted.

12.4 Keeping a Positive Attitude

As a running coach, I know how important a positive mental attitude is for athletic performance. It's much more than a winning attitude. I actively train my runners on *how* to focus on performance.

For performance, there is no right or wrong way to focus. For example, you might find a song you like that fits your marathon pace – just a few bars – and use that to readjust your pace. When you can't run any faster, you can focus on pumping your arms to increase your speed. You can focus on unnecessary muscle tension while running and get rid of it. When you're at a low spot in your marathon, you can focus on how happy you are to be there! Keeping a positive mental attitude is equally important for success in your running injury recovery program.

As a P.T., I can never say to my patients, "I can make you well and I'll never have to see you again." Likewise, in this book, I can't say, "Do what I tell you and you'll never have another running injury." Injuries happen, especially in the running world. What I can say is – if you keep a good attitude, stick with your recovery program, and focus on performing your exercises effectively – you should actually have a really good experience with your post-injury training. Learning the lessons in this book, and completing the steps of injury management in *The Running Injury Recovery Program Workbook*, will help you run better, and allow you to return to running with more enjoyment and greater confidence in your ability to reach for higher goals.

* * *

Chapter 13
Entering Phase Three:
Training Programs and Habits

The truth is, even the best athletes with the best coaching, the best training program, the best running shoes – the best everything possible – still get injured, even while their coaches are watching. As runners, we're always trying to challenge ourselves, to push ourselves beyond our limits, and that's when injuries occur. We fix them up, we learn from our mistakes, and we try to do better the next time.

I learned these lessons from my own coach, "Donna," a professional triathlete I met through the Miami Runners Club. I hired Donna to coach me through my first Ironman competition when I realized that I had no idea how to schedule that kind of time commitment and fit it into my work and family life. Donna taught me how to set goals and prepare a training program that made the best use of my time to get me where I needed to be for my race.

Not long after that Ironman, Donna and I met at another race where she was racing as a pro. After our training session, Donna told me she was suffering from iliotibial band (*ITB*) syndrome – which is pain on the

213

outside of the knee with weakness and tenderness that goes all the way up to the hip and buttock – and she didn't think she would be able to run her race the next day.

So I worked on her hip. I showed her where the weakness was. I released the muscles around her hip. I showed her how to ice to take the swelling out of the iliotibial band. The next morning, we ran together in the warmup, and she said her knee felt better. She ran a good race that day, and came in third – not bad considering that one day before she'd felt like she wouldn't be able to run at all. From that day on I became her therapist, and we worked together for many years. She taught me the habits that helped me manage my races, and I taught her the habits that helped her manage her injuries.

13.1 Running Habits and Running Injuries

More running injuries occur during training than in racing. Racing may be the goal of training, but no matter how you look at it, you spend way more hours training than racing, so there are just more opportunities for injuries while you're training. Running injuries can be caused by training too hard, or by not training hard enough, or by a combination of both that results in inconsistent training.

It takes many, many hours of running to become a really good runner. If you don't run enough, you're going to become injury-prone *because* you're not running enough. The idea that runners sometimes have to do more, not less, to reduce their risk of injury may seem like a strange concept, but I often see young athletes who are

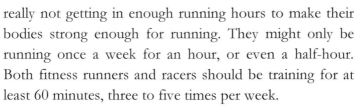
really not getting in enough running hours to make their bodies strong enough for running. They might only be running once a week for an hour, or even a half-hour. Both fitness runners and racers should be training for at least 60 minutes, three to five times per week.

On the other hand, you don't want to do too much training either. Overtraining just puts too much stress on your body. It's important to be consistent with the length of your training sessions, and to break up your training time over the week. I never like my runners to do more than half of their week's mileage in one run – that's just an invitation to injury. Spreading the training out promotes better running strength, and a certain amount of rest is essential for tissue repair and strengthening. How much rest you need depends on your individual body and your conditioning.

Overtraining is particularly risky for runners who are inexperienced. Most injuries occur during the first three years of running. That's how long it takes for your bones and muscles to reach peak condition. When an inexperienced runner puts in too much time – trying to do too much, too soon, too fast – his muscles will grow faster than his bones, and that increases the risk of a broken bone or stress fracture.

If you train correctly and consistently, put in the right number of running miles to condition your bones and muscles, and get through those first three years without an injury, then your risk of injury decreases. However, if an injury interrupts your training long enough – about six months – you'll have to start that three-year count all over again, and that can be frustrating.

A good post-injury training program will keep you going so you don't lose that conditioning and have to start over. This chapter introduces you to some of the basic concepts you'll use in Phase Three of your Running Injury Recovery Program. The details of how to perform the exercises will be found in upcoming chapters.

13.2 Elements of a Good Post-Injury Training Program

Individualized and Flexible: To deal with all your personal variables, a good training program must be individualized and flexible. Your program should be based on your individual needs and capabilities. A flexible program can be a moving target; it may change as your priorities change, or your physical condition changes. You should constantly monitor your progress and have objective checkpoints to help determine where you are in your program.

Set Goals: In a good training program, you have to set realistic goals. You have to ask yourself what you are training for, and how much work you have to do to reach that goal. Setting up goals helps you to optimize your time by doing the right amount of the right type of training. Each workout should also have a goal. For example, I can't just say, "Oh I'm just going to run today and do whatever my body tells me." Personally, my body never tells me to get out of bed and run. My body says stay in bed!

Balanced Quantity and Quality: One question that always factors into a training program is quantity versus quality. How much training should you do, and how hard or easy should you do it? Training too long or too often (or too little and too infrequently) is a quantity issue. A quality issue would be training too hard (too fast, or with too heavy a weight) or too easy. I see runners getting into trouble both ways, with unnecessary quality and unnecessary quantity. I think the answer is not in quantity versus quality, it's the right quantity *of* quality.

Balanced Rest and Training: Rest versus training is another important question when planning your training program. You have to rest enough to heal, and you have to train enough to progress; but the balance between the two changes as you move through the recovery phases. Phase One and Phase Two of the Running Injury Recovery Program emphasize rest and healing. Phase Three and Phase Four shift to progressive amounts of training for strengthening and recovery.

Consistency: Keeping up a consistent schedule is critical to your recovery training program. That's just the way it is. It doesn't have to be the same days of the week, but it has to be the same amount of weight-bearing exercise over a week or over a month.

Focus on Form: In Phase Three of the Running Injury Recovery Program you will have the opportunity to focus on your running form (stride) and correct bad habits. Everyone has bad running habits that they fall into automatically when they're tired or distracted – that's called **habituation**. In Phase Three, everyone will warm up with some *fitness walking*, which tends not to be habituated by runners, so it really helps focus your mind on your proper form before you start running.

Pacing: Pacing is an important element in running, and it's important in your rate of progress through the phases of the Running Injury Recovery Program. When I coach, I tie running pace in with form, and I try to set a pace that is very specific to each runner's goal. You have to pay attention to form, and you have to pay attention to rhythm. Pacing is built into the phases of your Running Injury Recovery Program, along with specific clearance checkpoints that will tell you when you are ready to progress to the next level.

Running: Ultimately, all training is about running, because the benefits of training only last as long as you are able to run. Cross-training such as swimming, biking, or weight-lifting is fine, but it doesn't have the same weight-bearing features. In Phase Three of your recovery program, you'll practice controlled running (*gliding*) – because only running trains you for running.

13.3 About Training Programs and Stress

The idea of an "injury-proof" training program is everywhere. It's all over the Internet, and in books and magazines. Everybody seems to think that, if they could just find the perfect formula, then they wouldn't get injured. Well, that perfect formula doesn't exist. There's a fine line between peak fitness and injured, and that line is always a moving target.

As a coach, there was a formula that I learned very early, which is "stress plus training equals overtraining." I'm not talking about the stress of training; I'm talking about other physical and psycho-social stresses that affect our bodies. For example, you might

Side Tracks: Biking and Stress Fractures (The "Sports Medicine Idiot Test")

This happens all the time: A patient comes to me with a **stress fracture** (hairline fracture) in his femur. I tell him that, until the bone heals, he can't run. I don't want him pounding on the fracture and making it worse. If he wants to do cardio exercise, I tell him it has to be zero impact, such as a stationary bike or spin class. Then he says "But my doctor (or other healthcare professional) told me I can ride my bike on the street." That's when I tell him his doctor just failed the "sports medicine idiot test."

Cycling injuries are the number one sports injury seen in emergency rooms in the United States, with about 200,000 emergency room visits each year. Every time you get on a bike, you have to be prepared to crash. So, if the pounding of high-impact exercise is dangerous, a bicycle crash in the street is like a lifetime of pounding in one second. Even a "minor" crash can open a healing fracture and result in a life-altering injury that requires surgery.

Bottom line: If there's even a possibility of a hairline fracture anywhere in your body, biking on the street is not a safe alternative to running. Stick with no-impact exercise until your injury heals and you can safely begin Phase Three Part Two in your Running Injury Recovery Program.

have done a great training session last week, but this week you put in extra hours at work or are emotionally distraught, and now it's breaking you down. That's a moving target we can't control, and it's a real factor to keep in mind during running-injury management.

13.4 Introduction to Phase Three

In Phase Two of the Running Injury Recovery Program, your flexibility will be improved with self-mobilization techniques and stretching exercises. As you progress through Phase Three, you'll be working harder and finding new areas of tenderness and stiffness to deal with, so you'll continue doing your mobilizations and stretches to maintain the gains you made in Phase Two.

In Phase Three, you'll develop a recovery training program that progressively adds more difficult weight-bearing exercises to address the weakness and dysfunction caused by your specific injury. Phase Three also introduces two new elements into your recovery program: *closed-chain exercises* will help you develop strength, balance, and posture while placing your body weight on the injured region, and a progressive *walk/glide program* will focus on form and technique as it strengthens your body for running.

In fact, these exercises will do much more than just strengthen your musculoskeletal system. They are part of **neuromuscular re-education**, which helps your nervous system control your body so that everything works together as an efficiently functioning unit. They will develop proper *mental focus* that helps you maintain a functional running form. They correct errors in your *technique* that contribute to running injuries. In other words, Phase Three develops the proper **training habits** that will make you a better, stronger, and safer runner.

When it comes to learning proper training habits, it's important to do it right. You can't rush neuromuscular re-education any more than you can rush the healing of muscle or bone. You have to progress carefully and mindfully through each phase of your recovery program. You have to focus on what you're doing. And it's important to monitor your progress and adjust your program as needed to make sure no Red Flags appear. Your injury recovery program is a serious commitment of time and effort, both physically and mentally – but it will ultimately reward you with a return to better running.

13.5 Phase Three Groups and Regions

In Phases One and Two of *The Running Injury Recovery Program Workbook*, you are sorted into one of two recovery groups based on the presence or absence of Red Flags. By the time you enter Phase Three, all Red Flags are gone, and these two groups are merged. Everyone starts Phase Three in the same group.

Phase Three will be divided into two parts, each with separate clearance checkpoints. Phase Three Part One (*Table 13-1*) consists of eight **Basic Closed-Chain Exercises** that everyone must do. These exercises are used to evaluate your overall strength and body awareness, to re-evaluate your injury, and to sort you into new recovery groups for Phase Three Part Two.

Table 13-1

Guidelines: Phase Three Part One

PHASE THREE PART ONE	All Groups
PT Time	1. Basic Closed-Chain Exercises, 40 minutes per day, every day (**Log Form B**) 2. Continue with *Stretch/Mobilization Cycles* (flexibility training), 20 minutes per day, every day (**Log Form M**).
Phase Three Part One Clearance *(Self-Assessment 3A)*	1. Able to perform all 8 Basic Closed-Chain Exercises correctly and symmetrically, with no increase in symptoms. **OR** 2. Completed 1 week of Basic Closed-Chain Exercises, but still *unable* to perform all 8 Basic Closed-Chain exercises correctly, symmetrically, or with no increase in symptoms.

In Phase Three Part Two, you'll be sorted into one of two groups based on two tests: (1) whether your original injury is simple or complex, and (2) how long it has been since you last ran in regular training.

Group 1(*Table 13-2*) includes only those who have simple injuries, and have been away from running for less than six weeks. Entering Phase Three Part Two, Group 1 will follow a **Self-Paced Plan** that will move them quickly through the clearance checkpoints.

Group 2 (*Table 13-3*) includes everyone else: those with complex injuries, and those who have been away from running for six weeks or longer. Entering Phase Three Part Two, Group 2 will follow a **Two-Week-Interval Plan** that will proceed more cautiously toward the clearance checkpoints.

Group 1 and Group 2 are each subdivided into two subgroups: Subgroup A is able to clear all Basic Closed-Chain Exercises in one week or less. Subgroup B is unable to clear all Basic Closed-Chain exercises after one week.

Within Group 1, Subgroup 1A proceeds directly to the *walk/glide program* during their Base Schedule, at the level determined by their *Self-Assessments*. Group 1B must *fitness walk* their Base Schedule (Level 0) until they have cleared all Basic Closed-Chain Exercises; then their group will be reassessed, and they will join either Group 1A or Group 2A, depending upon how long it has been since their last regular training run.

Everyone in Group 2 starts their Base Schedule at Level 0 (fitness walking). Group 2A can proceed to Level 1 (walk/glide program) after two weeks. Group 2B must clear all eight Basic Closed-Chain Exercises and complete two weeks at Level 0 before they can progress to Level 1 in their Base Schedule.

In addition to the Base Schedule, both groups in Phase Three Part Two will continue with one hour of P.T. Time, twice a week, consisting of closed-chain exercises, self-mobilizations and stretching exercises. Subgroups 1A and 2A will proceed directly to their list of Regional Closed-Chain Exercises for their specific affected region or regions. Those in Subgroups 1B and 2B, who have not cleared all eight Basic Closed-Chain Exercises, will continue with those basic exercises until they have cleared them, and then progress to their Regional Closed-Chain Exercises.

In addition to the ten regional injury groups (toe, arch, heel, shin, calf, band, knee, hamstring, hip, and buttocks), we can now add one more functional injury group: the **stress fracture**. A stress fracture is a hairline fracture that can occur in any region, but it is not assessed until Phase Three Part One. If you meet certain criteria after one week of doing Basic Closed-Chain Exercises, we'll presume that you might have a stress fracture, and you'll add specific Regional Closed-Chain Exercises to your training program to address that.

For each injury region, you'll find a detailed *Regional Plan* in *Appendix* R of *The Running Injury Recovery Program Workbook* that lists all of the criteria, goals, and exercises that apply to your specific injury region; plus additional instructions that apply to injuries with stress fractures. Some regional plans are also used to treat certain associated or **secondary regions**. For example, if your injury is in the inner thigh, you'll follow the *Regional Plan* for the hip region.

As a general rule, if your injury is complex and you need to follow *Regional Plans* for more than one region, always start with the worst injury in the most-affected region, and continue through all the prescribed treatments and exercises in order of severity. The *Self-Assessments* in *The Running Injury Recovery Program Workbook* will guide you through the process of setting up your exercise program and Base Schedule.

By the end of Phase Three in the *Workbook*, everyone in both groups should be able to complete their Base Schedule with a 50-minute glide for the specified amount of time with no increase in symptoms, and be able to perform all of their Regional Closed-Chain Exercises symmetrically and with no increase in symptoms in any affected region.

* * *

Table 13-2

Group 1 Guidelines: Phase Three Part Two

PHASE THREE PART TWO	GROUP 1	
Phase Three Part Two, Group 1 (Self-Assessment 3D)	1. Simple injury **AND** 2. Less than 6 weeks have passed since your last regular training run.	
	Subgroup 1A	**Subgroup 1B**
	Cleared all eight Basic Closed-Chain exercises in 1 week or less.	*Unable* to clear all eight Basic Closed-Chain exercises *after 1 week*.
Time Plan (Worksheet T)	Reduce PT Time to 2 days per week, and add your Base Schedule.	Reduce PT Time to 2 days per week, and add your Base Schedule.

(Table 13-2 cont.)

	Subgroup 1A	Subgroup 1B
Group 1 PT Time	1. Continue with *Stretch/Mobilization Cycles* (flexibility training), 2 days per week, 20 minutes per day (**Log Form M: Maintain Mobility**). 2. Begin Regional Closed-Chain Exercises for your one affected region, 2 days per week, 40 minutes per day (**Log Form R: Regional Closed-Chain**).	1. Continue with *Stretch/Mobilization Cycles* (flexibility training), 2 days per week, 20 minutes per day (**Log Form M: Maintain Mobility**). 2. Continue with Basic Closed-Chain Exercises, 2 days per week, 40 minutes per day, until you are able to perform all of them correctly and symmetrically, with no increase in symptoms (**Log Form B: Basic Closed-Chain**).

(*Table 13-2 cont.*)	Subgroup 1A	Subgroup 1B
Group 1 **Base Schedule** (*Self-Assessment 3E*)	Walk/Glide your Base Schedule (**Log Form S**) starting at the appropriate level, following the **Self-Paced Plan.**	1. Fitness Walk your Base Schedule (**Log Form S: Level 0**), following the **Self-Paced Plan** until you have cleared all Basic Closed-Chain Exercises. 2. When you have cleared all Basic Closed-Chain Exercises, do the *Group 1B Reassessment* below.

(Table 13-2 cont.)	**Subgroup 1B ONLY**
	Perform this reassessment on the day you clear all 8 Basic Closed-Chain Exercises:
	Look at the top section of today's **Log Form B: Basic Closed-Chain,** and find the box for "Days since last day you ran":
Group 1B Reassessment	A. If today is 42 days or less (6 weeks or less) since your last regular training run, you can now move to **Subgroup 1A** (Go to *Table 13-2, Group 1A PT Time* and *Base Schedule*).
	B. If today is 43 days or more (more than 6 weeks) since your last regular training run, you must move to **Subgroup 2A** (Go to *Table 13-3, Group 2A PT Time* and *Base Schedule*).

(Table 13-2 cont.)

	Subgroup 1A
Group 1: Phase Three Part Two Clearance *(Self-Assessment 3H)*	1. PT Time: Able to perform all regional closed-chain exercises for your one identified region, with symmetry and no increase in symptoms *(Self-Assessment 3F)*. 2. Base Schedule: Able to complete your Base Schedule with a 50-minute glide and glide drills for one week with no increase in symptoms *(Self-Assessment 3G1)*.

Table 13-3

Group 2 Guidelines: Phase Three Part Two

PHASE THREE PART TWO	GROUP 2	
Phase Three Part Two, Group 2 *(Self-Assessment 3D)*	1. Complex injury **AND/OR** 2. More than 6 weeks have passed since your last regular training run.	
	Subgroup 2A	**Subgroup 2B**
	Cleared all eight Basic Closed-Chain Exercises in 1 week or less.	*Unable* to clear all eight Basic Closed-Chain Exercises *after 1 week.*
Time Plan *(Worksheet T)*	Reduce PT Time to 2 days per week, and add your Base Schedule.	Reduce PT Time to 2 days per week, and add your Base Schedule.

(*Table 13-3 cont.*)	Subgroup 2A	Subgroup 2B
Group 2 PT Time	1. Continue with *Stretch/Mobilization Cycles* (flexibility training), 2 days per week, 20 minutes per day (**Log Form M: Maintain Mobility**). 2. Begin Regional Closed-Chain Exercises for all affected regions, 2 days per week, 40 minutes per day (**Log Form R: Regional Closed-Chain**).	1. Continue with *Stretch/Mobilization Cycles*, 2 days per week, 20 minutes per day (**Log Form M: Maintain Mobility**). 2. Continue with Basic Closed-Chain Exercises, 40 minutes per day, until you are able to perform all basic closed-chain exercises correctly and symmetrically, with no increase in symptoms (**Log Form B: Basic Closed-Chain**). 3. When you have cleared all Basic Closed-Chain Exercises, begin Regional Closed-Chain Exercises for all affected regions, 2 days per week, 40 minutes per day (**Log Form R: Regional Closed-Chain**).

(Table 13-3 cont.)	Subgroup 2A	Subgroup 2B
Group 2 **Base Schedule,** **Part 1:** **Fitness Walking** *(Self-Assessment 3E)*	Fitness Walk your Base Schedule, following the **Two-Week Interval Plan**, until you have completed a minimum of 2 weeks, *and* you can complete 60 minutes of fitness walking with no increase in symptoms (**Log Form S: Level 0**).	1. Fitness Walk your Base Schedule until you have cleared all eight Basic Closed-Chain Exercises (**Log Form S: Level 0**). 2. If you clear Basic Closed-Chain in less than 2 weeks, continue to Fitness Walk your Base Schedule, following the **Two-Week Interval Plan**, until you have completed a minimum of 2 weeks, *and* you can complete 60 minutes of fitness walking with no increase in symptoms.

(Table 13-3 cont.)	Subgroups 2A and 2B
Group 2 **Base Schedule, Part** **2: Walk/Glide**	Walk/Glide your Base Schedule, following the **Two-Week Interval Plan (Log Form S: Levels 1 through 5).**
Group2: **Phase Three Part** **Two Clearance** *(Self-Assessment 3H)*	1. PT Time: Able to perform all Regional Closed-Chain Exercises for each of your identified regions, with symmetry and no increase in symptoms *(Self-Assessment 3F).* 2. Base Schedule: Able to complete your Base Schedule with a 50-minute glide and glide drills for two weeks with no increase in symptoms *(Self-Assessment 3G2).*

Chapter 14
Closed-Chain Exercises for Strength and Balance

What happens when you have a running injury that is caused by a muscle imbalance, and it gets misdiagnosed? Your physical therapist treats the wrong injury, the real problem is never addressed, and you're headed way off the track of recovery.

Here's an example: "Sean" came to my P.T. clinic after months of failed rehab at another clinic. Every time he got 10 miles into his marathon training, his knee blew up and he couldn't run. Then, for days afterwards, he'd have trouble going up and down stairs (Stage 3 injuries). Sean's physician diagnosed him with chondromalacia and a patellar tracking problem. Based on that diagnosis, Sean's first therapist told him that he needed to strengthen his VMO muscle (the *vastus medialis oblique* muscle – a part of the quadriceps muscle on the inner side of his leg, above the knee cap.

Sean happily learned everything there was to know about his VMO, and spent weeks working with his therapist to strengthen it. Sean was diligent with his therapy (which included electrical stimulation and biofeedback in addition to gym exercises) and even spent extra time in the weight room after work doing his therapy exercises.

Unfortunately, even after strengthening his VMO muscle, Sean was no more able to run than he had been before he started therapy. His knee still blew up every time he ran, and he was still unable to climb stairs for days afterwards. His dysfunction hadn't changed.

When I examined Sean for the first time, I found tenderness and weakness at the outer side of his leg, below the kneecap. His problem wasn't chondromalacia with a tracking problem due to a weak VMO at all, it was chronic lateral patellar tendinosis. Every time Sean ran, his tendinosis turned into tendonitis (*"-osis"* refers to the chronic condition, while *"-itis"* refers to an acute inflammation), and his knee blew up.

Sean's difficulty with stairs was a big clue to his correct diagnosis. When I evaluated Sean on a step test and on the treadmill, his body wasn't balanced and he had poor control of his knee movement throughout his range of motion. He severely lacked body awareness and was moving with very little lower leg control (despite his newly-developed VMO). Sean desperately needed to increase his body awareness and correct his posture and knee mechanics.

Identifying Sean's specific running dysfunction allowed us to correct his muscle imbalance with neuromuscular re-education. Using closed-chain exercises, I worked with Sean to teach him how to control his knee and balance it in relation to the rest of his body. Once he was better able to control his knee and keep his body balanced for stepping, we transferred what he had learned into a walk/glide program, and eventually to his running. As a result, Sean not only overcame his injury, he became a better runner and went on to finish many marathons.

14.1 Neuromuscular Re-Education and Body Awareness

Muscles help us keep our balance by working together with our nervous system in a **neuromuscular control system**. Parts of our nervous system (**mechanoreceptors**) constantly monitor the tension in our muscles and ligaments and send that information to our **central nervous system (CNS)** for processing. The CNS constantly responds and sends back signals that adjust the muscles. Musculoskeletal running injuries often damage or destroy the mechanoreceptors in joints and/or ligaments, resulting in a loss or change in the information sent to the CNS. This contributes to neuromuscular dysfunctions such as poor postural control, delayed muscle reaction time, and muscle imbalances.

Rehabilitation focuses on restoring and improving the communication between our mechanoreceptors and our CNS to optimize posture, balance, and body positioning – with emphasis on the injured areas. In other words, we use **neuromuscular re-education** to improve our *body awareness.*

14.2 Muscle Imbalance

The popular press talk a lot about muscle imbalance, but they never really address muscle balance. As part of your recovery program, it's important to address any muscle imbalances that relate to your injury.

Muscle imbalances contribute to unstable posture, poor biomechanical alignment, and compensation mechanisms – all of which are running dysfunctions.

Muscle imbalances are usually caused by the tightening of a mobilizing muscle and the weakening of a stabilizing muscle. *Mobilizing muscles* are usually big muscle groups that produce movement and high power. *Stabilizing muscles* are usually smaller and control movement or joint position, working against gravity.

In running-injury management, we're working with whole muscle groups, not individual muscles, so it's not important for you to learn the names of specific muscles. For example, you don't really need to know the names of the muscles that control your kickback, you just need to learn how to kick back correctly. Getting your muscles in balance simply lets you work your legs properly for running.

14.3 Closed-Chain and Open-Chain Exercises

Biomechanically, running is like hopping from leg to leg in a balanced, forward movement – so balancing on one leg is important. In your recovery program, you're going to improve your body awareness and address muscular imbalance by doing certain **closed-chain exercises**, which are exercises that are performed slowly and thoughtfully, with your body weight balanced on one leg.

In comparison, **open-chain exercises** are exercises where you lift a weight in a specific way to strengthen one specific muscle (like the VMO muscle for knee problems). Lying on your back doing open-chain exercises doesn't work very well for running injuries because you really need to work the whole leg as a unit, not just one muscle. I don't use open-chain exercises for a running injury, except in Stage 5, while there's swelling and you're being iced.

Closed-chain exercises improve body awareness by optimizing certain sensory receptors (**proprioceptors** in muscles, tendons, joints, and the inner ear) which detect the motion and relative positions of body parts. When an area is injured and immobilized, muscles and proprioceptors "forget" their roles in coordinating body control with muscle activity. Closed-chain exercises help re-educate your proprioceptors and improve your stability.

Some closed-chain exercises are specific to a particular injury, and you can feel a difference in strength or range of motion when you compare the injured region with the same, uninjured region on the other side of your body. We can use these **Basic Closed-Chain Exercises** as an evaluation tool to locate the specific region that isn't working right (the **impairment**).

All closed-chain exercises will improve your balance while progressively strengthening the injured part and reinforcing your ability to place your weight directly through the injured region. In this chapter we introduce closed-chain exercises that address specific requirements for posture and balance. In the next chapter we'll move on to more difficult weight-bearing exercises, including fitness walking, progressive gliding, and gliding drills.

* * *

14.4 Closed-Chain Exercises for Balance and Strength

When it comes to posture and balance, there are four **Basic Form Requirements** *(Table 14-1)* that everyone should be able to do:

1. *Balance on one leg with your foot pointed straight forward.*
2. *Use your arms to balance your body.*
3. *Keep your body balanced while pushing off through the big toe.*
4. *Keep your body balanced while kicking straight back.*

To make sure that everyone can meet these *basic form requirements*, Phase Three Part One consists of eight *Basic Closed-Chain Exercises* that will be part of everyone's recovery plan. These eight basic exercises include two exercises to help you maintain stability over an aligned foot (exercises 1 and 2); two exercises that teach you to use the dynamics of your armswings to stabilize your body position (exercises 3 and 4); two exercises that teach you to keep straight and balanced while pushing off (exercises 5 and 6); and two exercises to keep you straight and balanced while running (exercises 7 and 8). Depending upon which areas are affected by your injury, your individual plan will also include specific **Regional Closed-Chain Exercises** that will further challenge your balance in Phase Three Part Two **[Box 14-2]**.

Closed-chain exercises also bring us to strength training. Closed-chain exercises strengthen the specific weaknesses of your running injury (the *muscle imbalance*) to bring your body back into balance. In fact, most of your strengthening will be done through these one-legged exercises.

Table 14-1

Form and Closed-Chain Exercises

Maintain Stability over the Aligned Foot:
14-1   Square Hops (*basic*)
14-2   Side Step-Down (*basic*)
14-9   Hip Abduction with Theraband
14-10   Lateral Straight-Leg Raise with Theraband
14-11   Straight-Leg Raise with Theraband

Control Armswing to Achieve a Balanced Body:
14-3   One-Legged Armswings, Barefoot (*basic*)
14-4   One-Legged Armswings, Single Pillow (*basic*)
14-12   One-Legged Armswings, Double Pillows
14-13   One-Legged Armswings, Side Incline
14-14   One-Legged Armswings, Double Weights
14-15   High Knees with Theraband

Controlled Weightbearing Through the First Ray:
14-5   Barefoot Push-Up (*basic*)
14-6   Quick Steps (*basic*)
14-16   Barefoot Push-Through
14-17   Shod Push-Up with Ankle Weights
14-18   Shod Push-Through with Ankle Weights
14-19   Box Step-Up

Maintain Stable Posture With Straight Kickback:
14-7   Weighted Kickback (*basic*)
14-8   Box Step Up and Over (*basic*)
14-20   Theraband Kickback

The ultimate goal will be to strengthen your legs by running – but before you can run, we have to find and correct any muscle imbalance. In Phase Three Part One, you'll use Basic Closed-Chain Exercises to break your injury down into different parts, and create an awareness of exactly where the stiffness and weakness is. You'll work with both legs to find the asymmetry between the more-impaired leg and the less-impaired leg. Once you have built up some strength and endurance in the injured area, you'll progressively and specifically attack any deficit in strength, symmetry, or running pattern you can find, using Regional Closed-Chain Exercises and a customized program of running drills in Phase Three Part Two.

14.5 Goals for Closed-Chain Exercises

In all closed-chain exercises, your goal is to duplicate the biomechanics of running in order to strengthen your body for running. You are striving for *symmetry* in form, pace, and duration of each exercise. For example, as you practice your one-leg armswings, it's important to concentrate specifically on what you're trying to accomplish. You'll be trying to put certain angles very specifically where they need to be, and trying to maintain that symmetry and balance from the beginning of each exercise to the end. That requires mental focus, body awareness, and a dedicated follow-through.

The importance of mental focus while you are performing these closed-chain exercises cannot be over-emphasized. The instructions for each exercise include a *Mental Focus Statement* that addresses one of our four *basic form requirements* for balance. As you perform each exercise, you can repeat this statement to yourself like a mantra to help keep your attention focused on what you're trying to accomplish. If you are not focusing on your form, you're probably doing it wrong.

Another important lesson when learning closed-chain exercises is to practice keeping your balance, not to practice losing it. You're working on areas of weakness and neuromuscular dysfunction, so you can expect to start out a bit wobbly or to become easily fatigued. When that happens, stop before you lose your balance, not afterwards. If you aren't able to hold your form, take a break and try again. You don't want to practice doing the exercise the wrong way.

14.6 Techniques for Closed-Chain Exercises

In all closed-chain exercises, you'll be challenged to maintain a specific posture and body alignment that is different from the way you normally run. This is an intentional technique to create *body awareness* and to improve your balance and *neuromuscular control.*

All closed-chain exercises must be done with a **straight posture**, including a good vertical alignment of the spine, shoulders back, head level, chin tucked back, and weight-bearing knee straight. Tighten all the muscles that support your central body (**trunk**), including the abdominal muscles. Keeping your body straight and your head aligned over your trunk through each set of exercises while balancing on one leg is not an easy task!

∗∗∗

Side Tracks: Pros and Cons (Cross Training and Trainers)

For runners, cross-training means any training other than running. Runners are always looking for a magic cross-training program that will prevent running injuries. In fact, any type of cross-training will do that, because as long as you're not running, you're not going to get a running injury. However, cross-training *can* cause other types of injuries that can contribute to a running injury when you do run – then you've got a complex injury that's more difficult to sort out and treat.

Remember, nothing strengthens your body for running as well as running. Exercise classes such as yoga and spinning are great for flexibility, strength, and endurance training; but they can reduce your exposure to running – and if you reduce your exposure to running *too* much, you don't get strong enough to run, and your risk of injury actually increases.

Unfortunately, I've seen some fads in cross-training that, in my opinion, are downright ludicrous. In one recent example, a runner who had calf pain from a running injury went to a personal trainer who advised the runner to strengthen his legs by pushing the trainer's car around the parking lot of the gym! As a result, the runner hurt his back as well as his calves. (As a medical professional, I can't even imagine the liability in recommending stunts like that.) And car-pushing is only one of many creative and untested ways some trainers come up with to exercise people.

(Side Tracks cont.)

The point is, there is no school that teaches running injury management, and trainers don't have any secret knowledge. Running-injury management is simply wide open to experimentation because there are no agreed-upon protocols. Learning to treat running injuries isn't easy. Personally, it took me four years of college, two years of P.T. school, 15 years of clinical practice, professional training for the Ironman, and many years of coaching runners before I really felt comfortable treating running injuries – and I've learned a lot in the years since then.

One thing I've learned in the coaching and fitness world is, there's a huge benefit to seeing a professional with a college education in their field. An educated person knows how much they don't know. They have learned certain things really well, and when they don't know something, they usually say so, and they don't make something up. I know some great, well-educated trainers but, sadly, they're not in the majority. It doesn't take a lot of credentials to become a running coach, personal trainer, or any other type of instructor in the fitness world. Whether it's in training, in running-industry magazines, or on the internet, watch out for "advice" from uneducated hustlers who don't know what they're talking about.

During closed-chain exercises, you'll be working on one leg, which we call the **weightbearing leg**, and keeping the other leg, called the **non-weightbearing leg**, in a particular position for balance. The hip of the weightbearing leg should always be aligned over the weightbearing foot.

Some closed-chain exercises will be done barefoot (**unshod**) to help you feel the balance through your foot. Other exercises that require greater support will be done in shoes (**shod**). In all closed-chain exercises, pay particular attention to the function of your toes in controlling your balance. In running, we focus on pushing off through the big toe, but all of your toes are involved in balance. In your barefoot exercises, think of your outer toes as suction cups that grip the floor and stabilize you. Don't let your toes curl up like claws! Once you are able to control your toes in barefoot exercises, try to feel the same thing in your shod exercises. That's one of the things that will help you learn to "run barefoot in your shoes." Whether shod or unshod, you'll be learning to use your foot to control your balance in all closed-chain exercises.

There are four basic leg positions in closed-chain exercises, which are combined with *straight posture*. One is a **straight leg position**, with the knee in line with the foot and hip (see CC#14-14). Second is the **high knees position** (also called the *90/90 position*) with the knee bent at 90 degrees and the leg raised to form a 90-degree angle at the hip, with the foot aligned directly below the knee (see CC#14-15). Third is the **kickback position**, with both knees even and one knee bent backward 90-degrees so the lower leg is parallel to the floor (see

CC#14-14). Fourth is the **glide position**, with knees even and the non-weightbearing knee bent back until the toe is just touching the ground, keeping the ankle in *neutral position*. Throughout Phase Three – including closed-chain exercises, fitness walking, and glides – your head, trunk, pelvis, and hip rotation remain essentially constant. Only the positions of your arms and legs will change.

In closed-chain exercises, visual feedback is important to reinforce the learning of balance skills and development of symmetry. You should do all of your balance exercises in front of a mirror – at least when you're starting out. As your skills improve, you can do your exercises away from a mirror.

When done correctly, closed-chain exercises can be deceptively difficult, so be careful. Before starting any closed-chain exercises in *The Running Injury Recovery Program Workbook*, review all the instructions accompanying each exercise [**Box 14-2**] and all the guidelines for Basic and Regional Closed-Chain Exercises [**Boxes 14-3 and 14-4**].

14.7 Timing for Closed-Chain Exercises

You should dedicate 10 minutes to each closed-chain exercise. That means you can do four exercises per day during your 40 minutes of P.T. Time. Since you will do eight Basic Closed-Chain Exercises in Phase Three Part One, and six or more Regional Closed-Chain Exercises in Phase Three Part Two, you'll follow the guidelines in the *Workbook* to determine which exercises you will do on any given day [**Boxes 14-3 and 14-4**].

The **pace** at which you perform each exercise will vary depending upon your physical condition and your individual goal as a **fitness runner** or **racer.** Your ultimate goal is to match the rhythm of your closed-chain exercises with your target *post-injury running* speed (**glide rhythm**), which should be slightly slower that your normal, pre-injury training pace. You'll start each exercise gradually, with a slow rhythm and short duration that allows you to maintain correct form and symmetry. Once you've achieved symmetry, you can **build** your time and pace as your strength and balance improve.

Each closed-chain exercise includes specific instructions for timing as well as form, so you'll need a stopwatch or runner's watch to time your exercises to the nearest second. In Phase Three Part One of your *Workbook*, you'll start each Basic Closed-Chain Exercise on the less-impaired leg first, and you'll record how long you can perform that exercise correctly, without breaking form or increasing pain. Then you'll do the same exercise on the more-impaired leg and compare the difference in time, to help measure symmetry (*Self-Assessment 3A* in the *Workbook*).

For each exercise in which you do *not* have symmetry, your goal is to build up your time on the more-impaired leg until you have achieved symmetry in time, form, and pace with your less-impaired leg. As I tell my patients, let the "smarter" leg teach the "dumber" leg to balance better. Spend more time working on the more-impaired leg, and less time on the less-impaired leg. For example, if you can hold your form for 20 seconds on your left leg, but only for 5 seconds on your right leg, then do more sets of that exercise on your right leg.

To clear Phase Three Part One, you must be able to perform each of the eight Basic-Closed Chain Exercises for the specified amount of time, on both legs (alternating left then right), symmetrically and painlessly for 10 consecutive minutes. The instructions for each exercise include specific *Basic Closed-Chain Clearance* requirements for symmetry in form, pace, and time.

When you begin Regional Closed-Chain Exercises, you'll again start slowly. First achieve symmetry at a glide rhythm, then *build* to your target time. Some exercises build time at a **glide rhythm**. Others will build as an **acceleration rhythm**, in which you start out slowly and gradually go faster, making sure that you stop accelerating before you lose form. The instructions for each Regional Closed-Chain Exercise include a specific **Final Target** time for your group, depending upon your goals as a *fitness runner* or as a *racer*.

You will notice that some closed-chain exercises are used in both Basic-Closed Chain and in Regional Closed-Chain. When following the instructions for these exercises, remember to follow the time goals that are appropriate for the phase you are in at the time (*Basic Closed-Chain Clearance* goals in Phase Three Part One, and the *Final Target* goals for the remaining phases).

As you progress through your recovery program, you'll continue to build the pace of your exercises while maintaining form and focusing on the weakness. You'll move a little faster when you're fitness walking, then increase your speed through glides. Then you'll develop more speed and power through plyometric exercises, until you are finally prepared for *post-recovery running*.

14.8 Closed-Chain Exercises through the Phases

Closed-chain exercises, along with stretches and self-mobilizations, will be part of your P.T. Time throughout your recovery program. In Phase Three Part One, everyone will be doing the same eight Basic Closed-Chain Exercises. Each of these exercises will help pinpoint certain areas of weakness and muscle imbalance that you'll work on in your regional recovery plan.

The clearance requirements for Basic Closed-Chain are somewhat independent of the Clearance requirements for Phase Three Part One. Some people will clear Basic Closed-Chain during Phase Three Part One. Other people will not clear Basic Closed-Chain until they are in Phase Three Part Two.

When you have cleared all eight Basic Closed-Chain Exercises in your *Running Injury Recovery Program Workbook*, you can switch over to your individual list of Regional Closed-Chain Exercises. However, the *length* of time it takes you to clear all eight Basic Closed-Chain Exercises will help determine which subgroup you will join in Phase Three Part Two. If you have *not* cleared all eight Basic Closed-Chain Exercises after one week, despite your best efforts, you will *not* be running or doing Regional Closed-Chain Exercises when you enter Phase Three Part Two. Everyone must clear all Basic Closed-Chain Exercises before they begin Regional Closed-Chain Exercises and Walk/Glide Sets in Phase Three Part Two of the *Workbook*.

When you complete your Basic Closed-Chain Exercises, you'll use the results to help you to pick your affected region(s) for Regional Closed-Chain Exercises

(*Self-Assessment 3B* in the *Workbook*). The fewer regions you choose to work on, the easier it will be for you to complete your recovery program. Follow the instructions in the *Workbook* and combine adjoining regions where possible. You should not end up with more than two injury regions in one leg, or three regions in two legs (not including stress fracture).

Everyone will assess their Basic Closed-Chain results to either eliminate or include the possibility of stress fracture. If you have not cleared Square Hop exercises (CC#1) after one week of Basic Closed-Chain Exercises, you will add stress fracture closed-chain exercises (Region 11) to your Regional Closed-Chain list.

You'll also use the results of your Basic Closed-Chain Exercises to prepare specific **Impairment Statements** that describe which of the four *basic form requirements* causes you the most difficulty, and the affected regions you will be working on to correct these problems (*Self-Assessment 3D* in the *Workbook*).

Once you have selected your injury region(s) and written your Impairment Statements, you'll find your Regional Closed-Chain Exercises in the *Regional Recovery Plan(s)* in *Appendix R* of the *Workbook*. These are the exercises you will do during P.T. Time for the rest of your recovery program.

Each plan lists six Regional Closed-Chain Exercises. Follow the guidelines in the *Workbook* for determining which four exercises to do first. As a general rule, always start with the most difficult exercises in your most-impaired region. If you are doing exercises for two or more regions in the same leg, you don't have to repeat any exercises that are duplicated on different lists . For example, if you are doing exercises for both the right hamstring (exercises 14-2, 14-7, 14-8, 14-12, 14-14, and 14-20) and the right band (exercises 14-2, 14-8, 14-9, 14-12, 14-13, and 14-20), your combined list would have eight exercises (14-2, 14-7, 14-8, 14-9, 14-12, 14-13, 14-14, and 14-20).

In Phase Three Part Two, your goal is to perform each of your Regional Closed-Chain Exercises for 10 minutes, according to the instructions – with correct form, symmetry, and no increase in symptoms. When you begin Regional Closed-Chain Exercises in P.T. Time, you will also start *walk/glide sets* in your *Base Schedule*, which we will learn about in the next chapter. This is the phase where most of your recovery work will actually take place. You must clear both Regional Closed-Chain Exercises and your Base Schedule before you can enter Phase Four.

$$* * *$$

Weight Guidelines for *Table 14-2*

Your Weight	Hand Weights[1]	Ankle Weights[2]
80-120 lb.	2 pounds	2.5 pounds
120-180 lb.	3 pounds	5.0 pounds
180+ lb.	5 pounds	7.5 pounds

Table 14-2
Equipment for Closed-Chain Exercises

Standard Equipment	Home Alternative
Full-length mirror	Full-length mirror, or window reflection, or someone watching you
Stopwatch	Runner's watch with interval and lap timer
Calculator	Phone with a calculator app
2 Hand weights [1]	2 Hand weights [1]
2 Ankle weights [2]	2 Ankle weights [2]
Low step, adjustable from 6" to 12"	Curb or stair step
Plyometric Box, adjustable from 12" to 24"	Two steps up on a flight of stairs; one step down on a flight of stairs
Square balance foam	2 Bed pillows
Slant board	21.5" X 17" X 0.75" plywood propped on half a cinder block
2.5 feet red (medium-resistance) Theraband tubing, tied in a loop	5 rubber-band loops (1 loop = 5 large rubber bands knotted together)

| Box 14-2 | *HOW TO:* Closed-Chain Exercises |

HOW TO: Closed-Chain Exercises

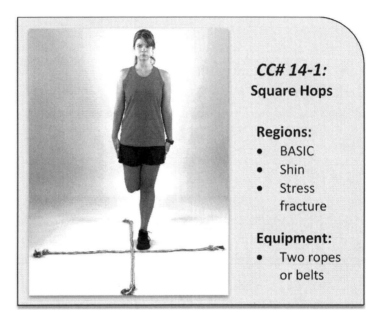

CC# 14-1:
Square Hops

Regions:
- BASIC
- Shin
- Stress fracture

Equipment:
- Two ropes or belts

Starting Position	1. Cross two ropes, belts, or chalk lines on the floor in front of a mirror, forming a 4-square grid. 2. Stand at the center of the grid in "straight" posture, with your feet parallel to the lines, hands down at your sides.
Action	1. Looking in the mirror, balance on one leg. Raise the other leg to "kickback" position.

(CC#14-1 cont.)

Action *(cont.)*	2. Keeping your toes pointed toward the mirror, hop flat-footed over each of the 4 lines in a clockwise pattern: front, side, back, and side. 3. Staying on the same leg, reverse to counterclockwise and hop side, forward, side, and back. 4. Continue on the same leg until you are fatigued or unable to maintain correct form. 5. Switch legs and repeat.
Goals	Try to maintain your posture and balance as you hop in four directions.
Focus Statement	"I will balance my body on a straight foot."
Basic Closed-Chain Clearance	1. Achieve symmetry at glide pace 2. *Target Time*: 10 repeats of 20 seconds on each leg with 10 second rest in between.
Final Target	Accelerate your pace as you build up to your target time: • Fitness Runners: 30 seconds each leg, with a 10 second rest • Racers: 90 seconds each leg, with a 10 second rest • Total of 10 minutes, with no break in form

CC#14-2: Side Step-Down

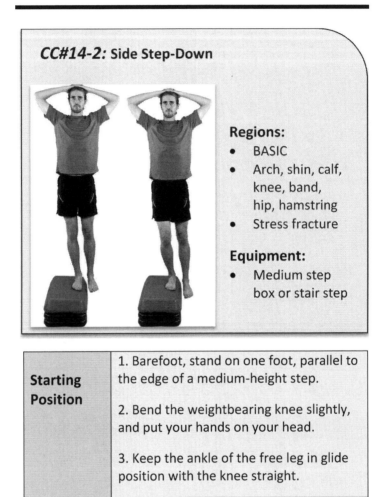

Regions:
- BASIC
- Arch, shin, calf, knee, band, hip, hamstring
- Stress fracture

Equipment:
- Medium step box or stair step

Starting Position	1. Barefoot, stand on one foot, parallel to the edge of a medium-height step.
	2. Bend the weightbearing knee slightly, and put your hands on your head.
	3. Keep the ankle of the free leg in glide position with the knee straight.

(CC#14-2 cont.)

Action	Alternately bend and straighten the knee and ankle of the weightbearing leg slightly, in small controlled movements, keeping the body straight.
Goals	1. Feel your weightbearing foot working while moving up and down, keeping your body straight. 2. Tighten your trunk to maintain your balance.
Focus Statement	"I will balance my body on a straight foot."
Basic Closed-Chain Clearance	1. Create symmetry. 2. *Target Time:* • 20 seconds on each leg • Total of 10 minutes, continuously, on a 6 inch step, with no break in form.
Final Target	Raise your step height as you build up to your glide rhythm and target time: • Fitness Runners: 30 seconds each leg • Racers: 90 seconds each leg • Total of 10 minutes, continuously, on a 12 inch step, with no break in form

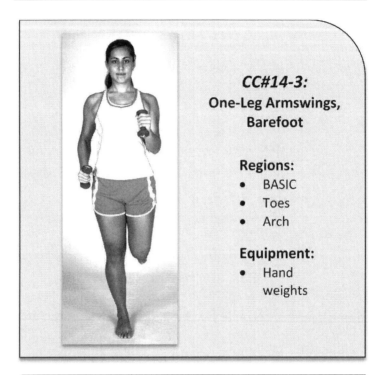

CC#14-3:
One-Leg Armswings,
Barefoot

Regions:
- BASIC
- Toes
- Arch

Equipment:
- Hand weights

Starting Position	1. Stand barefoot on a level surface, with "straight" posture. 2. Bend one knee 90 degrees so the lower leg is parallel to the floor (kickback position). 3. Holding a hand weight in each hand, bend elbows to 90 degrees.

(CC#14-3 cont.)

Action	1. Slowly swing your arms from the shoulder, keeping the elbows bent and close to the body. As one arm moves forward, the other arm moves backward. Use toes as suction cups to hold balance. 2. Alternate legs before you lose your balance.
Goals	1. Work the ground with your foot while using your arms to help maintain your body straight and balanced over the weight-bearing leg. 2. The only part of your body moving should be the balanced armswings.
Focus Statement	"I will use my arms to balance my body."
Basic Closed-Chain Clearance	1. Create symmetry. 2. *Target Time:* • 15 seconds on each leg with no rest • Total of 10 minutes, continuously, with no break in form.
Final Target	Build up to your glide rhythm and target time: • Fitness Runners: 30 seconds each leg • Racers: 90 seconds each leg • Total of 10 minutes, continuously, with no break in form.

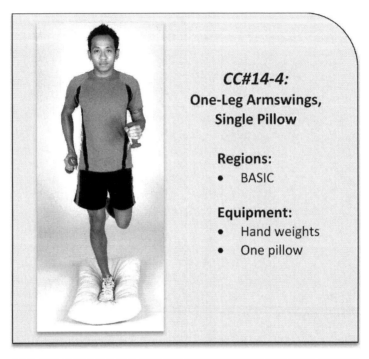

CC#14-4:
One-Leg Armswings,
Single Pillow

Regions:
- BASIC

Equipment:
- Hand weights
- One pillow

Starting Position	1. Wearing shoes, stand on one pillow with "straight" posture. 2. Bend one knee to kickback position. 3. Holding a hand weight in each hand, bend elbows to 90 degrees.

(CC#14-4 cont.)

Action	1. Slowly swing your arms from the shoulder, keeping the elbows bent and close to the body. As one arm moves forward, the other arm moves backward. 2. Alternate legs before you lose your balance.
Goals	1. Use your armswings to keep your body straight and balanced over the weight-bearing leg on the unstable surface. Feel your foot inside your shoe working to keep balance. 2. The only part of your body moving is your armswings.
Focus Statement	"I will use my arms to balance my body."
Basic Closed-Chain Clearance	1. Create symmetry. 2. *Target Time:* • 30 seconds on each leg with no rest in between. • Total of 10 minutes, continuously, with no break in form

CC#14-5:
Barefoot Push-Up

Regions:
- BASIC
- Toes
- Heel

Equipment:
- None

Starting Position	Barefoot, stand in "straight" posture, elbows bent 90 degrees.
Action	1. Raise one knee to the "high knees" position, keeping your foot aligned under the bent knee, and hold. 2. Move your arms to the coordinated position for balance, and hold.

(CC#14-5 cont.)

Action (cont.)	3. Push up through the big toe of the weightbearing leg, lifting the heel off the ground.
Goals	1. Try to maintain a small, smooth, controlled motion as you transition from the flatfoot position to the big toe, keeping the toes flat. 2. Try to keep your body straight and balanced while your weight moves forward and up into a pushoff position.
Focus Statement	"I will balance my body to push off through the big toe."
Basic Closed-Chain Clearance	1. Create symmetry at glide rhythm. 2. *Target Time:* • 15 seconds on each leg with no rest in between. • Total of 10 minutes, continuously, with no break in form
Final Target	Build up to your target time at glide rhythm: • Fitness Runners: 30 seconds each leg • Racers: 90 seconds each leg • Total of 10 minutes, continuously, with no break in form.

CC#14-6: Quick Steps

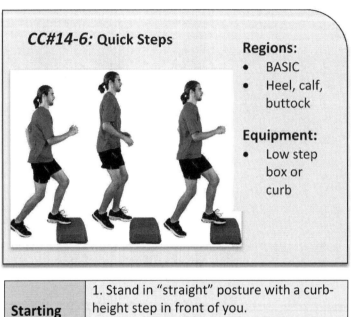

Regions:
- BASIC
- Heel, calf, buttock

Equipment:
- Low step box or curb

Starting Position	1. Stand in "straight" posture with a curb-height step in front of you. 2. Place one forefoot on the step, and evenly distribute your weight between both forefeet.
Action	1. Set your timer for 30 seconds. 2. Maintaining equal amounts of weight on the balls of both feet, push up strongly through the toes of both feet. 3. Quickly switch your legs forward and backward, keeping on your forefeet, both feet pointed straight forward.

(CC#14-6 cont.)

Action *(cont.)*	4. Coordinate your armswings with your leg motion. 5. Note how long you were able to perform each set. Do not exceed 20 continuous seconds. Start your next set when the timer reaches 30 seconds, and repeat.
Goals	Try to keep your motion quick, smooth, and coordinated as you scissor your legs forward in a skipping action.
Focus Statement	"I will balance my body to push off through the big toe."
Basic Closed-Chain Clearance	1. Create symmetry at glide rhythm. 2. *Target Time:* • Sets of 20 seconds with 10 second rest in between • Total of 10 minutes, on a 6 inch step, with no break in form.
Final Target	Build up to your target time, then accelerate your pace: • Fitness Runners: 50-second sets with a 10-second rest • Racers: 1minute-50-second sets with a 10-second rest • Total of 10 minutes, on a 6 inch step, with no break in form.

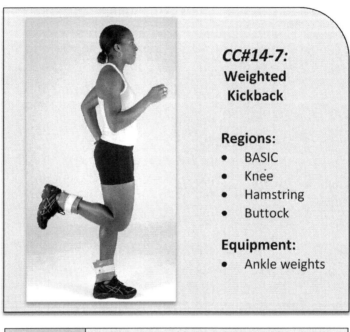

CC#14-7:
Weighted
Kickback

Regions:
- BASIC
- Knee
- Hamstring
- Buttock

Equipment:
- Ankle weights

Starting Position	1. Wearing ankle weights, stand in "straight" posture, toes pointed forward, elbows bent 90 degrees. 2. Keeping the knees even, bend the non-weightbearing knee until the toe is just touching down in the "glide" position.

(CC#14-7 cont.)

Action	1. Keeping the weightbearing knee straight, slowly bend the non-weightbearing knee to "kickback" position – raising the heel 90 degrees toward the glutes. 2. Continue to alternately bend and straighten the non-weightbearing knee, coordinating your armswings with your leg motion.
Goals	1. Try to maintain a smooth, controlled motion as you kick back. 2. Tighten your trunk to keep your body straight and balanced over the weight-bearing leg.
Focus Statement	"I will balance my body for a straight kickback."
Basic Closed-Chain Clearance	1. Create symmetry. 2. *Target Time:* • 60 seconds on each leg with no rest in between • Total of 10 minutes with no break in form.
Final Target	Build up to your glide rhythm and target time: • Fitness Runners: 2½ minutes each leg • Racers: 5 minutes each leg • Total of 10 minutes, continuously, with no break in form.

CC#14-8: Box Step Up and Over

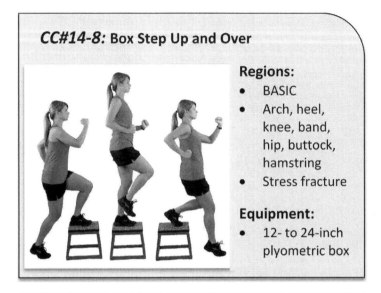

Regions:
- BASIC
- Arch, heel, knee, band, hip, buttock, hamstring
- Stress fracture

Equipment:
- 12- to 24-inch plyometric box

Starting Position	Wearing shoes, stand in "straight" posture with a knee-height box in front of you as you face the mirror; arms bent 90 degrees.
Action	1. Place one foot flat on the box, toes pointed forward in "high knees" position. 2. With the lower (second) foot, push up through the big toe. 3. Continuing your motion, step up and over the box, through "kickback" position, and land on the floor in front of you with the big toe of the second foot. 4. Coordinate your armswings with your leg motion.

(CC#14-8 cont.)

Action **(cont.)**	5. End by bringing the first foot down to the floor, from pushoff to flatfooted. 6. Walk around the box, making a gradual turn, and continue stepping over the box in the same direction.
Goals	1. Coordinate your armswings to maintain a smooth, controlled motion throughout. 2. Tighten your trunk to balance your body as you move from the high knees position to kickback position.
Focus Statement	"I will balance my body for a straight kickback."
Basic Closed-Chain Clearance	1. Create symmetry. 2. *Target Time:* • 60 seconds on each leg with no rest in between • Total of 10 minutes, on a 12-inch step, with no break in form.
Final Target	1. Gradually raise step height until hip and knee are bent at 90 degrees (high knees position). 2. Build up to your glide rhythm and target time: • Fitness Runners: 2½ minutes each leg • Racers: 5 minutes each leg • Total of 10 minutes, continuously, with no break in form.

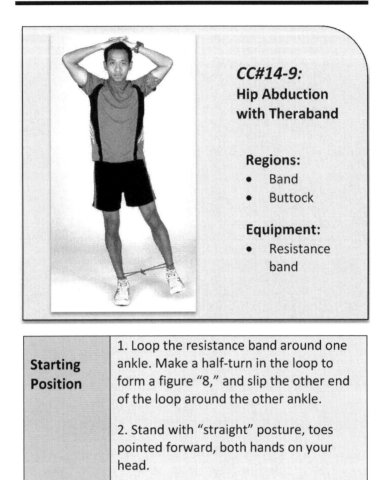

CC#14-9:
Hip Abduction
with Theraband

Regions:
- Band
- Buttock

Equipment:
- Resistance band

Starting Position	1. Loop the resistance band around one ankle. Make a half-turn in the loop to form a figure "8," and slip the other end of the loop around the other ankle. 2. Stand with "straight" posture, toes pointed forward, both hands on your head.

(CC#14-9 cont.)

Action	1. Keeping both knees straight, slowly raise one leg to the side, keeping the foot in neutral position. 2. Slowly return to the starting position, keeping the foot in neutral position.
Goals	1. Try to maintain a smooth, controlled motion. Keep the arms still, with elbows back. 2. Tighten your trunk to keep your body straight and balanced over the weight-bearing leg. 3. Create symmetry at glide rhythm.
Focus Statement	"I will balance my body on a straight foot."
Final Target	Build up to your target time at glide rhythm: • Fitness Runners: 60 seconds each leg • Racers: 2½ minutes each leg • Total of 10 minutes, continuously, with no break in form.

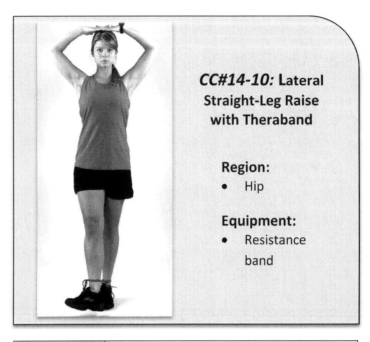

CC#14-10: Lateral Straight-Leg Raise with Theraband

Region:
- Hip

Equipment:
- Resistance band

Starting Position	1. Loop the resistance band around one ankle. Make a half-turn in the loop to form a figure "8," and slip the other end of the loop around the other ankle. 2. Stand with "straight" posture, toes pointed forward. 3. Place both hands on your head, elbows pointing out.

(CC#14-10 cont.)

Action	1. Rotate one leg at the hip so the toes point outward. 2. Keeping both knees straight, slowly raise the rotated leg straight forward, keeping the foot in neutral position. 3. Slowly return to the starting position, keeping the foot in neutral position.
Goals	1. Try to maintain a smooth, controlled motion. 2. Tighten your trunk to keep your body straight and balanced over the weightbearing leg without moving your arms. 3. Create symmetry at glide rhythm.
Focus Statement	"I will balance my body on a straight foot."
Final Target	Build up to your target time at glide rhythm: • Fitness Runners; 60 seconds each leg • Racers: 2½ minutes each leg • Total of 10 minutes, continuously, with no break in form.

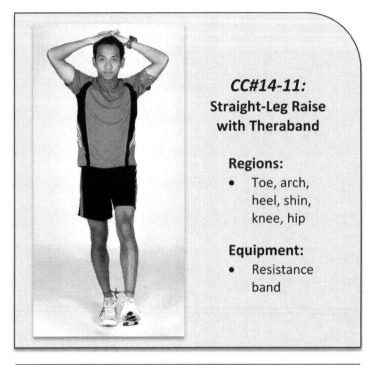

CC#14-11:
Straight-Leg Raise with Theraband

Regions:
- Toe, arch, heel, shin, knee, hip

Equipment:
- Resistance band

Starting Position	1. Loop the resistance band around one ankle. Make a half-turn in the loop to form a figure "8," and slip the other end of the loop around the other ankle.
	2. Stand with "straight" posture, toes pointed forward.
	3. Place both hands on your head, elbows pointing out.

(CC#14-11 cont.)

Action	1. Keeping both knees straight, slowly raise one leg straight forward, keeping the foot in neutral position. 2. Slowly return to the starting position, keeping the foot in neutral position.
Goals	1. Try to maintain a smooth, controlled motion while kicking forward. 2. Tighten your trunk to keep your body straight and balanced over the weight-bearing leg without moving your arms. 3. Create symmetry at glide rhythm.
Focus Statement	"I will balance my body on a straight foot."
Final Target	Build up to your target time at glide rhythm: • Fitness Runners: 60 seconds each leg • Racers: 2½ minutes each leg • Total of 10 minutes, continuously, with no break in form.

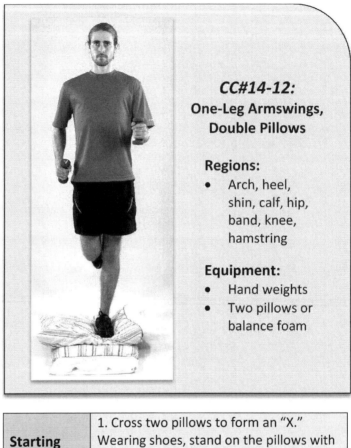

CC#14-12:
One-Leg Armswings,
Double Pillows

Regions:
- Arch, heel, shin, calf, hip, band, knee, hamstring

Equipment:
- Hand weights
- Two pillows or balance foam

Starting Position	1. Cross two pillows to form an "X." Wearing shoes, stand on the pillows with "straight" posture. 2. Bend one knee 90 degrees in the kickback position. 3. Holding a hand weight in each hand, bend elbows to 90 degrees.

(CC#14-12 cont.)

Action	1. Slowly swing your arms from the shoulder, keeping the elbows bent and close to the body. As one arm moves forward, the other arm moves backward. 2. Work up to progressively faster armswings as you accelerate to glide pace.
Goals	1. Work your arms to keep your body straight and balanced over the weight-bearing leg on this very challenging surface. 2. Achieve symmetry at glide pace.
Focus Statement	"I will use my arms to balance my body."
Final Target	Accelerate your pace after you build up to your target time: • Fitness Runners: 30 seconds each leg • Racers: 90 seconds each leg • Total of 10 minutes, continuously, with no break in form.

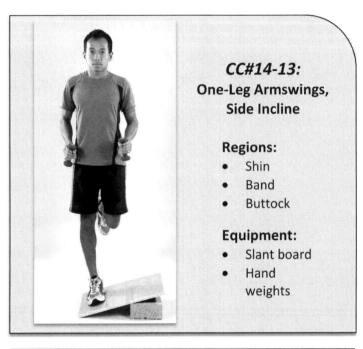

CC#14-13:
One-Leg Armswings,
Side Incline

Regions:
- Shin
- Band
- Buttock

Equipment:
- Slant board
- Hand weights

Starting Position	1. Set up an incline board so it slants to one side as you face the mirror. 2. Wearing shoes, stand on the incline board and bend the non-weightbearing knee 90 degrees to the kickback position, keeping a "straight" posture. 3. Holding a hand weight in each hand, bend elbows to 90 degrees.

(CC#14-13 cont.)

Action	1. Slowly swing your arms from the shoulder, keeping the elbows bent and close to the body. As one arm moves forward, the other arm moves backward. 2. Repeat on the other leg. 3. Change the incline board to the opposite side and repeat with both legs.
Goals	1. Use your armswings to keep your body straight and balanced over the weightbearing leg on the uneven surface. 2. Create symmetry at glide pace.
Focus Statement	"I will use my arms to balance my body."
Final Target	Accelerate your pace after you build up to your target time: • Fitness Runners: 30 seconds each leg • Racers: 90 seconds each leg • Total of 10 minutes, continuously, with no break in form.

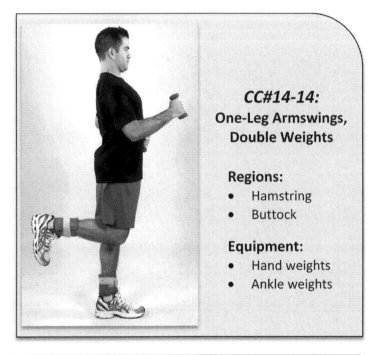

CC#14-14:
One-Leg Armswings,
Double Weights

Regions:
- Hamstring
- Buttock

Equipment:
- Hand weights
- Ankle weights

Starting Position	1. Wearing shoes and ankle weights, stand on a level surface with "straight" posture. 2. Bend one knee 90 degrees in the kickback position. 3. Holding a hand weight in each hand, bend elbows to 90 degrees.

(CC#14-14 cont.)

Action	Slowly swing your arms from the shoulder, keeping the elbows bent and close to the body. As one arm moves forward, the other arm moves backward.
Goals	1. Use your arms to balance your body while keeping the weightbearing leg straight and stationary in the kickback position. 2. Achieve symmetry at glide pace.
Focus Statement	"I will use my arms to balance my body."
Final Target	Accelerate your pace after you build up to your target time: • Fitness Runners: 30 seconds each leg • Racers: 90 seconds each leg • Total of 10 minutes, continuously, with no break in form.

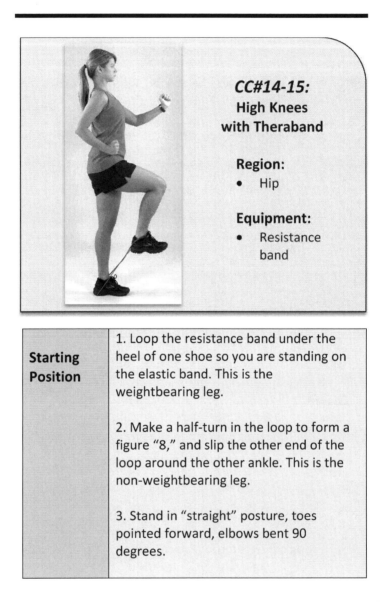

CC#14-15:
High Knees
with Theraband

Region:
• Hip

Equipment:
• Resistance
  band

Starting Position	1. Loop the resistance band under the heel of one shoe so you are standing on the elastic band. This is the weightbearing leg. 2. Make a half-turn in the loop to form a figure "8," and slip the other end of the loop around the other ankle. This is the non-weightbearing leg. 3. Stand in "straight" posture, toes pointed forward, elbows bent 90 degrees.

(CC#14-15 cont.)

Action	1. Keeping the weightbearing knee straight, raise the non-weightbearing knee directly forward to the "high knees" position, keeping the foot in neutral position. 2. Coordinate your armswings with your leg motion. 3. Slowly return to the starting position, keeping the foot in neutral position.
Goals	1. Try to maintain a smooth, controlled motion into the high knees position. 2. Tighten your trunk to keep your body straight and balanced over the weight-bearing leg. 3. Create symmetry at glide pace.
Focus Statement	"I will use my arms to balance my body."
Final Target	Build up to your target time at glide pace: • Fitness Runners: 60 seconds each leg • Racers: 2½ minutes each leg • Total of 10 minutes, continuously, with no break in form.

CC#14-16: Barefoot Push-Through

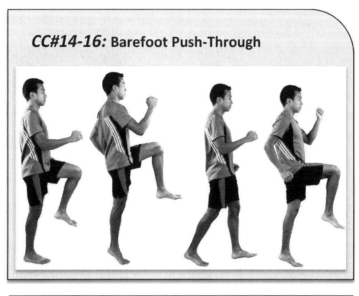

Regions	Toes, arch
Equipment	None
Starting Position	Barefoot, stand in "straight" posture, elbows bent 90 degrees.

(CC#14-16 cont.)

Action	1. Walk forward, raising the leading knee to the "high knees" position, keeping your foot aligned under the bent knee. 2. With each step, push up through the big toe of the weightbearing leg, lifting the heel off the ground, keeping the toes flat. 3. Coordinate your armswings with your leg motion.
Goals	1. Use your armswings to maintain a smooth, controlled motion. 2. Tighten your trunk to keep your body straight and balanced as you move forward from the flatfoot strike to the pushoff. 3. Create symmetry at glide pace.
Focus Statement	"I will balance my body to push off through the big toe."
Final Target	Build up to your target time at glide pace: • Fitness Runners: 4½ minute sets with 30 second rest. • Racers: One 10 minute set with no rest. • Total of 10 minutes with no break in form.

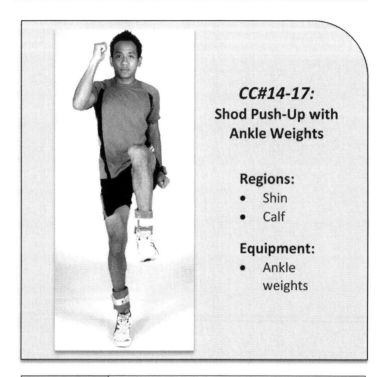

CC#14-17:
Shod Push-Up with Ankle Weights

Regions:
- Shin
- Calf

Equipment:
- Ankle weights

Starting Position	Wearing shoes and ankle weights, stand in "straight" posture, elbows bent 90 degrees.
Action	1. Raise one knee to the "high knees" position, keeping your foot aligned under the bent knee.

(CC#14-17 cont.)

Action *(cont.)*	2. Simultaneously, push up through the big toe of the weightbearing leg, lifting the heel off the ground. 3. Coordinate your armswings with your leg motion. 4. Return to the starting position and repeat.
Goals	1. Try to maintain a smooth, controlled motion throughout. 2. Tighten your trunk to keep your body straight and balanced over the weight-bearing leg. 3. Create symmetry at glide pace.
Focus Statement	"I will balance my body to push off through the big toe."
Final Target	Accelerate your pace after you build up to your target time: • Fitness Runners: 60 seconds each leg • Racers: 2 ½ minutes each leg • Total of 10 minutes, continuously, with no break in form.

CC#14-18:
Shod Push-Through with Ankle Weights

Regions	Toe, heel, calf, knee, stress fracture
Equipment	Ankle weights
Starting Position	Wearing shoes and ankle weights, stand in "straight" posture, elbows bent 90 degrees.

(CC#14-18 cont.)

Action	1. Walk forward, raising the leading knee to the "high knees" position, keeping your foot aligned under the bent knee. 2. With each step, push up through the big toe of the weightbearing leg, lifting the heel off the ground. 3. Coordinate your armswings with your leg motion.
Goals	1. Try to maintain a smooth, controlled motion to keep the weighted foot from slapping on the strike. 2. Tighten your trunk to keep your body straight and balanced as you move forward. 3. Create symmetry at glide pace.
Focus Statement	I will balance my body to push off through the big toe.
Final Target	Build up to target time at glide pace: • Fitness Runners: 4½ minute sets with 30-second rest • Racers: One 10 minute set with no rest. • Total of 10 minutes with no break in form.

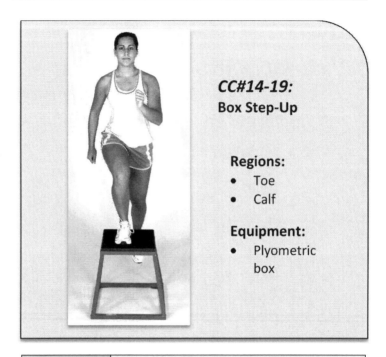

CC#14-19:
Box Step-Up

Regions:
- Toe
- Calf

Equipment:
- Plyometric box

Starting Position	Wearing shoes, stand in "straight" posture with a high box in front of you as you face the mirror; arms bent 90 degrees.
Action	1. Place one foot flat on the box, toes pointed forward. 2. With the lower (second) foot, push up through the big toe. 3. Continuing your motion, step up on the box with both feet.

(CC#14-19 cont.)

Action **(cont.)**	4. Coordinate your armswings with your leg motion. 5. Leaving the second foot on the box, step backward to the original position with the first foot.
Goals	1. Concentrate on a flatfoot stride and push through with a slow, smooth, controlled motion throughout. 2. Use slow, coordinated armswings to keep your body straight and balanced as you move up and down. 3. Create symmetry at glide pace.
Focus Statement	"I will balance my body to push off through the big toe."
Final Target	1. Gradually raise step height until hip and knee are bent at 90 degrees (high knees position). 2. Build up to target time at glide pace: • Fitness Runners: 2½ minutes each leg • Racers 5: minutes each leg • Total of 10 minutes, continuously, with no break in form.

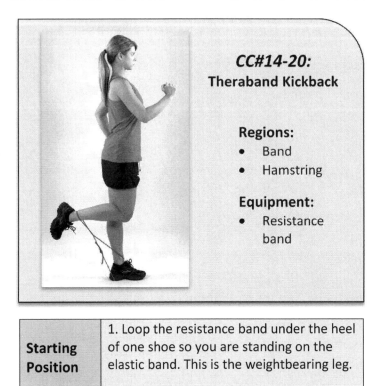

CC#14-20:
Theraband Kickback

Regions:
- Band
- Hamstring

Equipment:
- Resistance band

Starting Position	1. Loop the resistance band under the heel of one shoe so you are standing on the elastic band. This is the weightbearing leg. 2. Make a half-turn in the loop to form a figure "8," and slip the other end of the loop around the other ankle. This is the non-weightbearing leg. 3. Stand in "straight" posture, toes pointed forward, elbows bent 90 degrees. 4. Keeping the knees even, bend the non-weightbearing knee until the toe is just touching down in the "glide" position.

(CC#14-20 cont.)

Action	1. Keeping the weightbearing knee straight, slowly bend the non-weightbearing knee to the "kickback" position – raising the heel 90 degrees toward the glutes. 2. Alternately bend and straighten the non-weightbearing knee, coordinating your armswings with your leg motion.
Goals	1. Try to maintain a smooth, controlled motion as you kick back. 2. Tighten your trunk to keep your body straight and balanced over the weight-bearing leg. 3. Create symmetry at glide pace.
Focus Statement	"I will balance my body for a straight kickback."
Final Target	Accelerate your pace after you build up to your target time: • Fitness Runners: 60 seconds each leg • Racers: 2½ minutes each leg • Total of 10 minutes, continuously, with no break in form.

Box 14-3	*Guidelines:* Basic Closed-Chain Exercises

1. Assemble the required equipment, including a calculator and a stopwatch or timer (See *Table 14-2: Equipment for Closed-Chain Exercises*).

2. In your *Running Injury Recovery Workbook*, complete one **Log Form B: Basic Closed-Chain** for each day.

3. Carefully follow the instructions for each exercise in **Box 14-2**. Note that exercises 1 through 8 have instructions for both *Basic Closed-Chain Clearance* and *Final Target* (for Regional Closed-Chain). While you are using **Log Form B**, skip the instructions for *Final Target*.

4. Do *only* the eight Basic Closed-Chain Exercises (**Box 14-2** *Figures 14-1* through *14-8*) during Phase Three Part One P.T. Time. On your first day, choose four exercises and spend 10 minutes on each one. Do the other four exercises on your second day.

5. Each 10-minute exercise is broken into several **sets**. The maximum number of exercise sets you can complete in 10 minutes will vary, depending upon your fitness and the clearance goal for each Basic Closed-Chain Exercise. The *Target Time* for each exercise varies by exercise, from 15 to 60 seconds, and may or may not include a *Rest Between Sets*. (*Target Times* and *Rest Between Sets* are listed in the instructions on the line for *Basic Closed-Chain Clearance,* and on **Log Form B**.) Once you have reached the *Target Time* on the better leg, you can reduce the sets on that leg to a minimum of 3, and increase your sets on the other leg.

(Box 14-3 cont.)

6. For each exercise, start with your least-affected leg and time how long you can maintain correct form without increasing pain. *Example:* Square Hops. Starting on your better leg, hop clockwise around the square, and then counter clockwise. Keep going on the same leg for as long as you can stay balanced and accept load without increasing pain, or up to the *Target Time* of 20 seconds. Then repeat on the more-affected leg for comparison.

7. While performing each exercise, concentrate on the *Goals* for that exercise. Use the *Focus Statement* to help maintain correct form, create symmetry, and improve body awareness. Correct form means that you are able to hold the *Starting Position* as shown in the figure for that exercise, perform the described *Action*, and achieve the goals listed in the *Focus Statement*.

8. Stop each set when you feel fatigued, break form, or reach the *Target Time* for that exercise. It is better to do an exercise correctly for a shorter time than incorrectly for a longer time. Do not exceed the *Target Time* per set, even if you feel like you can. Record the time for each set on your **Log Form B** for that day.

9. Monitor your maximum pain level in each leg for each exercise, and enter those numbers on **Log Form B.**

10. For each exercise in Basic Closed-Chain, practice more sets on your weaker leg than on your stronger leg, even if the weaker leg in that exercise is not the injured leg. You must achieve **symmetry** in all exercises to clear Basic Closed-Chain before continuing to Regional Closed-Chain.

(Box 14-3 cont.)

Average set times on left and right legs are considered equal (symmetrical) if they are within 5% of each other (see *Symmetry Goals* in **Log Form B**).

11. *Special Instructions for CC#6 Quick Steps:* Because this exercise is performed with both legs at the same time, you will not be able to measure a separate time for each leg. Stop each set when you become fatigued or break form, and record that time on your log form. Do not do more than one set every 30 seconds (20 sets in 10 minutes). For this exercise, symmetry is defined as the ability to maintain correct form at glide rhythm, equal weight on both legs, with no increase in pain.

12. When you have completed your daily P.T. Time, complete the calculations on **Log Form B** to check for symmetry and clearance for those exercises (see **Instructions for Log Form B** in the Workbook.)

13. Continue rotating through the eight Basic Closed-Chain Exercises, doing four a day, 10 minutes each, for a total of 40 minutes. When you have cleared a particular Basic Closed-Chain Exercise, you can eliminate that exercise from your next rotation. When you have less than four exercises left to clear, you'll have some extra 10-minute sessions to fill. Select one of the Basic Closed-Chain Exercises you have already cleared at the *Basic* level, and try building your time and/or rhythm up to the *Final Target* level.

14. Continue to Regional Closed-Chain Exercises when you have cleared all eight Basic Closed-Chain Exercises.

Box 14-4 — Guidelines: Regional Closed-Chain Exercises

1. In your *Running Injury Recovery Workbook*, fill out one section of **Log Form R: Regional Closed-Chain** for each day of P.T. Time. (See *Self-Assessment 3B Part 2*, and **Instructions for Log Form R** in the Workbook.)

2. Continue to follow the same general guidelines for exercises that you used in Basic Closed-Chain [**Box 14-3**].

3. Carefully follow the instructions in **Box 14-2** for each individual exercise. Note that exercises 1 through 8 have instructions for both *Basic Closed-Chain Clearance* and *Final Target*. While you are using **Log Form R**, skip the instructions for *Basic Closed-Chain Clearance*.

4. Regional Closed-Chain Exercises progress in two stages. You must clear all of your Regional Closed-Chain Exercises in *Stage 1* (Symmetry and Clearance), before you progress to *Stage 2* (Build to Final Target).

5. On your first day of Regional Closed-Chain Exercises in Stage 1, follow the **Instructions for Log Form R** in the Workbook. Do the first four exercises on **Log Form R** (1st Injury Region), and complete your *Initial Assessment* for those exercises. Enter your Stage 1 *Symmetry Target* and *Symmetry Goal* for each exercise on **Log Form R**, and continue to use those numbers until you have cleared all Regional Closed-Chain Exercises in Stage 1.

(Box 14-4 cont.)

6. On your second PT day, continue with the next four exercises on your list, in order (the last two exercises for your 1st Injury Region, and first two exercises for your 2nd Injury Region). Complete your *Initial Assessment* for each exercise, and enter your Stage 1 *Symmetry Target* and *Symmetry Goal* on your **Log Form R.**

7. Continue with four new exercises and *Initial Assessments* in each PT session until you reach the end of your list, then start again at the top of the list with a new rotation.

8. When you begin a new rotation, copy the *Symmetry Target* and *Symmetry Goal* for each exercise from your first **Log Form R**. Do not repeat your *Initial Assessment*. For each exercise, do more repetitions on the more-impaired side, and fewer repetitions on the less-impaired side, until you have achieved symmetry (*Self-Assessment 3F* in the Workbook).

9. Follow the **Instructions for Log Form R** for Stage 1 and Stage 2. In Stage 1, when you have achieved symmetry in one exercise, you may skip that exercise in your next rotation and go on to the next exercise. As in Basic Closed-Chain, when you have less than 4 exercises remaining on your list, add back exercises that you have already cleared so that you always have 40 minutes of closed-chain exercises in Stage 1.

(Box 14-4 cont.)

10. Follow the instructions in *Self-Assessment 3F* in your *Running Injury Recovery Workbook* to clear Stage 1. You must achieve symmetry for all Regional Closed-Chain Exercises on your list before you begin Stage 2.

11. When you have cleared Stage 1, follow the **Instructions for Log Form R, Stage 2** to revise your **Log Form R** for Stage 2. In Stage 2, you must maintain symmetry in all Regional Closed-Chain Exercises, and work to *build* your time and pace toward the goals listed in the *Final Target* for each exercise (for fitness runner or racers). These will be your goals for Phase Four, not clearance requirements.

12. You must clear both Regional Closed-Chain Stage 1 and your Phase Three Part Two *Base Schedule* before you can proceed to Phase Four *(Self-Assessment 3H)* in *The Running Injury Recovery Workbook.*

* * *

Chapter 15
Fitness Walking and Glides

At this point in your recovery, the acute phase is over. You've controlled the inflammation, you've found the stiffness and mobilized it, and you've identified the weakness and strengthened it with closed-chain exercises. You understand the importance of mental focus, you've got the right shoes, and you're ready to begin your *post-injury running* exercises.

Post-injury running begins a phase of progressive weight-bearing that will continue until you have reached all of your weight-bearing goals. You'll warm up with **fitness walking**, which allows you to purposefully focus on your stride while loading your body-weight through the injured structure. In your **walk/glide program**, you'll gradually start building up your running base, and add more drills to improve your balance and strength.

Your ultimate goal is not just to return to running (*post-recovery running*), but to run better than you did before – stronger, smoother, and more efficiently. Performance-wise, that means running faster with less risk of injury.

As a P.T. and running coach, I really got into improving performance when I opened my running specialty store, *The Runner's High*, in Miami. We took over the management of the Miami Runner's Club, and I began working with lots of runners who wanted to improve their performance. One club member in particular, "Henry," was a serious runner who had run a few marathons but was always getting injured. If it wasn't one thing it was another, and he was getting desperate for a solution to his chronic running problems.

Henry first came to my P.T. office with runner's toe, and was in a great deal of pain. He'd had cortisone shots, he took medication, and he had orthotics and all kinds of stuff stuck in his shoes. He would do anything to run. I got him out of all that stuff and into a good running shoe. We corrected his injury problems, and then we improved his stride with a good post-injury running program. As a result, Henry became injury free, dropped an hour in his marathon time, and went on to run many great marathons. By carefully following his recovery program, Henry not only overcame his injury, he also retrained himself to run really well – and you can do the same.

15.1 Establishing Your Base Schedule

In Phase Three Part Two, you will continue with your P.T. Time (self-mobilizations, stretches, and regional closed-chain exercises) for one hour, two times per week. In addition, you're going to build a walk/glide program that establishes a strong and correct running base for when you are out of recovery and can return to your regular fitness program, or train for an event, or get back with your coaches. In other words, you're training to get back to training.

First, you'll need to establish a regular **Base Schedule** for your walk/glide program (*Self-Assessment 3F* in the *Workbook*). Your Base Schedule will consist of three elements that vary according to your individual goals and capabilities: duration, frequency, and distance.

Duration: A walk/glide program typically will go for one hour. That's a constant for most runners, depending upon your individual ability. A recovery training session that goes much longer than that starts to become regular training – but at this point we want to work just a little below that level.

Frequency: A runner will typically commit to daily training three, four, or five times a week, depending upon his goals. Six or more times a week for an hour is beyond the frequency for injury management, and two times a week is not enough running to strengthen your body. If your goal is fitness, you may train three to five times a week, depending upon your goals. If your goal is racing, you'll do post-injury training four or five times a week.

Distance: A typical pace for fitness walking is 3.5 to 4 miles per hour, which is faster than you normally walk. A typical pace for gliding might be anywhere from 4 to 7 miles per hour, which is slower than you normally run. Your Base Schedule should target between 10 and 25 miles per week of gliding, depending upon your goals and experience. Gliding less than 10 miles a week is really not enough, but gliding more than 25 miles a week while in recovery can cause problems. For optimum post-injury training benefits, you have to find that "sweet spot" somewhere in-between.

It's important to note that, while in recovery, a mileage goal of 10 to 25 miles a week does *not* mean 10 miles one week and 25 miles the next week. You have to be consistent. Determine the distance that works for you, and stick with it until you have recovered.

If you are a fitness runner, your *minimum* Base Schedule should be walk/gliding three times a week, building up to 3 to 4 miles of gliding per workout, for a total of 10 miles of gliding per week. If your goal is to train for racing, your *minimum* Base Schedule should be walk/gliding for one hour, four times a week, and building up to 4 to 6 miles of gliding per workout. Neither group should exceed a *maximum* of 6 miles of gliding sessions, five sessions per week, with a limit of 25 miles per week.

In some cases, when you first begin your walk/glide program you might not be able to reach your minimum goal, but that's okay. When you begin fitness walking, and again when you begin glides, your level of effort will increase, and you may feel some return of your original injury pain. Do not continue walk/gliding if this pain causes you to limp. In post-injury training, it's important to work at a **submaximal level** that doesn't increase your symptoms above Stage 2. If at any time you experience Stage 3 symptoms, or any Red Flags, you'll have to stop and go back to the previous Clearance Checkpoint – so don't overdo it. During recovery, doing less is sometimes better than trying to do too much.

Once you have established the duration, frequency, and distance for your Base Schedule, the most important thing is *consistency*. For example, you might train for two or three days, then take two days off. Some people can only train four days in a row, then take three days off, because that's their work schedule. That's fine, as long as you're consistent.

Table 15-1
How To Estimate Your Base Schedeule

Last Regular Training Schedule:	Fitness Runners	Racers
Less than 10 mi/wk	3 to 4 miles, 3 times per week	3 to 4 miles, 4 to 5 times per week
10 to 25 mi/wk	Previous mileage divided into 3 or 4 times per week	Previous mileage divided into 4 or 5 times per week
More than 25 mi/wk	No more than 5 miles, 5 times per week	No more than 5 miles, 5 times per week

15.2 Post-Injury Running Posture

As a PT, one of the things I look at a lot is posture. There are lots of books that promote different styles of running, involving different degrees of lean, modifications in stride and armswing, and specific footwear (or lack thereof). Each style has its own posture. Some have you leaning or bending forward, or twisting your arms in a particular way – but they're all altering your stride and your balance point.

Although most of these books talk about "injury prevention," they're not intended to deal with injury management. Leaning forward has a place in some styles of *post-recovery running*, but not in *post-injury running*. For post-injury running, I don't want you to lean forward because that prevents you from centering your balance over your injury – and weight-bearing through your injured region is the whole point of the exercise.

Wherever your injury is, I want your weight centered over it during post-injury running. I don't want your weight forward, backward, or to one side. We practice post-injury running under a very tight balance point. We're purposely trying to put the load directly through the injury – finding the impairment, and finding the weakness. That's what we're paying attention to. So, no forward leaning, and no wobbling.

15.3 Focus on Stride and Technique

The natural result of an injury is imbalance. We favor the region that's injured. We avoid placing weight evenly on the injured side. We cheat on the weakened area by leaning forward, or by leaning sideways. If we continue doing that, several things happen: we lose strength and function on the injured side, we get out of balance, and we get habituated to a **compensatory pattern** of movement that can cause a running injury later on if it's not identified and corrected. Addressing these problems as quickly as possible is one of the main goals of your recovery program.

Now is the time to begin focusing on your stride (or **gait**, as we call it in physical therapy). You're going to take what you learned in your closed-chain exercises about balance and body awareness, and apply it to three different strides as you progress from fitness walking and gliding to accelerations and plyometrics.

People say that it's hard to change your stride – that it's hard to force changes in the musculo-skeletal functions that control walking or running. Well, yeah, but that's an important part of physical therapy – improving your stride. Physical therapists use many different approaches to correct a patient's stride, and one important thing I've learned is, there's no such thing as a perfect stride. To start out, all we'll be looking for is a stride that will help you make progress in getting over your injury. It's not a perfect way to run, it's just a way to progress back to running.

To do that, we're going to have to modify your stride and correct any habituated techniques that you've developed, that cause you to put a dysfunctional load through your injury. We're really focusing on posture, balance, and awareness of body positioning. Forcing you to walk (since fitness walking has not been habituated) makes you regroup and think about what you are doing.

We're looking for a balanced, efficient stride that allows you to get stronger and safely transition back to running. That's the ultimate goal of your walk/glide program.

In this phase, each exercise includes a general *Mental Focus Statement* that you should concentrate on. Mental focus is important throughout your recovery program, and it's particularly important in fitness walking and glides. As you are exercising, think about your injury: the weaknesses, the stiffnesses, and all the things you've learned in your recovery program. Observe your body in all three planes of body position. Try to loosen up the stiffness and become stronger and more aware. As you progress through your walk/glide program, concentrate on your form and body awareness, not on trying to go fast. Focus on staying smooth, upright, and balanced.

15.4 Biomechanics: From Foot-Strike to Pushoff

Before you begin your walk/glide program, we have to discuss the runner's foot-strike, which translates into three basic running strides (*Table 15-2*). There's always been a lot of controversy over which part of the foot we're supposed to land on. Do we land on our forefoot, or on our midfoot, or on our hindfoot?

Forefoot running is very important in sprinting and accelerations. You have to be on your forefoot to go super-fast over short distances. Some running-book authors recommend that people run slowly on their forefeet, but I don't – I see that as prancing. We'll talk more about forefoot running in Phase Four when we start working on accelerations.

When people discuss landing on the *midfoot*, I always translate that in my mind to *flatfoot*, because the midfoot is an anatomically impossible region to land on. (*P.T. Note:* The outer midfoot is your cuboid bone. The forefoot begins at the metatarsals, which begin farther back than most people realize; and the hindfoot is the calcaneous, which extends farther forward than most people think.)

Most distance runners strike on their hindfoot. For some reason, much of the popular press portrays striking on the hindfoot as a bad thing, yet it clearly works for lots of great runners.

There was an interesting study that recorded the strides of elite runners in the middle of a half-marathon. In that study, only one percent were running on their forefoot in the middle of the race. Twenty-four percent were landing on what was called the midfoot, and seventy-five percent were striking on their hindfoot. My point is, during any distance race you can find elite runners who are forefoot strikers, flatfoot strikers, and hindfoot strikers, all running together at the same pace. When it comes to running, there is no right or wrong stride – as long as you're not injured.

That said, while you're recovering from a running injury, you're going to have to do things differently. You're wearing supportive shoes, and you're working toward a stable, efficient stride. You're not trying to find the stride where you're the fastest, you just want to find a stride that moves you forward in your *post-injury running* and gets you to *post-recovery running*. Then you can work on your performance!

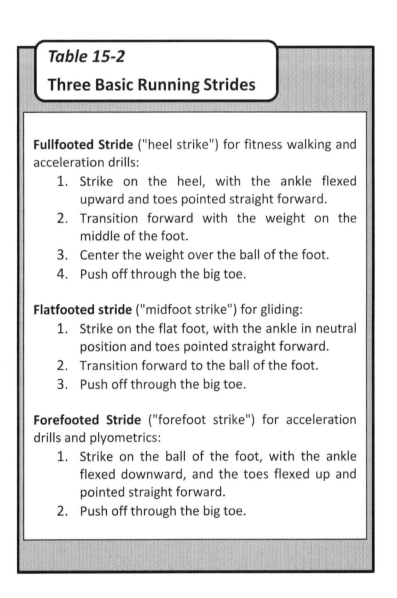

Table 15-2

Three Basic Running Strides

Fullfooted Stride ("heel strike") for fitness walking and acceleration drills:

1. Strike on the heel, with the ankle flexed upward and toes pointed straight forward.
2. Transition forward with the weight on the middle of the foot.
3. Center the weight over the ball of the foot.
4. Push off through the big toe.

Flatfooted stride ("midfoot strike") for gliding:

1. Strike on the flat foot, with the ankle in neutral position and toes pointed straight forward.
2. Transition forward to the ball of the foot.
3. Push off through the big toe.

Forefooted Stride ("forefoot strike") for acceleration drills and plyometrics:

1. Strike on the ball of the foot, with the ankle flexed downward, and the toes flexed up and pointed straight forward.
2. Push off through the big toe.

This is how I do it: When you come to my office with a running injury, I slow you down. We select a post-injury shoe that gives you proper support and is properly fitted. For fitness walking, you're going to land way back on your hindfoot, then move forward in a straight line, heel-to-toe, in a **fullfoot stride**. This puts you into a smooth landing position to prepare you for gliding.

For the glides, you're going to land **flatfooted**, with your ankle pretty well neutral. I don't want you landing firmly on your heel. We're looking for a smooth, balanced stride throughout your walk/glide exercises. In *post-injury running*, the focus is on control and balance. You have to control where you land. You have to pay attention to the specific impairments of the injury region, and to strengthen those impairments. You want your stride to be light and smooth and even. We're purposely manipulating your stride for that outcome – and being more flatfooted on the glide helps you balance your weight-bearing through the injury.

Ultimately, where you land is not as important as where you push off. All runners have to push off through the big toe (the **first ray**) – not to the outside of the first ray, and not to the inside. Whether you run fullfooted, flatfooted, or forefooted, the pushoff through the first ray is the same. Runners may argue about the best place to land, but no one argues about the best place to push off – and your goal is a strong and balanced pushoff.

15.5 Two Recovery Groups

As you begin your walk/glide program in Phase Three Part Two, you will again be sorted into one of two recovery groups based on the complexity of your injury and other factors (*Self-Assessment 3F* in the *Workbook*). Each group is then divided into two subgroups (A and B), based on your ability to clear Basic Closed-Chain Exercises in one week or less *(Table 15-3A)*.

Group 1 includes only those who have simple injuries (as defined in *Self-Assessment 2B* in the *Workbook*), and have been away from regular training for less than six weeks. In this group, the goal is to progress as quickly as possible, following an individualized, **Self-Paced Plan**. If you are in Group 1, this means you will enter the progressive series of walk/glide sets at the highest level that is safe for you, which in turn will depend upon how long you were able to run with your original injury before you started feeling pain *(Table 15-3B)*.

This Self-Paced Plan will move Group 1 through the walk/glide sets as fast as their symptoms will allow. Subgroup 1A (those who have cleared Basic Closed-Chain Exercises in one week or less) will proceed directly to their walk/glide program, following their individual Base Schedule. Subgroup 1B (those who have *not* cleared Basic Closed-Chain Exercises in one week or less) will Fitness Walk their Base Schedule until they have cleared Basic Closed-Chain Exercises. At that point, Group 1B will reassess their group status and join either Group 1A (away from regular training for *less* than six weeks) or Group 2A (away from regular training for *more* than six weeks). Group 1A will progress through their walk/glide sets until cleared, and finish Phase Three with one week of 50-minute glide sets.

Table 15-3 A: Base Schedule Startup
All Groups

Group 1A Self-Paced Plan	
Start with appropriate level of Log Form S (See *Table 15-3 B*)	

Group 1B Self-Paced Plan	
Start with Log Form S, Level 0 (fitness walking)	Reassess Group after clearing Basic Closed-Chain Exercises

Group 2A Two-Week Interval Plan	
Start with Log Form S, Level 0 (fitness walking)	Begin walk/glides after 2 weeks

Group 2B Two Week Interval Plan	
Start with Log Form S, Level 0 (fitness walking)	Begin walk/glides after clearing Basic Closed-Chain AND 2 weeks of fitness walking

Table 15-3 B: Base Schedule Startup Group 1A, Self-Paced Plan

With your original injury, if you had pain after running:	Start with Log Form S:
Less than 10 minutes, or 1 mile	Level 0
10 to 20 minutes, or 1 to 2 miles	Level 1
20 to 30 minutes, or 2 to 3 miles	Level 2
30 to 40 minutes, or 3 to 4 miles	Level 3
40 to 50 minutes, or 4 to 5 miles	Level 4
More than 50 minutes or 5 miles	Level 5

Group 2 includes all those who have complex injuries, and those who have been away from regular training for six weeks or more. Everyone in Group 2 will follow the **Two-Week-Interval Plan**, which begins with two weeks of fitness walking. Group 2A (those who cleared Basic Closed-Chain Exercises in one week or less) will then progress to walk/glide sets. Group 2B (those who have *not* cleared Basic Closed-Chain Exercises) will continue fitness walking until they have cleared all Basic Closed-Chain Exercises, then progress to walk/glide sets. Everyone in Group 2 will begin walk/glide sets at Level 1 (1-4 sets), and take a *minimum* of two weeks at each level before progressing to the next higher level (2-3, 3-2, 4-1, and 50-minute glide sets). Yes, that does add up to at least 10 weeks in the walk/glide program. If you are in Group 2, we're purposely slowing you down to make sure that every trace of your injury is healed and strengthened before you continue.

15.6 Fitness Walking

Fitness walking is a controlled, high-energy form of fullfooted (heel-to-toe) walking **[Box 15-2]**. Everyone (both Group 1 and Group 2) will *always* start with a 10-minute fitness walk to warm up before they run one step. I just can't emphasize that enough. Warmup is about vasodilation – getting blood to specific muscles, tendons and other structures used in running – to prepare them for a more intense effort. Other exercises, such as biking, don't do that – they use different muscles. Even in triathlon, where we transition from bike to running, the

315

bike doesn't count as a warm-up for running because the blood is distributed in different regions.

Warmup fitness walking is also a daily check-up for gliding. You'll walk to loosen up the injury, and to make sure you can walk painlessly before gliding. If your injury doesn't loosen up in ten minutes, that's a Red Flag and you'll have to take a step back in your recovery process.

If you are in Group 2, your goal is to fitness walk your Base Schedule for two weeks without raising any Red Flags. Depending upon the severity of your injury, you may have to work up to it a little at a time. If you begin limping while fitness walking, or if your symptoms go to Stage 3 on the Injury Stage Scale, that's a Red Flag to back up.

Once you've finished with your injury-management program, you are free to get rid of the 10-minute fitness walk if you want to. However, a lot of my runners find that those ten minutes really help them warm up, and they never give it up. In other words, you can stop fitness walking in *post-recovery running*, but you must do it during *post-injury running*.

15.7 Glides

The walk/glide program is structured as a progressive series of increasingly challenging running exercises. These are the exercises that are going to strengthen your weaknesses and prepare you for running. It's not the stretching, it's not the balancing, it's not the self-mobilization, and it's not the shoes – those just get you to where you can safely train on your injury.

Ultimately, the only way you'll get strong enough for running is to run.

I describe **glides** as a very smooth, controlled running motion **[Box 15-3]**. It's not a maximum effort; it's an efficient effort, kind of like a long-distance training stride. You won't be trying for speed or distance here. You're just starting out with very short intervals of gliding, alternating with periods of fitness walking. Switching between fitness walking and gliding helps you focus on the signs and symptoms of your injury, while helping you progressively strengthen your weaknesses. We want forward momentum in the process of recovery, and a good mental focus will help you avoid sliding backwards on the injury stage scale. As you progress through your walk/glide sets, you'll gradually be eliminating fitness walking and adding more glides. The actual progression of interval training will differ somewhat among individuals, depending upon which recovery group you are in and your ability to progress.

Keep in mind that you won't really feel all the effects of a workout until it's over, or maybe even until the next day. It's okay if you still feel like you can do more at the end of your training session. It's more important to progress carefully and take the time to evaluate your condition so you don't get reinjured. If at any time you find that your injury doesn't loosen up during the warmup, or if you're having pain that relates to the injury while fitness walking, *don't* try to glide on it – go back to fitness walking, and be extra careful with your progression next time!

15.8 Glide Drills for Balance

Keeping your balance while running is harder than keeping your balance while walking. In your walk/glide program, you're going to build on the balance skills you learned in closed-chain exercises by practicing armswing and stride control (**glide drills**) during your glides – trying to feel the connection between your elbows and your pelvis, or your feet and your pelvis, and trying not wobble. You'll purposely lose your balance by moving your arms in or out, or to the front or to the back; then use your arms to find your balance. You'll purposely lose your balance by running with your feet in or with your feet out, then straighten your feet to find your balance. All of this is hard to do. When I train runners, I can tell how hard it is by the looks of concentration on their faces!

There are five variations of glide drills that you will insert into the glide portion of your walk/glide program [**Box 15-4**]: two drills for finding your balance using your arms, two drills for finding your balance using your feet, and one for balancing your upper body over your pelvis. Each drill should be performed for about 15 seconds while gliding, with about 1 minute in-between drills. If you are doing 1-4 sets (1 minute gliding and 4 minutes fitness walking), you can insert one drill into a 1 minute glide. If you are doing 2-4 sets, you can insert one or two glide drills, and so on. Your goal is to do each of the five glide drills three times (a total of 15 glide drills) during your 50-minute glide sets without breaking form or losing your balance (*Table 15-4*).

It's important to maintain correct form as you transition between gliding and glide drills. Remember, you don't want to practice doing any of these exercises the wrong way. At first, you may have to slow down your pace to achieve symmetry and balance, then gradually build your speed back up to your normal glide rhythm while maintaining that symmetry and balance.

15.9 Moving Ahead

The Clearance Checkpoint at the end of Phase Three is the same for both Groups 1 and 2. You must be able to complete your Base Schedule with 50-minute glide sets (including gliding drills) for the required amount of time with correct form and no increase in symptoms. You must also be able to perform all of your Regional Closed-Chain Exercises with symmetry and no increase in symptoms.

At the end of Phase Three, your injury symptoms should be completely gone. You will have corrected any dysfunction in your stride. You'll be strong, balanced, and mentally focused. At this point, most recovery programs would clear you to return to running – but that's actually where they go wrong. Right after an injury is the time when you are most susceptible to reinjury. You have come a long way and made great gains, and you don't want to lose that by being in too much of a hurry, so just be patient for a little while longer. In Phase Four you will be challenged to your limits, and that's where you will truly become a better, stronger, and safer runner.

***

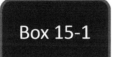

Box 15-1

HOW TO: Build Your
Walk/Glide Program

The formula for a 60-minute training session is
**10 minutes fitness walking + [5 minutes (Glide + Walk) x
10 sets] = 60 minutes.** I keep walk/glide sets in units of
5 minutes because it's easy to set your timer.

1. *Warm Up:* Always begin with 10 minutes of **fitness
walking** to warm up. If you are not able to fitness walk
for 10 minutes without pain or breaking form, do not
proceed to walk/glide sets.

2. *Walk/Glide Sets:* After the warm-up, begin your series
of 5-minute walk/glide sets. There are five progressive
levels of walk/glide sets, each consisting of one or more
minutes of **gliding** followed by four or fewer minutes of
fitness walking *Table 15-4*]. Follow the instructions for
Group 1 (Self-Paced Plan) or Group 2 (Two-Week-
Interval Plan).

3. *Glide Drills:* There are five variations of **glide drills
[Box 15-4]**.
- For 1-4 sets, insert one 15-second glide drill into
  each 1-minute glide for a total of 10 glide drills (do
  each of the five glide drills twice).
- For 2-3 sets and higher, do each of the five glide
  drills three times for a total of 15 glide drills per
  training session.

4. *Cool Down:* At the end of each walk/glide session,
fitness walk for at least five minutes to cool down.

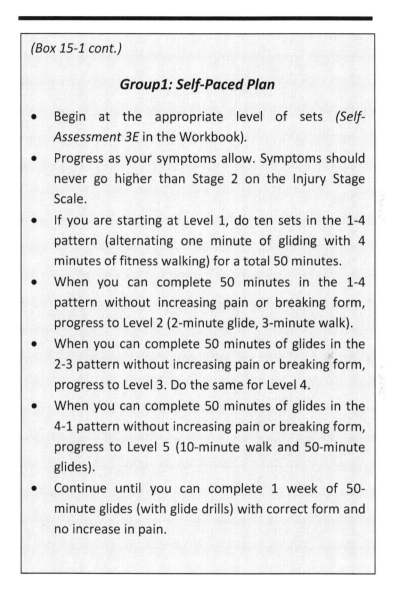

(Box 15-1 cont.)

Group1: Self-Paced Plan

- Begin at the appropriate level of sets *(Self-Assessment 3E* in the Workbook).
- Progress as your symptoms allow. Symptoms should never go higher than Stage 2 on the Injury Stage Scale.
- If you are starting at Level 1, do ten sets in the 1-4 pattern (alternating one minute of gliding with 4 minutes of fitness walking) for a total 50 minutes.
- When you can complete 50 minutes in the 1-4 pattern without increasing pain or breaking form, progress to Level 2 (2-minute glide, 3-minute walk).
- When you can complete 50 minutes of glides in the 2-3 pattern without increasing pain or breaking form, progress to Level 3. Do the same for Level 4.
- When you can complete 50 minutes of glides in the 4-1 pattern without increasing pain or breaking form, progress to Level 5 (10-minute walk and 50-minute glides).
- Continue until you can complete 1 week of 50-minute glides (with glide drills) with correct form and no increase in pain.

(Box 15-1 cont.)

Group 2: Two-Week-Interval Plan

- Fitness walk your Base Schedule for a *minimum* of two weeks (Log Form S Level 0). You must clear all Basic Closed-Chain Exercises before progressing to walk/glide sets.
- Begin walk/glide sets at Level 1 (1-4 sets) for a total of 10 sets in 50 minutes. Do 1-4 sets for a *minimum* of two weeks, continuing until you can complete the 50 minutes with correct form and no increase in symptoms. Your symptoms should never go above Stage 2 on the Injury Stage Scale.
- When you have cleared the 1-4 sets, you can progress to Level 2 (2-3 sets). Do 2-3 sets for a *minimum* of two weeks, continuing until you can complete 50 minutes with correct form and no increase in symptoms.
- Do the same for Level 3 (3-2 sets) and Level 4 (4-1 sets), for a *minimum* of two weeks each, continuing until you can complete 50 minutes with correct form and no increase in symptoms.
- When you have cleared 4-1 sets with no increase in pain or break in form for two weeks, begin Level 5 (50-minute glides with glide drills).
- Complete at least two weeks at Level 5. Continue until you can complete at least two consecutive workouts with correct form and no increase in pain.

Table 15-4 A
Base Schedule: Level 1

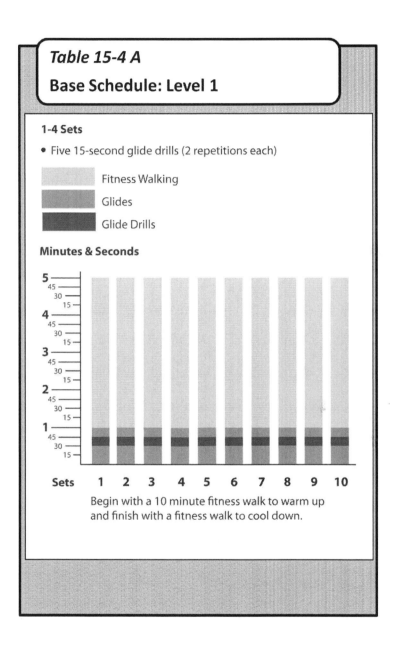

1-4 Sets

- Five 15-second glide drills (2 repetitions each)

  Fitness Walking

  Glides

  Glide Drills

Minutes & Seconds

Sets   1   2   3   4   5   6   7   8   9   10

Begin with a 10 minute fitness walk to warm up and finish with a fitness walk to cool down.

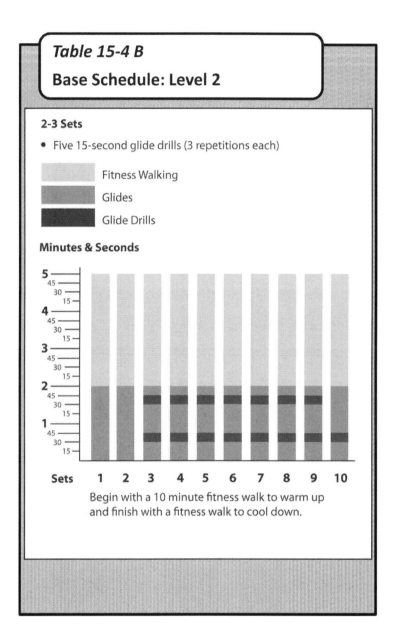

Table 15-4 B

Base Schedule: Level 2

2-3 Sets

• Five 15-second glide drills (3 repetitions each)

Fitness Walking

Glides

Glide Drills

Minutes & Seconds

Sets: 1 2 3 4 5 6 7 8 9 10

Begin with a 10 minute fitness walk to warm up and finish with a fitness walk to cool down.

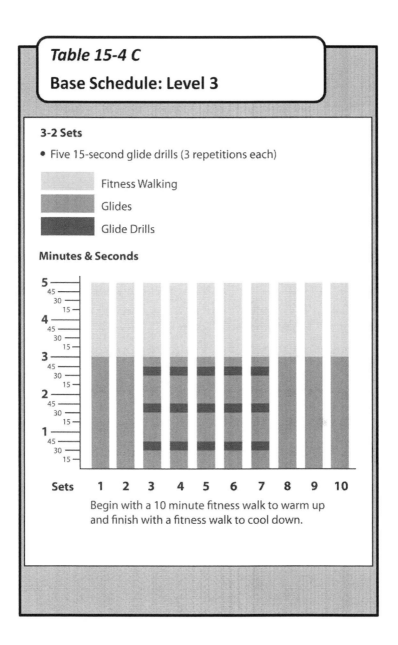

Table 15-4 C
Base Schedule: Level 3

3-2 Sets

• Five 15-second glide drills (3 repetitions each)

[light] Fitness Walking
[medium] Glides
[dark] Glide Drills

Minutes & Seconds

Sets: 1 2 3 4 5 6 7 8 9 10

Begin with a 10 minute fitness walk to warm up
and finish with a fitness walk to cool down.

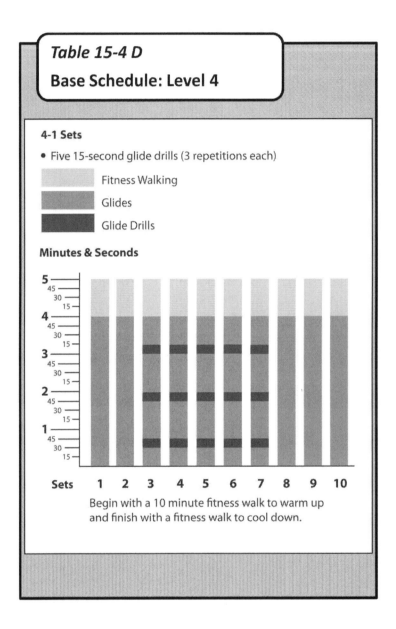

Table 15-4 D

Base Schedule: Level 4

4-1 Sets

• Five 15-second glide drills (3 repetitions each)

Fitness Walking

Glides

Glide Drills

Minutes & Seconds

Begin with a 10 minute fitness walk to warm up and finish with a fitness walk to cool down.

Table 15-4 E
Base Schedule: Level 5

50-Minute Glides

- Five 15-seconds glide drills (3 repetitions each)

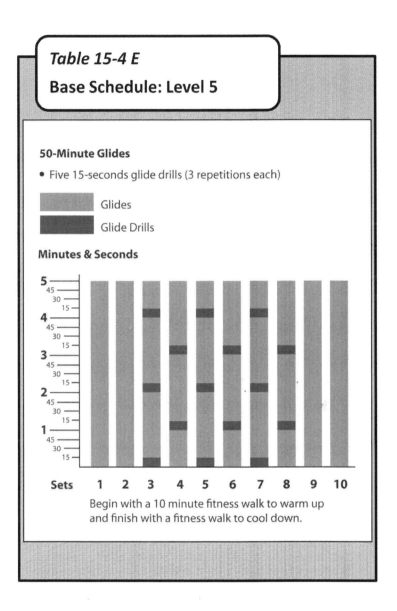

Glides

Glide Drills

Minutes & Seconds

Sets   1   2   3   4   5   6   7   8   9   10

Begin with a 10 minute fitness walk to warm up
and finish with a fitness walk to cool down.

| Box 15-2 | *HOW TO:* Fitness Walking |

Starting position	1. Stand with "straight" posture. 2. Bend your elbows 90 degrees, keeping your arms close to your body.
Action	1. Walk forward with a **fullfooted stride**, keeping your body balanced and coordinated. 2. Maintain "straight" posture and balance.

Figure 15-1: **Fitness Walking**

(Fitness walking cont.)

Action (cont.)	3. Coordinate your armswings with your walking motion.
Goal	1. Maintain form, balance, and symmetry. 2. Your effort level should be high enough to raise your heart rate to a moderate exercise level.
Focus Statement	"I will use my arms to balance my body on a straight foot, and push off through my big toe."

HOW TO:
Box 15-3 | Glides

Starting position	1. Stand with "straight" posture.
	2. Bend your elbows 90 degrees, keeping your arms close to your body.
Action	1. Using a **flatfooted stride**, run forward slowly and smoothly.
	2. Maintain "straight" posture and balance.

Figure 15-2: **Glides**

(Glides cont.)

Action (cont.)	3. Keep your kickback straight, in line with your hip. 4. Coordinate your armswings with your running motion.
Goals	Achieve smooth and efficient forward motion, balance, and symmetry.
Focus Statement	"I will use my arms to balance my body on a straight foot, and push off through my big toe for a straight kickback."

HOW TO:
Box 15-4 Glide Drills

Figure 15-3: Glide Drill #1: Arms In

Action	1. During glides, purposely overswing your arms in front of your body until you begin to feel out of balance. 2. Bring your arms back into correct armswing position to find your balance.
Goal	Notice how the position and motion of your arms affects your balance.

Figure 15-4: Glide Drill #2: Arms Out

Action	1. During glides, purposely rotate your armswings outward, away from your body, until you begin to feel out of balance.
	2. Bring your arms back into correct armswing position to find your balance.
Goal	Notice how the position and motion of your arms affects your balance.

Figure 15-5: Glide Drill #3: Feet In

Action	1. During glides, purposely rotate your leg inwards, toes pointing in, just until you begin to feel out of balance. (Don't rotate so much that it causes you to stumble.) 2. Rotate your legs back into a normal, forward position to find your balance.
Goal	Notice how the alignment of your legs and feet affects your balance.

Figure 15-6: Glide Drill #4: Feet Out

Action	1. During glides, purposely rotate your legs outwards, toes pointing out to the sides, just until you begin to feel out of balance. (Don't rotate so much that it causes you to stumble.) 2. Rotate your legs back into a normal, forward position to find your balance.
Goal	Notice how the alignment of your legs and feet affects your balance.

Figure 15-7: Glide Drill #5: Hands on Head

Action	1. During glides, place both hands on top of your head. 2. Keep the elbows pointed straight out to the sides. Do not twist the upper body. 3. Tighten the muscles of the trunk to help control your balance. 4. Run with your body straight, feet straight, and chin tucked. 5. Running motion should be straight forward, not side to side.
Goal	Maintain the alignment of the trunk over the pelvis while keeping the arms stationary.

When life looks easy street, there is danger at your door.
  – Grateful Dead

Chapter 16
Entering Phase Four:
Accelerations and Hills

You are now entering Recovery Phase Four: the safe return to functional running. Whether you're a fitness runner or a racer, your recovery plan must prepare you for your return to regular training, which will bring new challenges to your strength, balance, and endurance. In Phase Four, your goal is to make your body stronger and better prepared for running than it was before your injury. That's going to make your real-world training safer and easier, and when a challenge does come up, your body will be ready to handle it.

In this chapter you're going to learn about two types of challenges – accelerations and hills – which deal with changing momentum, and changing the angle and direction of applied forces. Everyone who races has to deal with acceleration, so getting up to speed is a familiar part of competitive training. Personally, my biggest challenge was learning how to run on hills. I grew up on Long Island, then I moved to Miami – and they're both flat! My wake-up call came the first time I ran the Boston Marathon. I knew there would be hills, but I was training in Miami and I just did my regular old routine. However, once I started racing in Boston, it didn't take long for me to realize that my body wasn't up to the added challenge of hills. At the finish line, my tail was really dragging!

In the year after that race, I dedicated myself to learning about hills, both in running and on the bike. My triathlon coach in Miami began educating me about hills, and then I kicked it up a notch. I went to Boulder, Colorado, for advanced training, and I got to train and spend time with a bunch of amazing coaches and triathletes. By the time I was done, I had really learned a lot about how to bike and run on hills!

I finally felt I was ready for a hill challenge. I signed up for a really hard, hilly race – the inaugural Ironman in Lake Placid – at a place where I used to hike when I was a kid in New York. Three days before the race, I was all prepared and ready to go. I hadn't been to Lake Placid for years, and I was really looking forward to being there. Unfortunately, life had another sort of challenge in mind. My wife, Sherry, had had a suspicious mammogram, and the biopsy came back the day before we were to leave. They were expecting it to be nothing, but it came back positive. Needless to say, we didn't go to the race.

My point is, you never know what running or life has in store for you, so it's important to prepare as well as you can, both physically and mentally. As I remind my patients, mental focus is essential both in training and in recovery from an injury or illness. My family got through a difficult period with surgery and chemo and radiation –

and I continued training for my Ironman. I was able to race at Lake Placid the following year, and during that race I found myself thinking about hills, and how hard they are. I really felt like I had conquered hills in life, as well as in racing. I had the kind of Ironman I had been hoping for, where I felt well prepared and able to deal with anything the race might throw at me. That's what training in Phase Four is really all about!

16.1 Introduction to Phase Four

At this point in your recovery program, your injury has healed and your running dysfunctions have been corrected. You may think you're ready to begin regular training, but you're not. Now you have to strengthen yourself even more for the challenges of *post-recovery running*. These are the exercises that can make the difference between running safely or getting reinjured and having to start your recovery program all over again.

As you increase your level of effort, the main difference between post-recovery running and post-injury running is still going to be your straight posture and your balance points. Before you return to regular training, you must be able to do accelerations, hills, and plyometrics in an upright posture that places the full force of these strenuous exercises directly through your injured region. In regular training, you typically lean into accelerations and hills, which is a different set of biodynamics. In post-injury running, you'll have to make a conscious effort to do these exercises with a straight, upright posture – which is much more difficult.

In Phase Four, the focus of your post-injury training changes from fixing your problems to achieving your goals, which will vary depending upon the type of running you normally do. I divide runners into two general groups: those who run for fitness (**fitness runners**), and those who race competitively (**racers**). Everyone will do the same Phase Four exercises, but the target level of effort will be higher for racers than for fitness runners.

As you enter Phase Four, mental focus becomes an increasingly important factor. You'll be writing a Specific Mental Focus Statement (*Self-Assessment 31* in the *Workbook*) that will help you focus on your individual impairment and injury region as you increase the difficulty of your workouts. Keeping a sharp mental focus throughout Phase Four will help improve your mind-body control and speed your recovery.

You'll begin Phase Four with **acceleration drills**, where you'll work on your stride, your armswing, and your balance while progressively working on speed. For example, in one acceleration drill you'll pump your arms faster, letting the armswing imbalance accelerate you. You'll naturally run faster, getting the rhythm, while focusing on maintaining form.

You'll continue with your P.T. Time, one hour twice a week, including your self-mobilizations, stretches, and Regional Closed-Chain Exercises. You'll also be adding two new closed-chain exercises [**Box 16-2**] which will prepare you for hill training. In Phase Four, you'll build your Regional Closed-Chain Exercises toward a *Final Target* which varies by exercise, and by the type of running you do: either fitness running or racing. For each exercise, you'll build your time, either at a *glide pace* or an *acceleration pace*, according to the instructions for that particular exercise. For step-up and step-over exercises, you'll also build up the height of your box until you have reached "high-knees" position.

When you've cleared your closed-chain exercises for hills, you can start hill training, where you will learn separate techniques for uphill and downhill running. Once you have mastered both accelerations and hills, you'll be ready to face the ultimate challenge of Phase Four: the explosive world of plyometrics (*Table 16-1*).

16.2 Techniques for Acceleration Drills

Acceleration means running progressively faster. The faster you run, the less of your foot you use, and the more you're on your forefoot. The more you run on your forefoot, the more your foot is angled downward. That happens naturally as you accelerate. That means you'll be transitioning from the flatfooted stride we used in the glides to a forefooted stride.

The **forefooted stride** is a sprinting stride that is used both for acceleration drills and in plyometrics. In this stride, you strike on the ball of your foot, with the ankle flexed downward, and the toes flexed up and pointed straight forward. Then you push off normally through the big toe. In *post-injury running*, your goal is to do that while maintaining your upright glide posture and balance.

You'll be doing three types of acceleration drills [**Box 16-1**]: In the first drill, you'll run progressively faster without leaning forward, maintaining a smooth and upright glide form. In the second drill, you'll run progressively faster by using your armswings to accelerate and control your balance. In the third drill, you'll start with a fullfooted stride and progressively run faster while smoothly transitioning into a flatfooted stride, then into a forefooted stride.

You'll use the same reference points for acceleration drills as you did for gliding drills. In your gliding drills you focused on a very straight, balanced movement, and you'll still be in a very straight, upright, posture in acceleration drills. It's about control. You'll gradually start going faster, but at first it's important to limit your rate of acceleration to control your balance.

16.3 Techniques for Hill Training

As I mentioned, training for hills in Miami is a challenge. For road work, I have to take my running club to a bridge. In my office, I put runners on an adjustable treadmill to simulate running uphill and downhill. It's not identical to hills in the real world, but it helps you learn the proper techniques under controlled conditions. While you're in post-injury training, I want you to avoid *atypical* hills (hills that are different from what you are used to) until you've cleared your glides and accelerations.

The techniques for running uphill are different from the techniques for running downhill. Running downhill moves your balance point back, and makes you accelerate faster. Running uphill moves your balance point forward, and slows you down. You'll be learning more about your body's specific balance points, and how to hold your arms to control your balance for both uphill and downhill running. Your goal in post-injury hill training is to do this while balancing on your injury region and paying attention to the form you learned in glides and accelerations.

First you must do **Hill Closed-Chain Exercises [Box 16-2]**, to practice balancing on one leg on an incline. On the downhill incline, you'll lower your center of gravity by bending your knees, keep your elbows out, shorten your armswing, and increase your rhythm. On the uphill incline, your balance point is more forward. You'll change your balance point by keeping your elbows in, and swinging your arms more to the front than to the back. It's important to focus on staying vertical, and not be moving forward and backward.

When you've mastered the Hill Closed-Chain Exercises, you'll begin working on your balance while running on hills **(Hill Drills, Table 16-3)**. You'll practice keeping your body as straight as you did in gliding, and use the techniques you learned in Hill Closed-Chain Exercises to change your balance points for uphill and downhill runs. When running downhill, try to avoid rocking from side to side as the downhill momentum accelerates you. As in accelerations, compensate by shortening your stride, and increasing your step rate.

16.4 Adding Accelerations and Hills to Your Base Schedule

Acceleration drills and hill training will be incorporated into your Base Schedule along with your warmup, glides, and cooldown. Don't forget to use your new *Specific Mental Focus Statement*. You'll start with short intervals of accelerations and hills that will allow you to progress without your form falling apart. There's no fixed formula for this, because each individual has too many unique variables.

You'll insert the three types of *acceleration drills* into your 50-minute glides (*Table 16-2*). If you're working on a treadmill, you can simulate acceleration drills by repeatedly pushing the speed button to keep going faster. As a general guideline, fitness runners will do 10 minutes of glides; then do each acceleration drill for 30 seconds, repeating each drill three times; then finish gliding their normal Base Schedule. Racers will do the same, but build up to three 90-second accelerations for each of the three acceleration drills.

Up to this point in your recovery program, you've been working on a fairly level surface. For hill training, you'll be doing *Hill Drills* on an adjustable treadmill or street grade with a little more incline than whatever you are normally accustomed to. It should be just a little challenging to work on your balance. If you are running on the street, you can fit Hill Drills into your 50-minute glides by running uphill, then turning around and running back downhill (or vice versa), with no break in between; then do a short glide interval on a level surface to recover before repeating. Fitness runners will do three repeats of 3 minutes each (90 seconds uphill and 90 seconds downhill). Racers will build up to three repeats of 9 minutes each (4.5 minutes uphill and 4.5 minutes downhill) (*Table 16-3*). Your warmup, glides, and cooldown should always be done on a level surface.

If you are doing hill training on a treadmill, the treadmill should be at grade 3 to 8, depending upon your ability and what you're accustomed to. Most treadmills can incline uphill, but not downhill. To simulate downhill running on a treadmill that does not decline, keep the treadmill flat, start running at your gliding speed, then add speed to accelerate. While accelerating, practice using your downhill techniques to adjust your balance point.

When you first begin acceleration drills and hill training, you may have to slow down your pace a little to make sure you maintain correct form and balance. Focus on your body symmetry and upright posture. Accelerate slowly to maintain that symmetry. In hill training, increase your incline gradually to maintain upright posture. Build up your speed slowly until you can do acceleration drills and hill training at your glide rhythm, without breaking form. When you are able to complete your Base Schedule, including Acceleration Drills and Hill Drills, with correct form and no increase in symptoms, you are ready to move on to plyometrics.

* * *

Table 16-1

Guidelines: Phase Four

	All Groups
PT Time	Continue with Stretch/Mobilization Cycles, 2 days per week, 20 minutes per day **(Log Form M)**. 1. Continue with your Regional Closed-Chain Exercises, 2 days per week, 40 minutes per day **(Log Form R)**. 2. Add Hill Closed-Chain Exercises and clear the *Symmetry Target* before progressing to Hill Drills in your Base Schedule.
Base Schedule	Continue your Base Schedule.

(Table 16-1 cont.)	All Groups
Acceleration Drills *(Self-Assessment 4A)*	Add Acceleration Drills into your Base Schedule (**Log Form S: Level 6**).
Hill Drills *(Self-Assessment 4B)*	Add Hill Drills into your Base Schedule (**Log Form S: Level 7**).
Plyometric Exercises *(Self-Assessment 4C)*	Add Plyometric Drills into your Base Schedule (**Log Form S: Level 8**).
Clearance to Start Regular Training *(Self-Assessment 4D)*	Able to perform all Phase Four exercises correctly for the specified amount of time with no increase in symptoms.

Table 16-2 A (Fitness Runners)
Base Schedule: Level 6, Accelerations

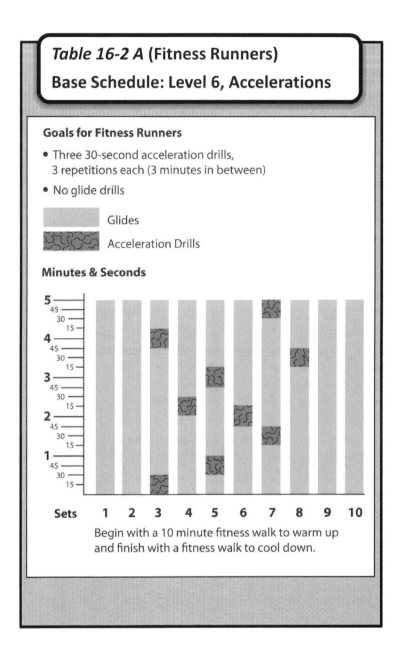

Goals for Fitness Runners

- Three 30-second acceleration drills,
  3 repetitions each (3 minutes in between)
- No glide drills

Glides

Acceleration Drills

Minutes & Seconds

Sets   1   2   3   4   5   6   7   8   9   10

Begin with a 10 minute fitness walk to warm up
and finish with a fitness walk to cool down.

Table 16-2 B (Racers)
Base Schedule: Level 6, Accelerations

Goals for Racers

- Three acceleration drills, 3 repetitions each
- Begin with 30-second accelerations (3 minutes in between)
- Build up to 90-second accelerations (2 minutes in between)
- No glide drills

  Glides

  Acceleration Drills

Minutes & Seconds

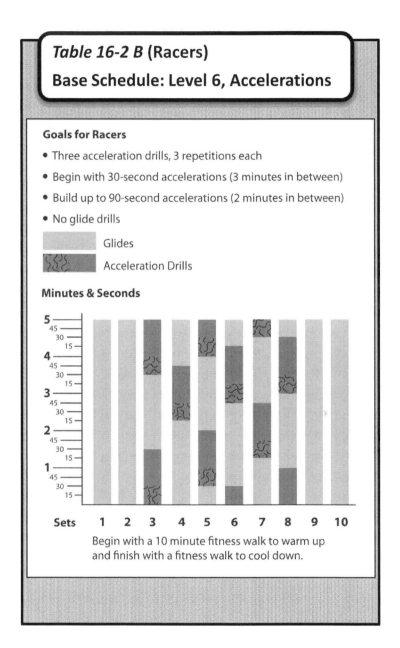

Begin with a 10 minute fitness walk to warm up
and finish with a fitness walk to cool down.

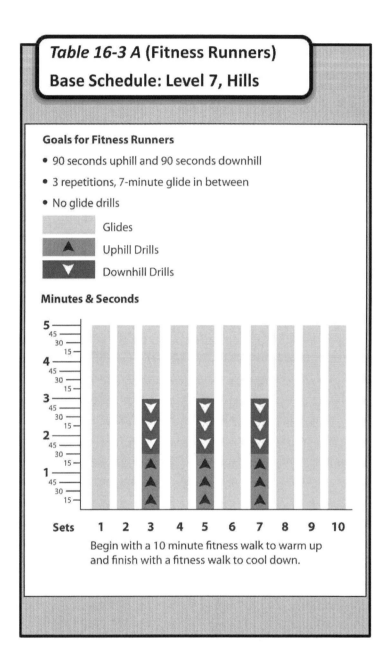

Table 16-3 A (Fitness Runners)
Base Schedule: Level 7, Hills

Goals for Fitness Runners

- 90 seconds uphill and 90 seconds downhill
- 3 repetitions, 7-minute glide in between
- No glide drills

	Glides
	Uphill Drills
	Downhill Drills

Minutes & Seconds

Sets 1 2 3 4 5 6 7 8 9 10

Begin with a 10 minute fitness walk to warm up
and finish with a fitness walk to cool down.

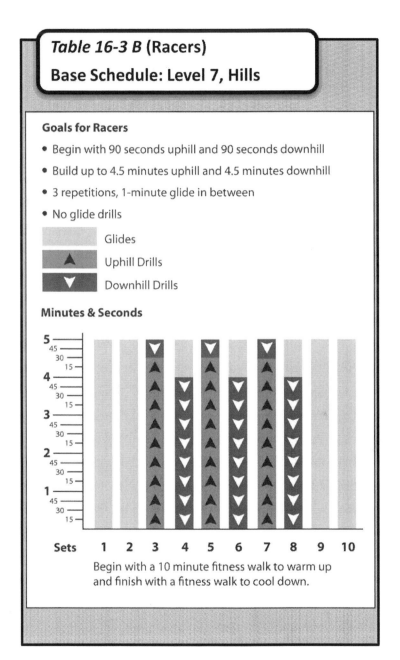

Table 16-3 B (Racers)
Base Schedule: Level 7, Hills

Goals for Racers

- Begin with 90 seconds uphill and 90 seconds downhill
- Build up to 4.5 minutes uphill and 4.5 minutes downhill
- 3 repetitions, 1-minute glide in between
- No glide drills

Glides

Uphill Drills

Downhill Drills

Minutes & Seconds

Sets 1 2 3 4 5 6 7 8 9 10

Begin with a 10 minute fitness walk to warm up
and finish with a fitness walk to cool down.

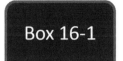

Box 16-1

HOW TO:
Acceleration Drills

Figure 16-1: Accelerations

Acceleration Drill #1

Starting position	Gliding with "straight" posture
Action	1. Increase your speed gradually through your Target Time while maintaining glide form and balance. 2. Glide for 2 minutes. 3. Repeat 3 times.
Goal	Try to accelerate without leaning forward.
Focus Statement	Use your specific mental focus statement (*Self-Assessment 3H* in the *Workbook*)

Acceleration Drill #2

Starting position	Gliding with "straight" posture
Action	1. Accelerate through your Target Time while pumping your arms harder and faster to drive acceleration. 2. Glide for 2 minutes. 3. Repeat 3 times.
Goal	Use your armswings to accelerate and control your balance.
Focus Statement	Use your specific mental focus statement (*Self-Assessment 3H* in the *Workbook*)

Acceleration Drill #3

Starting position	Gliding with "straight" posture and flatfooted stride
Action	1. Accelerate to a slightly faster **fullfooted stride**, then to a faster **flatfooted stride**, then to an even faster **forefooted stride** [*Table 15-1*]. 2. Glide for 2 minutes. 3. Repeat 3 times.
Goal	Use correct foot position for each of the three strides.
Focus Statement	Use your specific mental focus statement (*Self-Assessment 3H* in the *Workbook*)

HOW TO:
Hill Closed-Chain

Hill Closed-Chain #1:

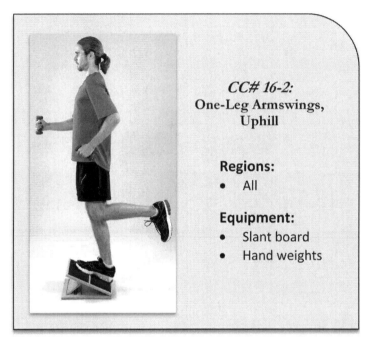

CC# 16-2:
One-Leg Armswings, Uphill

Regions:
- All

Equipment:
- Slant board
- Hand weights

Starting Position	1. Set up an incline board so that it slants uphill as you face the mirror. 2. Wearing shoes, stand on the incline board with "straight" posture. 3. Bend one knee 90 degrees to kickback position. 4. Holding a hand weight in each hand, bend elbows to 90 degrees.

(Hill Closed-Chain #1 cont.):

Action	1. Slowly swing your arms from the shoulder, keeping the elbows bent and close to the body. 2. Find your uphill balance point by swinging your arms a little farther forward than backward. 3. Build up to your glide rhythm, then accelerate your pace to your target time. 4. Repeat on each leg to create symmetry.
Goal	Use your armswings in a more forward position to keep your body straight and balanced over the weightbearing leg.
Focus Statement	"I will use my armswings to balance my body."
Clearance Target (to begin Hill Drills)	Create symmetry: • Accelerate to 20 seconds on each leg with no rest in between. • Total of 10 minutes, continuously, with no break in form.
Final Target	Accelerate your pace after you build up to your target time: • Fitness Runners: 30 seconds each leg • Racers: 90 seconds each leg • Total of 10 minutes, continuously, with no break in form.

Hill Closed-Chain #2:

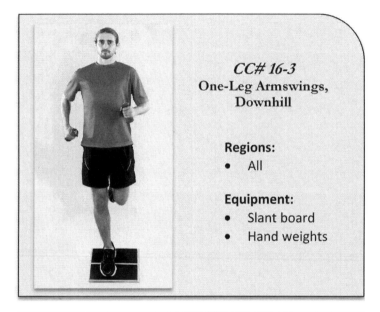

CC# 16-3
One-Leg Armswings,
Downhill

Regions:
* All

Equipment:
* Slant board
* Hand weights

Starting Position	1. Set up an incline board so that it slants downhill as you face the mirror. 2. Wearing shoes, stand on the incline board with "straight" posture. 3. Bend one knee 90 degrees to kickback position. 4. Slightly bend the weight-bearing knee. 5. Holding a hand weight in each hand, bend elbows to 90 degrees.

(Hill Closed-Chain #2 cont.)

Action	1. Slowly swing your arms from the shoulder, keeping the elbows a little farther from the body to improve balance. 2. Find your downhill balance point by swinging your arms a little farther backward than forward. 3. Build up to your glide rhythm, then accelerate your pace to your target time. 4. Repeat on each leg to create symmetry.
Goal	Hold your elbows farther away from your body and use a more rapid rhythm to keep your body straight and balanced over the weight-bearing leg.
Focus Statement	"I will use my armswings to balance my body."
Clearance Target (to begin Hill Drills)	Create symmetry: • Accelerate to 20 seconds on each leg with no rest in between. • Total of 10 minutes, continuously, with no break in form.
Final Target	Accelerate your pace after you build up to your target time: • Fitness Runners: 30 seconds each leg • Racers: 90 seconds each leg • Total of 10 minutes, continuously, with no break in form.

"A coach is someone who tells you what you don't want to hear, who has you see what you don't want to see, so you can be who you have always known you can be."
  – Tom Landry, Head Coach, Dallas Cowboys

Chapter 17
Plyometrics: Building Endurance, Power, and Efficiency

Your final goal in Phase Four is to maximize the endurance, power, and efficiency of your running muscles. We accomplish this through **plyometrics**, which can be defined as high-intensity exercises that use explosive movements such as bounding, hopping, and jumping to develop muscular power. Plyometrics are a powerful way to train – the most intense type of exercise you can do – and will quickly strengthen your legs for running.

Depending upon how severe your injury was when you started, and how fast you are progressing, you may actually get to start plyometrics fairly soon after your injury. In fact, some of my patients are quite surprised by how quickly they can progress through plyometrics and return to their regular training. For example, "Eric" was a long-distance runner who had been running with pain in the bottom of his foot and outer toes for several months. He first started noticing the pain when he was about 20 miles into his runs. However, since he hadn't done anything about it, it was getting worse and he was now feeling the pain after running only 10 miles. Although the pain would stop when he stopped running, it was severe; and it was taking all the joy out of his running experience.

Eric was showing the classic signs of a Stage 1 running injury brought on by fatigue, which was causing him to break his form. When I observed his running, I saw that when he got tired he dropped his head down, leaned forward, and rotated his foot outward. That caused him to slap the outside of his foot, which caused the pain in his outer toes. The outward rotation was also causing him to push off from the inner edge of his foot rather than straight through his big toe, which brought on the pain in the bottom of his foot.

Following his recovery plan, Eric quickly moved through the four phases of rehabilitation. In the first week, we mobilized his toes and arch, and corrected his stride. In the second week, he began more strenuous plyometric exercises to make him strong enough to maintain correct form – not just in the first few miles, but all the way through to the end of his run, with something left over in reserve. After a week of plyometrics, Eric was pain free and able to return to training.

That's what plyometric exercises can do for you. They give you that extra strength and endurance to keep you running with correct form and balance all the way through your run, which will make you a safer and healthier runner.

17.1 Focusing on Plyometrics

Plyometrics are the highest-level exercises you will do. In fact, these drills are purposely harder than your normal running. Plyometrics place a greater force on the weakness than running, and you're intentionally pushing this force directly through the injured region. You're also directing a lot more force onto your forefoot during landing. You're smashing the weakness. You're going to master these hard things in practice, under controlled conditions, so that running in the real world will be easier.

In *post-injury running*, you're not actually going to be doing plyometric exercises in an explosive manner. You should be doing them in a smooth, balanced manner. You're learning to control your explosive movements and improve the reactivity of your nervous system through the mind-body connections you're developing. You're not going as hard as you can – you're only going as hard as you can while maintaining control. That means you have to be mentally focused on what you're doing. Of course mental focus is important in all of your exercises, but it's absolutely essential in plyometrics. Focus on doing each exercise correctly, and save the really explosive training for your *post-recovery running*.

In all of the illustrations in this book, I've tried to show every exercise being executed with perfect, straight posture and upright positioning, which is particularly challenging for runners who are accustomed to traditional track and field exercises. However, I'm telling you now, exact perfection of these techniques is not essential in plyometrics. The outcome we're looking for isn't perfect technique – it's balancing on the weakness, progressively putting more force on the weakness, and using these last few exercises to push maximum strength through the healing injury. As long as you are progressing toward that goal, there's room for some interpretation in your technique.

That said, always try to do a good job. Stop and think about what you are doing. Try to understand the nature of each plyometric exercise and how it relates to your earlier exercises. Find the weakness. Find your personal balance points. With each exercise, move forward progressively with your weight-bearing through the injured region. That's the real goal.

17.2 Shoes for Plyometrics

In plyometric exercises, you're running on your forefoot. It's about power. Runners generate the power to lift their bodies and propel themselves forward by pushing off from the ground through the big toe, and your shoe selection plays an important role in achieving that.

Runners have always debated about the merits of running on soft surfaces versus hard, and about wearing shoes with cushioning versus shoes with support. The thing to remember is, the same physical principles apply to both running surfaces and shoes. Whenever you push off against something soft, you lose some power. The softer the surface or shoe, the more muscular power your body has to generate in order to push off with the same amount of force. It's the same thing with your landing – a softer surface or shoe reduces the shock by absorbing some of the energy that you generated in your pushoff.

So, you don't want a shoe that's *too* soft – but a shoe that's too hard on your injury isn't helpful either. You definitely should *not* do plyometrics in racing flats or track spikes – those are designed for performance, not protection. Because plyometric exercises generate greater forces than running, it's important to wear a protective shoe with a stable heel. I don't want you intentionally landing on your heel in plyometrics – everything is on the forefoot – but in case you do land a bit awkwardly, you don't want to hurt yourself.

Each of our plyometric exercises has you working on your injury a bit differently, and you can feel that in your shoe. As you generate force to propel your body forward, I want you to concentrate on controlling your balance from the landing through the pushoff, straight through the big toe. Feel the weight of your body centered through the toe and pushing against the shoe. The training shoe you select should allow your toes and forefoot to flex freely, and have adequate padding to protect your forefoot against the increased force.

17.3 Techniques for Plyometric Drills

You will be working progressively through four types of plyometric exercises: *high kickbacks, high knees, bounding,* and *skipping.* Note that, although you can do fitness walking, glides, glide drills, and drills for accelerations and hills on a treadmill or fairly level surface, *plyometric exercises must be done on a level surface ONLY, and never on a treadmill.*

All plyometric exercises are done on the forefoot, while maintaining the same balance and straight posture you've practiced in all of your earlier exercises. As you move from foot to foot, your weight should be evenly distributed on the balls of both feet. Focus on your specific balance point for each exercise, using your armswings for coordination and balance while maintaining momentum.

High kickbacks is about powering your running. In high kickbacks, you'll be running on your forefoot, kicking back so that your heel touches or nearly touches your butt, while holding your balance and upright position. It's important to use your armswing for balance in order to achieve a straight kickback.

High knees is a classic running drill that focuses on the alignment of the landing, maintaining a straight posture, and having your foot positioned under your knee. The balance point for high knees is farther forward than in high kickbacks. You're on your forefoot throughout, rapidly balancing, focusing on pushing your weight evenly through the toes of both feet. Keep your weight centered, and come down straight over your feet. It's important not to lean forward, because that will cause your foot to slap during the foot-strike.

Bounding is a very powerful exercise in which you run and take little leaps, balancing as you're bounding. As you're running on your forefoot, you'll push off, extend the leading leg, and leap – landing on your forefoot with your foot straight and balanced. This one can be a real challenge to your ability to control both the pushoff and the landing.

Skipping means balanced skipping on your toes, with coordinated armswings, while focusing on the injured region. (If you're not familiar with skipping, it's a rhythm in which you land on your forefoot, then take a small hop forward on your toes before pushing off.) Skipping is purposely the last exercise in this book. It takes a lot of coordination to learn to skip while remaining straight and balanced. I figure that, if you can coordinate the complexity of skipping while maintaining your form, running has got to be easier!

17.4 Adding Plyometrics to Your Base Schedule

In this final part of Phase Four, you'll continue with your regular P.T. time (one hour, twice a week, including all of your stretches, self-mobilizations, and regional closed-chain exercises) and your Base Schedule. Once you have cleared accelerations and hills, you're finished with those exercises, and you can now dedicate that time in your Base Schedule to plyometrics and glide drills. (Glide drills were temporarily suspended while you were working on accelerations and hills).

Plyometric exercises are hard if you do them right, so you don't have to spend a lot of time doing them. Fitness runners will do each plyometric drill for 15 seconds. Racers will begin by doing each plyometric drill for 15 seconds, then build up to 45 seconds per drill as they feel able. The goal for both groups is to do three repetitions of each of the four plyometric drills. Don't forget, if you have been doing your walk/glides and drills on a treadmill up until now, it's time to move to a level track or street. You should never do plyometric exercises on a treadmill.

Begin your Base Schedule as usual, with 10 minutes of fitness walking, followed by 10 minutes of glides to warm up for plyometric drills. Then do the first plyometric drill for 15 seconds, followed by 1 to 2 minutes of glides. Then do the second plyometric drill for

15 seconds, followed by 1 to 2 minutes of glides, and so on (*Table 17-1A*). Racers will gradually build up to 45-second plyometric drills over several workouts (*Table 17-1B*). Alternate your plyometric drills with short glides until you have completed each of the four plyometric drills three times, for a total of 12 plyometric drills. Because plyometrics tire the legs, you'll want to get the plyometric drills out of the way earlier rather than later in your workout.

Once you have done your 12 plyometric drills, complete the remaining time in your Base Schedule, alternating between glides and 15-second gliding drills. Do each of the five gliding drills twice, with at least one minute of gliding in-between. As usual, finish with at least 5 minutes of fitness walking to cool down.

17.5 Reaching Your Goal: Return to Running

Once you are able to complete your P.T. Time and Base Schedule – including all Regional Closed-Chain Exercises, plyometric drills, glides, and gliding drills – without breaking form and with no increase in symptoms, you're done with *post-injury running*! We're declaring you recovered, and you're cleared for *post-recovery running*.

Whatever type of post-recovery running you do, your goals will change, and so will your technique. You will no longer be focused on finding the weakness and strengthening it; you'll be focusing on your own running goals. If you have learned any techniques in *The Running Injury Recovery Program* that you liked, you can keep them. If you don't like them, you don't have to keep them. However, you'll still want to pay attention to the Running

Injury Stage Scale. In your post-recovery running, you'll be working hard and you may provoke some of your running-injury pain. In post-recovery training, your symptoms are allowed to reach Stage 3, but Red Flags are never allowed. Monitor your symptoms and use the techniques you have learned in this book to keep them under control.

Also remember that, although you've recovered from your injury and done some specific strengthening, no program or technique can magically *prevent* future running injuries. That's not a realistic expectation. All runners make mistakes when they're tired and vulnerable. Even very fit runners can push past their boundaries and keep running harder until they push so hard that they end up with an injury that requires injury management and further training. It happens to the best runners working with the best coaches, and it still happens to me. Learning from your mistakes, and constantly reworking your training plans and goals, is the secret to achieving all great goals.

The important lesson here is that all the things you have learned in this book are going to make you a more knowledgeable and skillful runner. Using this knowledge will help you manage any problems you may encounter quickly and effectively. That means you actually *will* be a better runner, and your new skills may help you reach goals that you were unable to attain before you were injured.

* * *

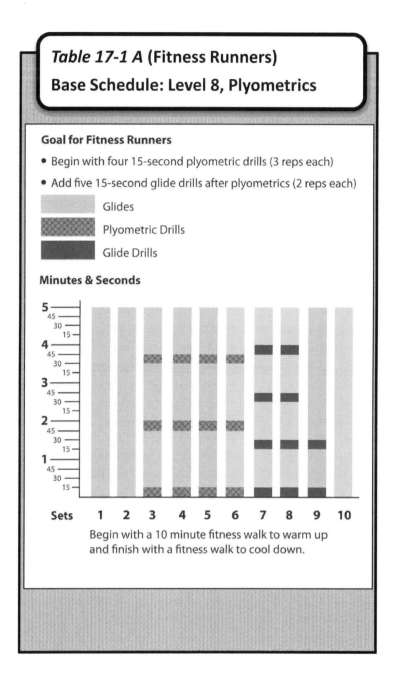

Table 17-1 A (Fitness Runners)

Base Schedule: Level 8, Plyometrics

Goal for Fitness Runners

- Begin with four 15-second plyometric drills (3 reps each)
- Add five 15-second glide drills after plyometrics (2 reps each)

Glides

Plyometric Drills

Glide Drills

Minutes & Seconds

Begin with a 10 minute fitness walk to warm up and finish with a fitness walk to cool down.

Table 17-1 B (Racers)
Base Schedule: Level 8, Plyometrics

Goal for Racers

- Begin with four 15-second plyometric drills (3 reps each)
- Build up to 45 seconds per exercise (3 reps each)
- Add five 15-second glide drills after plyometrics (2 reps each)

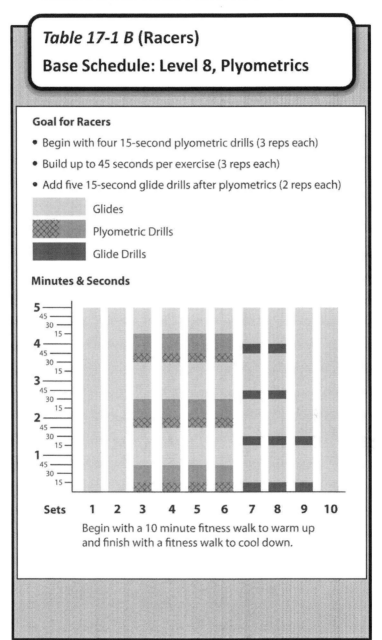

Glides

Plyometric Drills

Glide Drills

Minutes & Seconds

Sets 1 2 3 4 5 6 7 8 9 10

Begin with a 10 minute fitness walk to warm up
and finish with a fitness walk to cool down.

HOW TO:
Plyometric Drills

Box 17-1

Plyometric Drill #1: Plyometric High Kickbacks

Starting position	Gliding with "straight" posture and flatfooted stride on a level surface (not a treadmill).
Action	1. Keep your weight on your forefeet throughout the exercise. The balance point is farther back than in *high knees*. 2. Using a fast gliding motion, kick your rear foot up as far as you can toward your butt as you run, keeping the knee pointed down and the foot in straight alignment.

Figure 17-1:
High Kickbacks

(Plyometric Drill #1 cont.)

Action (cont.)	3. When kicking back, coordinate your armswings by snapping the opposite arm back. 4. Flex the weight-bearing foot and ankle downward (plantar flexed) and push up through big toe, keeping your body balanced. 5. When you land, bring the front leg down straight over your foot (forefooted), keeping your weight centered.
Goals	1. Focus on balance, maintaining a straight posture, and having your foot positioned under your knee. 2. Focus on pushing your weight equally through the toes of both feet, and the alignment of the landing. 3. Focus on performing equal kickbacks through both legs.

Plyometric Drill #2: Plyometric High Knees

Starting position	Gliding with "straight" posture and flatfooted stride on a level surface (not a treadmill).
Action	1. Keep your weight on your forefeet throughout the exercise. The balance point is farther forward than in *high kickbacks*. 2. Using a fast gliding motion, tighten your trunk muscles and drive each knee upward toward your chest as you run, keeping the foot aligned under the raised knee ("high knees" position). 3. Coordinate your armswings with your leg motion.

Figure 17-2:
High Knees

(Plyometric Drill #2 cont.)

Action (cont.)	4. Flex the weightbearing foot and ankle downward (plantar-flexed) and push up through the big toe. 5. When you land, bring the front leg down straight over your foot (forefooted), keeping your weight centered.
Goals	1. Focus on balance, maintaining a straight posture, and keeping your foot positioned under your knee. 2. Focus on pushing your weight equally through the toes of both feet. 3. Focus on straight alignment of the landing.

Plyometric Drill #3: Plyometric Bounding

Starting position	Gliding with "straight" posture and flatfooted stride on a level surface (not a treadmill)
Action	1. Keep your weight on your forefeet throughout the exercise. The balance point is farther forward than in *high knees*. 2. Using a fast gliding motion, push off strongly through the big toe and leap forward, leading with the front knee.

Figure 17-3: Bounding

(Plyometric Drill #3 cont.)

Action (cont.)	3. Extend the leading leg and land on the forefoot with your weight centered, keeping your foot straight and balanced. 4. Coordinate your armswings with your leg motion.
Goals	1. Focus on balance, maintaining a straight posture, and the alignment of the landing. 2. Focus on pushing your weight equally through the toes of both feet. 3. Focus on performing bounds equally through both legs.

Plyometric Drill #4: Plyometric Skips

Starting position	Gliding with "straight" posture and flatfooted stride on a level surface (not a treadmill).
Action	1. Keep your weight on your forefeet throughout the exercise. The balance point is centered over your pelvis. 2. Using a fast gliding motion, flex the weight-bearing foot and ankle downward (plantar flexed), push off strongly through the big toe, and skip forward, keeping your body upright and balanced. 3. When skipping, coordinate your armswings by snapping the opposite arm back.

Figure17-4: Skips

(Plyometric Drill #4 cont.)

Action (cont.)	4. Land on the same foot, keeping your foot straight and your weight centered. 5. Continue your forward motion onto the opposite foot, and repeat.
Goals	1. Focus on balance, maintaining a straight posture, and the alignment of the landing. 2. Focus on pushing your weight equally through the toes of both feet. 3. Focus on performing skips with equal force through both legs.

Chapter 18
Life Decisions and Lifelong Running

How you deal with a personal crisis, including your mental attitude and the decisions you make, can determine the success or failure of your recovery. This is true in life, and it's true in injury management. For most runners, what happens in life affects our running, and what happens in running affects our life.

In my life, one of my biggest crises developed from a series of events that revolved around running, and eventually led to the writing of this book. I was working full time at my P.T. practice, constantly bent over a table and getting all twisted up by the end of the day. At the same time, I was also training for an Ironman triathlon, producing races for the Miami Runners Club, leading group training for club members, managing my running store, and trying to find time for my family. It was a perfect storm for stress and injury.

So, how many things can possibly go wrong? After I finished the Ironman, my wife Sherry and I were leaving on vacation when I got a panicked phone call. A race I was producing for the Miami Runners Club was having a meltdown. The sponsor was pulling out of the race at the last minute – and while we were travelling, I was frantically shutting down the race and minimizing our damage. Then, when I got back, I learned that the club's non-profit status had been violated due to an error in our state paperwork, which led to a great deal of unpleasantness among our leadership group. There were some major arguments over the future of the Miami Runners Club, and I reacted badly and lost some longstanding friends and training companions.

Seething with feelings of betrayal and resentment, I started training for my next triathlon when a small (literally millimeters) mechanical problem between my bike pedal and the crank created an abnormal shear force on my knee that developed into a Stage 5 injury. By the time I identified it I was having trouble getting out of a chair, and I couldn't run for six weeks. Now I was angry *and* crippled! Then, just in case there wasn't enough going on, we had a flood in my P.T. office. A water pipe broke on a holiday weekend, our second-floor office was flooded, and we flooded out the whole bottom floor. It took the whole office building down.

That was a rough period of time. I realized I had to take charge of the attitude, the injury, and the problems with the running club. To recover from the knee injury, I used the guidelines and principles in this book. I knew the source of the injury and I knew how to get it under control. I helped reorganize the Miami Runners Club to focus on educational programs to promote running and safe training instead of producing races, and (abandoning the non-profit status) I folded the club management into my running store, *The Runner's High*, just so the club could continue to exist.

As for the attitude, that's always a work in progress. Psychologically, my family and work always keep me firmly centered. I can get straightened out and relieve my physical stress with one hour of P.T. Time, doing my self-mobilizations, stretches, and closed-chain exercises. As in any type of recovery, I find that setting goals and maintaining mental focus help keep all aspects of my busy life in balance.

For any lifelong runner, it's important to protect your running through proper habits and goal setting. Much of what I try to teach is how to establish good habits, including body awareness. By protecting your running lifelong you'll also be protecting your life. Many early warning signs of distress in your body and your life can first be seen in your running. Awareness of your running, and early intervention at the first signs of distress, can improve your entire life.

18.1 *Carpe Diem*

To undertake a recovery program that is as detailed and time-consuming as this one is, you really need to be motivated. As a P.T. and running coach, I've worked with runners for more than thirty years, and I've seen the beginnings and the endings of many running careers. Looking back, the best advice I can give to any runner is, make the most of the time you have, while you can still run. For some endurance athletes, running is only a brief moment in their life, and then it's over. Many distance runners fear being stopped by a running injury but, in real life, it's often an illness that finally stops you. The important thing is to fix your running injury now, because you never know what the future may bring.

A good example of this principle is my friend "Steve." When Steve first came to me as a patient, he was a mess. He was a lifelong endurance athlete, and part of his diagnosis was runner's heel. With runner's heel, the Achilles tendon microscopically and progressively rips, resulting in overstriking and a dysfunctional pushoff.

One day, toward the end of his treatment, Steve was in my office looking at all my race-finisher medals there on the wall, and said, "Bruce, I'd love to do an Ironman." As it happened, I had just signed up for two events in the upcoming year, a half Ironman and a full Ironman, so I invited him to sign up and train with me. Of course, this was a big commitment. You have to sign up for these things a year in advance, so for a year you know this is on your schedule, and the training for an Ironman is very time consuming.

We had very little time to get Steve well and trained for the first event. After he completed rehab, he joined my club's running classes, and we incorporated closed-chain exercises, glides, glide drills, accelerations, hill training, and plyometrics into his training. The plyometrics particularly helped with the rapid training. Steve learned to modify plyometrics for injury management, and he learned to focus on strengthening his tendon for pushoff. In less than six months, he went from being crippled to being ready for a half Ironman.

So, we went off to the half Ironman, and then a funny thing happened. The day before the race, Steve started asking me how these things work, and revealed to me that he had never done any kind of triathlon! But he did great; he was nervous, but it turned out fine. Of course we had already signed up for the full Ironman, so we continued training and had a successful race there as well.

However, Steve's story doesn't end there. Soon after, Steve became very ill and was no longer able to run. As it turned out, if Steve had not done his rehab with me, and if he hadn't done his first Ironman races with me that year, then he would never have been able to do them.

The message is, no one knows where life will take you, so recover from your injuries now and move forward. And if you're fit to race, and you want to race, take every opportunity – because you only live once.

18.2 Entering Post-Recovery Running

When you move from *post-injury running* to your regular *post-recovery running*, lots of things will change. You'll be building up your pace from a glide pace to your normal fitness-running or racing pace. You'll change your body position from the upright position we used in training to your individual running or racing style. Your strike zone and balance points may change. Also, you may be running in different footwear that affects your stride. As you make these transitions, be cautious. Always monitor your Running Injury Stage, and use the principles you've learned to maintain the gains you've made during your recovery.

One difference between *post-injury running* and *post-recovery running* is that, in post-recovery, you're allowed to have some Stage 3 symptoms. The pain pattern of training after an injury is different than the pain pattern of normal training, and there may be a little bit of your injury that lingers in the background. That doesn't mean you're injured. You're increasing your effort level, and your body is dealing with it. It can always feel a little different at different times. However, Red Flags are never acceptable. Stage 3 is allowed in small and infrequent doses, but less than 30 percent of your workouts should elicit Stage 3 symptoms.

Remember that running injuries result from repeating bad habits over and over again. In running, as in every other repetitive activity, doing something over and over again the same way does not make you better at it – it makes you stupid. So I say, practice does not make perfect, practice makes stupid. Only "perfect" practice makes perfect. You can't always be perfect, and you can't always be thoughtful, so you'll need to create moments in your running to be thoughtful and mix it up. That's part of training.

You can also use different closed-chain exercises to avoid repetitive activity. During your recovery program, you habituated your personal list of Regional Closed-Chain Exercises, but you didn't habituate the Basic Closed-Chain Exercises, and you didn't habituate all the other Regional Closed-Chain Exercises that were not on your list. In your future training, that gives you a whole bunch of closed-chain exercises that are not habituated, which you can rotate through and mix up for improved performance.

The one thing that you should habituate is your flexibility training. Do use your stretching exercises to look for asymmetry. Do know all of the self-mobilization exercises. Use these stretches and self-mobilizations to monitor yourself. Any sudden change could be an early warning sign of an injury that you can identify before emerging symptoms appear. If something suddenly stiffens up, or gets super tender, and you address it quickly and make modifications, you might never even get to emerging symptoms.

A 10-minute fitness walk to warm up can reduce your risk of reinjury, and it's just a good idea in general. A lot of my runners maintain a period of fitness walking as a warmup for the rest of their running careers. It's not unreasonable for you to do the same, at least for the first year of your recovery, because of the greater risk for a running injury during the first year after an injury – and failing to properly warm up raises that risk.

Finally, don't forget your glides. Glides are useful both for recovery training and for distance training. Recovery training means that, after a hard workout, your legs need to recover. A recovery run would be gliding until your legs feel better, then stopping before you feel bad again. Endurance training means only the distance – the time on your feet – is fatiguing, not the effort. Gliding is the best way to build your endurance.

To become a better runner, there has to be some pushing. There have to be some hard workouts. There has to be some risk-taking. However, beware of running over-aggressively at the beginning – that's a common training error when people first return to running. It really is a learning process to deal with increasing your speed and distance training without constantly hitting worsening symptoms. Remember, it's not miles that make champions, it's injury-free miles that make champions. In post-recovery running, you should enjoy running and work to reach your internal and external goals. If you can accomplish those goals for one year without injury, and for three continuous years without a 6-month gap in running, then you will have succeeded.

18.3 Goal-Setting for Racers

One of my main points in designing an individualized running injury recovery program is that racers and fitness runners have to train differently. If you are a racer, 20 to 30 percent of your time and effort will be spent in racing or race-specific training. Elite distance runners are doing 100-mile-plus weeks just to get in the volume of training that they need.

Like all human activities, racing pace and style are really different for everybody. The only way I can help my athletes find their lean, find their cadence, and find their race-pace strike zone and balance, is at racing pace. I work with them while they're doing it, and then work with them to maintain that style and pace. And, yes, it's difficult, so it's hard to habituate. Whatever your style, the important thing is to use what you have learned to maintain your balance and control your stride.

Racing is meant to be hard and 100-percent effort. Of course, when we give 100-percent effort, we expect some recovery time. Our bodies just can't give 100 percent all the time, or we break down (some of us more than others). When you are preparing to race – to give 100-percent effort – you want to go in there fresh, not fatigued, so you really need to plan for it.

As a racer, you need to train intelligently and set specific goals. You can't allow every race to be a symptom-worsening experience. I teach my athletes to rate their races as *A*, *B*, or *C*. An *A* race is one of great importance, when you really have to be at your best. You prepare for it for six months, which means you're only allowed to have two or three of these a year. For a top athlete, that's a tough thing; you've really got to pick and choose. With an *A* race, you'll have a longer taper before the race, and a longer recovery period after the race. *B* races have lesser importance, and have a shorter taper and a shorter recovery. *C* races are basically at a high training level – you train up to them – it's kind of a test of your training. Whether you rate a race as an *A*, *B*, or *C*, you'll always have to expect some recovery time with worsening symptoms because, if you're racing, there is still going to be 100-percent effort at some point.

After a race, the requirements for recovery are the same as the requirements for recovering from an injury. You can't have medication. You have to be able to hop; you have to be able to do steps; and you have to be able to glide. You have to be able to do plyometric exercises at a submaximal level. Post-race symptoms may not be an actual injury, but you can use the same criteria to work through them and build up again to your racing potential.

18.4 Shoes for Running Faster

If your goal is to run faster, pay close attention when you transition from a supportive post-injury training shoe to your lightweight trainers or racing flats. Be careful when you're doing race-specific shoe selection. Make sure that the shoe you select is going to be appropriate for your condition, your needs, and your weight-bearing pattern. It's not a pie-in-the-sky goal.

The reason I'm making this point is, a racing flat is a flat, unsupportive shoe. If there is any possibility that you might end up walking – then understand that racing flats are awful for fitness walking. When you fitness walk, you need that heel. I see that in races all the time; when athletes end up walking and they're in racing flats, it's not good.

When in doubt, this is how I coach my runners: If they might not be able to hold their form for their race-specific length of time, I keep them in trainers until they can do it. I would rather they lose a little bit in microseconds from the weight of the shoe than to get into a pattern where they're not supported throughout their running. That's what I tell my patients, and that's how we sell it at my store.

For racers, I also want to discuss shoeing down for performance. You know that, while you're shoeing down, a lighter, more responsive shoe will improve your performance – and that has a place. However, when you habituate shoeing down, it's no longer lighter. You get used to it very quickly, and you lose any advantage of shoeing down. So, for training shoes, I teach my athletes that strengthening comes from pushing your body against a firmer shoe that is less responsive, that the firmer shoe forces you to balance on your foot, and that lifting the weight of the shoe makes you stronger.

In my own experience, whenever I do a marathon and feel fatigued, it's never from lifting the weight of the shoe! Lighter makes a difference, but it's not that big of a difference, and you may lose more in the tradeoff than you gain. In fact, I run very poorly in racing flats. Whenever I go into racing flats, I can't control my stride, no matter how hard I try. I can't stay on my forefoot very long, and my foot slaps. So, I train in supportive shoes, then I race in lightweight trainers that are less supportive. For me, that's shoeing down. It's all relative.

At the time this book was written, there was a trend in the running-shoe industry to address running problems by progressively shoeing people down to "barefoot" shoes. For many runners, that turned out to be a serious mistake, and a lot of people developed serious injuries. In fact, if my first running store had done that to me, I wouldn't be running today. The truth is, we get fitter in our training shoes so we can shoe down to go faster. We don't put on racing shoes and get fitter. It's running that makes us stronger, not lighter shoes.

18.5 Barefoot Running and Triathlon

For many years as a triathlete and coach, I've practiced and taught barefoot running for triathlon. It's a skill, and it's part of what we do in races. In the first transition (T1), we come out of the water barefoot, and we've got to get to where we set up our bikes. The bikes aren't waiting for us there on the sand of the beach! In triathlon, that place can be far away – a half-mile or more – so we may be running barefoot longer than most people might think.

This is how I coach barefoot running for T1: I use an extremely balanced glide, and I practice the same glide drills that I teach in this book, barefoot, on a safe surface. In Miami, it's on the beach by the shoreline. I also practice the same closed-chain exercises barefoot, in front of a mirror. We do these very same drills in preparation for triathlon, and in preparation for T1, because they address the same need for balance and stability.

In triathlon, often our barefoot transition is on concrete or asphalt, and not even nice concrete or asphalt. There are cracks and uneven surfaces, so it's important to be balanced. I would not use a heel-striking style of running, because I want to be balanced; and I would not use a forefoot-striking style of running, because of the uneven surfaces. I would use a very balanced, flatfooted gliding movement that's not hammering.

Another reason for using a balanced glide for T1 is that one of the challenges of the transition is vasodilation, which we discussed in a previous chapter. For T1, the blood starts out in our swimming muscles, and we need to shunt it over to our cycling muscles. In the period of running between the swim and the bike, we don't want to be doing an all-out hard run that would shunt blood to our running muscles. That's just going to slow things down and hurt our performance. So we practice running barefoot with a nice, smooth, flatfooted glide.

18.6 Lifelong Running

One of the greatest joys in my life has been watching my daughters, Tracy and Rachel, grow up and become runners, although there were times when I thought it might never happen. Rachel started running, and ran with the Miami Runner's Club, when she was in elementary school – but not for fun. Rachel was a good student, and she tried hard, but her P.E. teacher was about to flunk her because she hadn't mastered certain P.E. skills. Thinking back to my own P.E. days, I was sympathetic. I spoke with her P.E. teacher and got her to give Rachel extra credit for working on running, and coming out to races, and training with a running club.

So, Rachel ran with the Miami Runners Club and got extra credit to pass elementary-school P.E.. Then, in her tweens and adolescence, she rebelled from fitness and did other things. Happily, I watched her turn into a runner as a young adult, and had the pleasure of helping her and coaching her to her first marathon. I got to watch her do her first and second NYC marathons, and it was just great fun to sit at the finish line, waiting for her, and watching so many runners of every shape and size reach their goals. Now, when I see Rachel running, I see her developing good lifelong running skills.

Knowing how to deal with running injuries is one lifelong skill that every runner should have. By definition, an injured runner is still a healthy human being. However, a crippled runner is at risk for life-altering complications because they can get caught up in the medical system, which can expose them to all kinds of medical complications. Any running injury can become a severe and complex running injury if you don't recognize it and take the proper steps to correct it. My advice is, learn the skills that will make you a smart, mindful, and fit runner for life.

Always keep in mind that injury-free miles make champions. For fitness runners, try to maintain your base, and don't drop down below 10 miles per week. For racers, try to maintain a healthy base of at least 25 miles per week, and achieve that base before you try to go faster, farther, or longer. Mistakes come from fatigue and from not absorbing those miles. Time and time again, I have found that trying to do too much too soon is the most common cause of reinjury in my patients.

Despite our best precautions, injuries still happen. Take the time to figure out what works best for you, and what keeps you moving forward in your recovery. This book is a guidebook that you can customize to your individual needs, not a static, nonchanging protocol. You should never mindlessly follow any exercise book as if it were a cookbook. That said, if you follow the principles in this book, there is no doubt in my mind that you will come out a stronger runner.

Finally, this book is about optimism. Lifelong running is a lifelong quest. If you want to run for your whole life, you've got to make time for it. You've got to learn about it, and you've got to respect it. Embrace the joy of running, and never take it for granted.

* * *

COURSE MAP

KEY

Educational Goals	White boxes contain educational goals from the *Running Injury Recovery Program*.
Action Required	Light-shaded boxes require you to take a specific action in the *Running Injury Recovery Program Workbook*.
Checkpoints	Dark-shaded boxes are Checkpoints for moving through phases in the *Workbook*.

Note: Read all of the chapters in the *Running Injury Recovery Program* before starting your *Running Injury Recovery Program Workbook*.

PHASE ONE: Education and Self-Help

Section I. History and Self-Assessment (Chapters 1 -4)

CH 1: Do I Really Have a Running Injury?

1.1	I've read Chapter 1.
1.2	I've determined that I have an injury caused by running (*Self-Assessment* 1A).
1.3	I've completed my *Running History* (*Self-Assessment 1B*) and entered the last day I ran on Worksheet 1D.
1.4	I've made a list of *intrinsic* and *extrinsic factors* that might affect my running (Worksheet 1B1) and I am taking steps to correct them.
1.5	I've completed my *Medical History* (*Self-Assessment 1C*) and recorded any relevant pre-existing medical conditions (Worksheet 1C1).

CH 2: Introduction to the Four Phases of Recovery

2.1	I've read Chapter 2.
2.2	I've decided to undertake a phased recovery plan for my running injury.

CH 3: How Bad is my Injury?

3.1	I've read Chapter 3.
3.2	I've documented my pain pattern and any visible swelling associated with my running injury (*Self-Assessments* 1D1 and 1D2).
3.3	I've determined the severity of my injury on the Running Injury Stage Scale, and whether or not I have any Red Flag symptoms (*Self-Assessment* 1D3).
3.4	I've summarized my original injury by *possible affected region* (*Self-Assessment* 1D4).
3.5	I've determined which treatment group I am in for Phase One (*Self-Assessment* 1D5).

CH 4: What Type of Injury Do I Have?

4.1	I've read Chapter 4.
4.2	I understand the difficulties in the diagnosis of running injuries, and why we focus on injury regions in running-injury management.
4.3	I understand the differences between *simple* running injuries and *complex* running injuries, and why they are treated differently.
4.4	I will assess my running injury and implement self-management for all affected regions.

Section II: Education and Self-Help (Chapters 5 - 9)

CH 5: Entering Phase One, Self-Help

5.1	I've read Chapter 5.
5.2	I understand the goals of Phase One.
5.3	I understand PRICE and how it applies to me.
5.4	I've followed the instructions for Protection and

	Recovery.
5.5	I've determined that I do not need to ICE (Group 1). **OR** I've begun to ICE (Ice, Compression, and Elevation) and I am filling out my *Log Form I* (Group 2).

CH 6: The Right Recovery Plan

6.1	I've read chapter 6.
6.2	I understand when to seek professional help [**Box 6-1**].
6.3	I understand how to evaluate professional help [**Box 6-2**].
6.4	I understand that my management program must include both active treatment and education.
6.5	I've obtained medical clearance to self-manage my running injury. **OR** I am following medical advice to resolve any medical issues before starting self-management.

CH 7: What to Watch out For

7.1	I've read chapter 7
7.2	I understand the importance of not running while taking medication for pain or inflammation.
7.3	I understand the importance of active treatment and weight-bearing exercise in running-injury management.
7.4	I can distinguish between effective treatments and "tricks" for running-injury management.
7.5	I will undertake an active recovery program, without medication for my running injury.

CH 8: Running Shoes and Running Injuries

8.1	I've read chapter 8.
8.2	I understand the relationship between running shoes and running injuries.

| 8.3 | I understand the importance of wearing a well-fitted, supportive training shoe for running-injury management. |
| 8.4 | I will do my post-injury training in a proper training shoe. |

CH 9: Choosing the Right Shoe

9.1	I've read chapter 9.
9.2	I've undergone a professional *gait analysis* to determine what type of functional support I need. **OR** I understand what type of functional support I need.
9.3	I've chosen a pair of *post-injury training shoes* based on function, fit, and feel [**Box 9-1**].
9.4	I have inspected my shoes for defects [**Box 9-2**].

CHECKPOINT TO ENTER PHASE TWO:

| I am taking steps to protect and recover from my running injury. |
| Group 2 ONLY: I am icing and filling out Log Form I. |
| I've completed my *Phase One Self-Assessment.* |

PHASE TWO: Regaining Mobility (Chapters 10 through 12)

CH 10: Phase Two, Manual Therapy and Self-Mobilization

10.1	I've read chapter 10.
10.2	I understand the goals for Phase Two.
10.3	I understand the Goals, Techniques, and Guidelines for Self-Mobilization.
10.4	I understand how to perform *Self-Mobilizations by Region* [**Box 10-2**].
10.5	I've obtained the necessary *Tools for Self-Mobilization* [***Table 10-1***].
10.6	I will find the tenderness and restricted regions that affect my running, and improve my mobility.

CH 11: Keep it Moving

11.1	I've read chapter 11.
11.2	I understand the concept of P.T. Time.
11.3	I understand how to perform a *Mobility Self-Assessment* [**Box 11-1**], and how each self-mobilization is associated with one specific injury region [***Table 11-3***].
11.4	I understand *Stretch/Mobilization Cycles* for affected and unaffected regions [**Box 11-2**].
11.5	I understand how to perform *Stretching Exercises* [**Box 11-3**], and how each exercise is associated with one or more specific injury regions.
11.6	I've obtained all the equipment I need to perform *Stretching Exercises* [***Table 11-4***].
11.7	I've completed my *Mobility Self-Assessment* (*Self-Assessment 2A* and Worksheet 2A1).
11.8	I've determined my affected and unaffected region(s) for this injury, and the order in which I will do my stretches and self-mobilizations in Phase Two (*Self-Assessment 2A*).
11.9	I've recorded my program of Stretch/Mobilization Cycles for Phase Two on my first *Log Form C: Stretch/Mobilization Cycles.*
11.10	I've determined my treatment group for Phase Two, and whether I will follow guidelines for *simple* or *complex* injuries (*Self-Assessment 2B*).
11.11	I 've started a daily schedule of Phase Two P.T. Time, following the instructions for my treatment group (*Table 11-1*) and my complexity subgroup (*Table 11-2*); I am recording the results on *Log Form C*; and I am evaluating my daily *Log Form C* for symmetry requirements for my complexity subgroup (*Self-Assessment 2C*).
11.12	I've cleared Phase Two symmetry requirements for my complexity subgroup (*Self-Assessment 2C*), and I will now use *Log form M: Maintaining*

	Mobility to record my stretch/mobilization cycles during P.T. Time.
11.13	I've evaluated my *Log Form C* for regional tenderness (*Self-Assessment 2D*).

CH 12: The Psychology of Running Injuries

12.1	I've read chapter 12.
12. 2	I understand the mental challenges of running-injury management.
12. 3	I understand the importance of focusing on the instructions in this book while self-managing my running injury.
12. 4	I will follow my post-injury training program with proper mental focus.

CHECKPOINT TO ENTER PHASE THREE PART ONE:

I have achieved the degree of symmetry and range of motion required for my (simple or complex) injury.
(Group 2 only) I have completed two weeks of icing and all inflammation is cleared.
I have completed *Phase Two Self-Assessment.*
I am continuing with my individualized list of self-mobilizations and stretches, and I am recording the results on *Log form M: Maintaining Mobility.*
I am now following the Guidelines for Phase Three Part One in *Table 13-1.*

PHASE THREE: Improving Strength and Balance (Chapters 13 through 15)

CH 13: Entering Phase Three, Training Plans and Habits

13.1	I've read chapter 13.
13.2	I understand the goals for Phase Three.
13.3	I understand the importance of an individualized *Regional Training Plan*.

13.4	I understand how *Basic Closed-Chain Exercises* are used for self-assessment in Phase Three Part One.
13.5	I understand how *Regional Closed-Chain Exercises* are used to improve strength and balance, and how they fit into P.T. Time in Phase Three Part Two.
13.6	I understand all of the factors used to determine which treatment group I will enter in Phase Three Part Two *[Table 13-2]*.
13.7	I understand the concept of the *Base Schedule*, and its division by groups into *self-paced plans* and *two-week-interval plans*.
13.9	I've determined the amount of time that I intend to commit to my Base Schedule.

CH 14: Closed-Chain Exercises

14.1	I've read chapter 14.
14.2	I understand how different *Basic Closed-Chain Exercises* are used to assess basic balance requirements in Phase Three Part One.
14.3	I understand how my specific *Regional Closed-Chain Exercises* are used to improve strength and balance in Phase Three Part Two.
14.4	I understand the correct techniques for performing all Basic and Regional Closed-Chain Exercises **[BOX 14-2]**.
14.5	I've assembled the exercise equipment required for closed-chain exercises *[Table 14-3]*.
14.6	I am continuing with my individualized list of self-mobilizations and stretches, and I am recording the results on *Log form M: Maintaining Mobility*.
14.7	I have added Basic Closed-Chain Exercises to my daily P.T. Time, and I am recording the results on *Log Form B: Basic Closed-Chain*.
14.8	I am monitoring my progress to make sure my symptoms do not increase higher than Stage 2.

14.9	I have completed *Self-Assessment 3A: Basic Closed-Chain Clearance.*
14.10	I have completed my *Regions and Stress Fracture Self-Assessment* (*Self-Assessment 3B*).
14.11	I have determined my Regional Closed-Chain Exercise plan for my Injury Regions (*Self-Assessment 3C*) and prepared my first *Log Form R: Regional Closed-Chain.*
14.12	I have written my Impairment Statements (*Self-Assessment 3D part 1*) and understand the weaknesses that I need to work on throughout my recovery program.
14.13	I have determined my treatment group for Phase Three Part Two (*Self-Assessment 3D part 2*).

CHECKPOINT TO ENTER PHASE THREE PART TWO:

I am able to perform all *Basic Closed-Chain Exercises* correctly and symmetrically, with no increase in pain. OR I have completed one week of *Basic Closed-Chain Exercises*, but I am still *unable* to perform all eight *Basic Closed-Chain Exercises* correctly, symmetrically, or with no increase in pain.
I have completed *Self-Assessments 3A* through *3E*.
I am now following the Guidelines for Group 1A or 1B (Table 13-2) or Group 2A or 2B (Table 13-3).

CH 15: Fitness Walking and Glides

15.1	I've read chapter 15.
15.2	I understand the importance of gradually building a running base to prepare for post-recovery running, and using a Base Schedule to maintain the correct level and consistency of effort during post-injury training.
15.3	I understand the importance of working at a submaximal level to keep my symptoms below Stage 3.

15.4	I understand the importance of maintaining erect posture to load body weight through my injury.
15.5	I understand the *Three Basic Running Strides* [*Table 15-1*] and the importance of pushing off correctly through the big toe.
15.6	I understand the importance of fitness walking for warmup and cooldown, and the correct technique for fitness walking **[BOX 15-2]**.
15.7	I understand the importance of glides to strengthen my injury for running, and the correct technique for glides **[BOX 15-3]**.
15.8	I understand the importance of glide drills for balance, and the correct techniques for glide drills **[BOX 15-2]**.
15.9	I understand the use of progressive walk/glide sets, and how to build my individualized walk/glide program **[BOX 15-1]**.
15.10	I understand the importance of mental focus to maintain correct form.
15.11	I've established a *Base Schedule* based on my running experience and goals, and I've reduced my P.T. Time to two times per week (*Self-Assessment 3E*).
15.12	I've completed my *Worksheet T: Training Plan for Phase Three Part Two*.
15.13	I will now follow the *Course Map* below for **Group 1 (A or B)** or **Group 2 (A or B)**.

GROUP 1 (A and B) ONLY

15.13A	I understand the goals of the *Self-Paced Plan*.	
15.14A	I am continuing with Stretch/Mobilization Cycles during P.T. Time, and recording the results on *Log Form M: Maintaining Mobility*.	
15.15A	**Group 1A:** 1. I have cleared all *Basic Closed-Chain*	**Group 1B:** 1. I have **not** cleared all *Basic Closed-Chain*

	Exercises in 7 days or less. 2. I am following the guidelines for **Group 1A** in **Table 13-2**.	*Exercises* in 7 days or less. 2. I am continuing with *Basic Closed-Chain Exercises* during P.T. Time, and I am recording the results on *Log Form B: Basic Closed-Chain*. 3. I am following the guidelines for **Group 1B** in **Table 13-2.** 4. I have completed ***Group 1B Reassessment***.
15.16A	I have progressed to *Regional Closed-Chain Exercises* during P.T. Time; I am recording the results on *Log Form R: Regional Closed-Chain;* and I am evaluating my *Log Form R* for Stage 1 clearance (*Self-Assessment 3F*).
15.17A	I have started my walk/glide program at the level determined in *Self-Assessment 3E*; I am following the Self-Paced Plan; and I am recording the results at the correct level in my *Log form S: Base Schedule*.
15.18A	I am using *Self-Assessment 3G1 for Self-Paced Plan* to evaluate my *Log Form S*.
15.19A	I have successfully incorporated the glide drills for my level into the glide portion of my walk/glide program **[*Table 15-4*]**.
15.20A	I am focusing on correct form for fitness walking, glides, and glide drills **[BOX 15-2, Box 15-3, and Box 15-4]**.
15.21A	I am increasing my pace and distance gradually to prevent my symptoms from going above Stage 2.
15.22A	I have progressed through each level of walk/glide sets with correct form and with no increase in symptoms **[*Table 15-4*]**

15.23A	I have progressed to Base Schedule Level 5 (50-minute glides and glide drills) *[Table 15-4E]*.
15.24A	PT Time: I am able to perform all *Regional Closed-Chain Exercises* for each of my injury regions with symmetry and no increase in symptoms *(Self-Assessment 3F)*.
15.25A	Base Schedule: I have completed my Base Schedule at Level 5 for one week with no increase in symptoms *(Self-Assessment 3G1)*.
15.26A	I have Cleared Phase Three P.T. Time and Base Schedule, written my *Specific Mental Focus Statement*, and prepared my log forms for Phase Four *(Self-Assessment 3H)*.

GROUP 2 (A and B) ONLY

15.13B	I understand the goals of the *Two-Week-Interval Plan*.	
15.14B	I am continuing with Stretch/Mobilization Cycles during P.T. Time, and recording the results on my *Log Form M: Maintaining Mobility*.	
15.15B	**Group 2A:** 1. I have cleared Basic *Closed-Chain Exercises* in 7 days or less. 2. I have progressed to *Regional Closed-Chain Exercises* during P.T. Time, recording the results on *Log Form R: Regional Closed-Chain*, and evaluating *Log Form R* for Stage 1 clearance (*Self-Assessment 3F*). 3. I am following the guidelines for **Group 2A** in **Table 13-3**.	**Group 2B:** 1. I have *not* cleared *Basic Closed-Chain Exercises* in 7 days or less. 2. I am continuing *Basic Closed-Chain Exercises* during P.T. Time, and recording the results on my *Log Form B: Basic Closed-Chain*. 3. I am following the guidelines for **Group 2B** in **Table 13-3**.

15.16B	I've started fitness walking my Base Schedule, following the Two-Week-Interval Plan, and I am recording the results on Level 0 of *Log form S: Base Schedule*.
15.17B	I am using *Self-Assessment 3G2 for Two-Week-Interval Plan* to evaluate my Log Form S.
15.18B	I am focusing on correct form for fitness walking **[BOX 15-2]**.
15.19B	I am increasing my pace and distance gradually to prevent my symptoms from going above Stage 2.
15.20B	**I have completed fitness-walking my Base Schedule for at least two weeks.**
15.21B	**I can fitness walk my Base Schedule for 60 minutes with no increase in symptoms, and I am cleared to begin the walk/glide program (*Self-Assessment 3G2*)**
15.22B	**Group 2B ONLY: I've progressed to *Regional Closed-Chain Exercises* during P.T. Time, I am recording the results on *Log Form R: Regional Closed-Chain*, and I am evaluating *Log Form R* for Stage 1 clearance (*Self-Assessment 3F*).**
15.23B	I 've started my walk/glide program at Level 1, following the Two-Week-Interval plan, and I am recording the results on *Log Form S, Level 1*.
15.24B	I have successfully incorporated the glide drills for Level 1 into the glide portion of my walk/glide program **[*Table 15-4A*]**.
15.25B	I am focusing on correct form for fitness walking, glides, and glide drills **[BOX 15-2, Box 15-3, and Box 15-4]**.
15.26B	I am increasing my pace and distance gradually to prevent my symptoms from going above Stage 2.
15.27B	I have completed my Base Schedule, Level 1, for at least two weeks, with correct form and no increase in symptoms **[*Table 15-4A*]**.

15.28B	I have completed my Base Schedule, Level 2, for at least two weeks, with correct form and no increase in symptoms *[Table 15-4B]*.
15.29B	I have completed my Base Schedule, Level 3, for at least two weeks, with correct form and no increase in symptoms *[Table 15-4C]*.
15.30B	I have completed my Base Schedule, Level 4, for at least two weeks, with correct form and no increase in symptoms *[Table 15-4D]*.
15.31B	I have completed my Base Schedule, Level 5 (50-minute glides and glide drills) for two weeks with correct form and no increase in symptoms *[Table 15-4E]*.
15.32B	**P.T. Time: I am able to perform all *Regional Closed-Chain Exercises* for each of my injury regions with symmetry and no increase in symptoms (*Self-Assessment 3F*).**
15.33B	**Base Schedule: I am able to complete my Base Schedule with a 50-minute glide and glide drills for two weeks with no increase in symptoms (*Self-Assessment 3G2*).**
15.34B	**I have cleared Phase Three P.T. Time and Base Schedule, written my *Specific Mental Focus Statement*, and prepared my log forms for Phase Four (*Self-Assessment 3H*).**

CHECKPOINT TO ENTER PHASE FOUR (all Groups)

| I have achieved symmetry in *Basic Form Requirements:*
1. I can balance on one leg with my foot pointed straight forward.
2. I can use my arms to balance my body.
3. I can keep my body balanced while pushing off through the big toe.
4. I can keep balanced while kicking straight back. |
| I have completed all Phase Three Self-Assessments. |

PHASE FOUR: Return to Functional Running
(Chapters 16 - 18)

CH 16: Entering Phase Four, Accelerations and Hills

16.1	I've read chapter 16.
16.2	I understand the goals of acceleration drills and hill training.
16.3	I understand the use of the forefooted stride in accelerations and plyometrics.
16.4	I understand the techniques for the three types of Acceleration Drills **[BOX 16-1]**
16.5	I am continuing with Stretch/Mobilization Cycles during P.T. Time, and I am recording the results on my *Log Form M*.
16.6	I am continuing with my *Regional Closed-Chain Exercises* during P.T. Time; I am increasing the difficulty and time per exercise according to my running goals *[Table 16-1]*; and I am recording the results on my *Log Form R*.
16.7	I have added *Hill Closed-Chain Exercises* to my P.T. Time **[Box 16-2]**, and I am recording the results on my *Log Form R*.
16.8	I have added *Acceleration Drills* to my Base Schedule *[Table 16-2]*, and I am recording the results on my *Log Form S, Level 6*.
16.9	I am using my Specific Mental Focus Statement and focusing on straight posture and balance points in acceleration drills.
16.10	I am increasing the time per acceleration drill according to my running goals *[Table 16-1]*.
16.11	I am monitoring my progress to make sure my symptoms do not go higher than Stage 2.
16.12	**I have cleared Base Schedule Level 6 *Acceleration Drills* and *Hill Closed-Chain Exercises* (*Self-Assessment 4A*).**

16.13	I understand the *Techniques for Hill Training*, either on the street or on a treadmill.
16.14	I have added *Hill Training Drills* to my Base Schedule *[Table 16-3]*, and I am recording the results on my *Log Form S, Level 7*.
16.15	I am focusing on straight posture and balance points in hill training.
16.16	I am increasing the time per hill drill according to my running goals *[Table 16-1]*.
16.17	I am monitoring my progress to make sure my symptoms do not go higher than Stage 2.
16.18	**I have cleared Base Schedule Level 7** *Hill Training Drills (Self-Assessment 4B)*

CH 17: Plyometrics

17.1	I've read chapter 17.
17.2	I understand the goals of plyometric drills.
17.3	I understand the techniques for the four types of plyometric drills **[BOX 17-1]**.
17.4	I understand that plyometric exercises must be done on a level surface ONLY, never on a treadmill.
17.5	I have added plyometric drills and glide drills to my Base Schedule *[Table 17-1A]*, and I am recording the results on my *Log Form S, Level 8*.
17.6	I am focusing on straight posture and balance points in plyometric drills.
17.7	I am increasing the amount of time per plyometric exercise as determined by my group (Fitness Runner or Racer) *[Table 16-1, Table 17-2B]*.
17.8	I am gradually increasing the force exerted in each plyometric exercise, but I am still working *submaximally*.
17.9	I am monitoring my progress to make sure my symptoms do not go higher than Stage 2.
17.10	**I have cleared Base Schedule Level 8** *Plyometrics (Self-Assessment 4C).*

CH 18: Life Decisions and Lifelong Running

18.1	I have read chapter 18.
18.2	I understand the importance of a careful transition from *post-injury running* to *post-recovery running*.
18.3	In *post-recovery running*, I will monitor my Injury Stage and avoid Red Flags.
18.4	I will mix up my running activities as part of my regular training.
18.5	I will maintain symmetry in my flexibility and watch for early warning signs of injury.
18.6	While running, I will focus to maintain my balance and control my stride.
18.7	I will maintain a proper Base Schedule in my regular training.
18.8	**I have completed *Self-Assessment 4D: Clearance for Post-Recovery Running*.**

CHECKPOINT TO RETURN TO RUNNING:

I am able to perform all of my P.T. Time exercises correctly for the specified amount of time with no increase in symptoms.
I am able to complete my Base Schedule with plyometric exercises and glide drills with correct form and no increase in symptoms.
I have completed all of my *Phase Four Self-Assessment*.
I have learned running habits that will help me become a smarter and safer runner.
I am ready to return to functional *post-recovery* running.

GLOSSARY

Acceleration drills: Training exercises done while running at a progressively faster pace. Part of your Base Schedule in the *Running Injury Recovery Program Workbook*.

Acceleration rhythm: In the *Running Injury Recovery Program*, doing closed-chain exercises by starting out slowly, then increasing the pace, while limiting the top speed according to your ability to hold correct form.

Activate (muscle contraction): Physical therapy techniques used to tighten and stabilize soft tissue impairments.

Active treatment: An injury management program in which you play an active role in working with a health professional to treat your injury. Not passive treatment.

Activities of daily living (ADLs): The physical motions that you perform during a normal day.

Acute injury: An injury that improves and lasts for a relatively short time.

Acute phase: After an injury, the time period in which you have the most severe symptoms, often including pain and swelling (inflammation).

Affected regions: The body areas that are directly impaired by a running injury.

Avoidance: Not doing something.

Base Schedule: Used in the *Running Injury Recovery Program Workbook*, the training part of your recovery program. Includes fitness walking, glides, glide drills, and drills in accelerations, hills, and plyometrics.

Basic Closed-Chain Exercises: Used in the *Running Injury Recovery Program Workbook*, closed-chain exercises that you need to perform properly in order to make clearance to begin glides.

Basic Form Requirements: Four standard criteria for balance that everyone should be able to do.

Body awareness: Self-perception of your body, its position, the interactions between body parts, and neuromuscular control.

Build exercise: Progressively doing an exercise for a longer period of time, or with a higher level of difficulty, without breaking form.

Central nervous system (CNS): Brain and spinal cord.

Chondromalacia: Softening of the cartilage in the knee.

Chronic injury: An injury that lasts for a long time with little or no improvement.

Clearance: Permission to move on to the next level in your injury recovery program.

Clearance Checkpoints: Used in the *Running Injury Recovery Program Workbook*, a specific set of requirements in your *Course Map* and/or *Self Assessments* to receive clearance to move to the next level in your injury recovery program.

Closed-chain exercises (general): Exercises done with your body weight on one leg, carrying your weight upward from the foot to the trunk.

Compensatory pattern: A dysfunctional walking or running movement used to reduce the pain or compensate for the weakness caused by an impairment.

Complex running injury: An injury that involves more than one region, or that has a traumatic or pre-existing medical factor.

Cortisone: A powerful steroid used as an anti-inflammatory medication.

Course Map: Your primary guide through the *Running Injury Recovery Program*.

Deep vein thrombosis (DVT): A life-threatening blood clot in the leg.

Defects (in shoes): Any part of a shoe that is improperly manufactured and can contribute to a running injury.

Direct, dynamic, and progressive: Description of the types of methods used in an active recovery program.

Dorsiflexed (foot): Upward movement of the foot at the ankle joint that that raises the toes.

Dysfunctional running: Running in a manner that weakens your body and interferes with your ability to reach your running goals.

Dysfunctions: Factors in your running that interfere with your ability to reach your running goals.

Efficiency (efficient running): Running without excessive (damaging) strain (force) on the body to reach *functional goals.*

Evaluation: An assessment by a qualified healthcare professional.

Extrinsic factor: Anything that originates outside of you and creates a possible risk for injury.

Final Target: In *The Running Injury Recovery Program,* the length of time a fitness runner or racer will set as a goal for each exercise in Phase Four.

First ray: The big toe.

Fitness runner: A runner whose goal is to run for fitness, not for competition.

Fitness walking: Walking with a balanced, fullfoot stride with no single-leg stance (both feet always touching the ground), with a pace that is faster than normal walking.

Flatfoot stride (flatfooted): Running so that the foot strikes with the ankle in neutral position (landing on the flat foot).

Forefoot stride (forefooted): Running so that the foot strikes with the ankle plantar-flexed (landing toes first).

Fullfoot stride (fullfooted): Walking or running so that the foot strikes with the ankle dorsiflexed at initial contact (landing heel first).

Functional goals: Measurable things that you want to achieve (for *functional running*).

Functional outcome: Achieving the ability to perform better in a measurable way.

Functional running (efficient running): Running in a way that lets you achieve your *functional goals.*

Functional strengthening: Strengthening for an outcome that relates to a measurable activity.

Gait: Stride.

Gait analysis: Stride assessment by a qualified observer.

Gait disorders: Problems that cause you to alter your normal stride.

Gait dysfunction: Problems with your stride caused by gait disorders.

Gate control theory: The theory that sensory stimulation blocks the perception of pain.

Gestalt: A combination of two or more factors which produces a result that is greater than the sum of the individual parts.

Glide drills: Specific balance exercises done while gliding. Part of your Base Schedule.

Glide (gliding): A form of balanced running with straight posture, using a flatfooted stride that is slower than normal.

Glide position: Standing with knees and hips even; one leg slightly bent, with ankle in neutral position and toes touching the ground behind you.

Glide rhythm: The cadence of your arm and leg movements during glides.

Habituation: Repeating the same activity over and over again until it can done without thinking about it

High knees position (90/90 position): Standing with one knee raised to form a 90 degree angle at the hip and a 90 degree angle at the knee, with the ankle in neutral position (*Example: Figure CC# 14-15*).

Hill Closed-Chain Exercises: Used in the *Running Injury Recovery Program Workbook*; closed-chain exercises used to improve your ability to balance on an incline.

Hill Drills: Running exercises used to improve your ability to balance on a hill. Part of your Base Schedule in the *Running Injury Recovery Program Workbook*.

Hyponatremia: Condition of low blood sodium.

ICE: Self-help for injuries with Red Flags, swelling, or inflammation. Consists of specific requirements for Icing, Compression, and Elevation of the injured body part.

Iliotibial band (ITB) syndrome: A common running injury that involves the area that connects the gluteus maximus muscle and tensor fascia to the tibial bone.

Impairment: Anything that reduces your ability to normally function and perform activities.

Inflammation: The nonspecific immune response to any injury, resulting in redness, swelling, and pain.

Inhibited: Being unable to perform an activity due to pain and/or weakness.

Intrinsic factors: Anything that originates within you and creates a possible risk for injury.

Intrinsic muscles (of the foot): The small muscles of the foot.

Kickback position: Standing with knees and hips even; the knee of the non-weightbearing leg bent to 90 degrees, with the ankle in neutral position. (*Example:* Figure CC# 14-14.)

Kinetic chain: The weightbearing function of the leg that supports the body weight from the foot upward to the entire body.

Log Forms: Used in the *Running Injury Recovery Program Workbook* to keep track of your recovery exercises and progress.

Macroscopic injury: An injury that is large enough to be visible.

Manual therapy: The professional use of hands as part of treatment for an injury or dysfunction.

Mechanoreceptors: Sensory organs that allow our bodies to perceive movement and position.

Mental focus: What you think about while exercising.

Mental focus statement: In the *Running Injury Recovery Program Workbook*, a repeated thought to help maintain concentration, used to perform an exercise properly.

Metatarsal heads: The ends of the bones of the foot before the toes.

Microscopic injury: An injury that is too small to see.

Mobility: Measurement of flexibility of movement.

Mobilizing muscle: One of the larger muscles that move the body.

Motion control shoe: Type of shoe with the most added support.

Multifactorial causes: When many different issues contribute to a running injury.

Muscle imbalance: A dysfunction resulting from improper amounts of mobility and stability.

Neuromuscular control system: The information pathways from the central nervous system to the voluntary muscles that move your body.

Neuromuscular re-education: Techniques to identify movement disorders and improve neuromuscular control.

Neutral shoe: Type of shoe with no added cushioning or support that affects your balance.

Nontraumatic activity: Something you do that can cause an injury due to forces originating within your body, *i.e.* lifting a box.

Non-weightbearing leg: While doing closed-chain exercises, the leg that is *not* carrying your body weight.

NSAIDS (non-steroidal anti-inflammatory drugs): Medication that reduces pain and inflammation and does not contain cortisone or other steroids

Open-chain exercises: Exercises that do *not* place the body weight directly through the leg to the floor.

Osteoarthritis (OA): The degenerative breakdown of a joint.

Overpronation: The foot rolls excessively inward during the mid-point of the weight-bearing phase of your stride.

Pace: Your speed while walking or running.

Pain pattern: Self-description of pain location.

Patellar tendinosis: Degenerative breakdown of the tendon around the kneecap.

Patellofemoral pain syndrome (PFPS): A disorder of the kneecap due to abnormal movement.

Plantar: Relating to the bottom of the foot.

Plantarflexed (foot): Downward movement of the foot at the ankle joint that that points the toes.

Plyometrics (plyometric drills): Running exercises done with a forefoot stride, used to challenge impairments in a complex manner. Part of your Base Schedule in the *Running Injury Recovery Program Workbook*.

Post-injury running: Running used for injury recovery. All glides and drills used in your Base Schedule in the *Running Injury Recovery Program Workbook*.

Post-injury training: All exercises used for injury recovery in the *Running Injury Recovery Program Workbook*.

Post-recovery running: Running that you do after completing the *Running Injury Recovery Program*.

PRICE: The method of self-help for running injuries used in the *Running Injury Recovery Program Workbook*: Protection, Recovery, Icing, Compression, and Elevation.

Pronation: The foot rolls inward when walking or running.

Proprioceptors: Sensors that our nervous systems uses to perceive body movement and location.

Protocols: A set of agreed-upon procedures for the proper way to do something.

PT Time: Used in the *Running Injury Recovery Program Workbook*; the time spent in your recovery program doing physical therapy (P.T.) exercises to improve flexibility, strength, balance, and body awareness – not walking or running.

Racer: A runner whose internal or external goal is to compete for speed and/or distance.

Red Flags: In the Running Injury Stage Scale, an intensity-specific list of signs of possible severe injury.

Regional Closed-Chain Exercises: Used in the *Running Injury Recovery Program Workbook*; specific closed-chain exercises done during recovery for specific impaired regions, including stress fracture.

Regions: Used in the *Running Injury Recovery Program Workbook*; parts of the body associated with running injuries.

Release (muscle relaxation): Physical therapy techniques used to loosen up restrictions in soft tissues.

Roll (rolling): Self-mobilization technique using a mobilization tool with downward pressure and a twisting motion.

Running Injury Stages: Used in the *Running Injury Recovery Program Workbook*; a method used to evaluate and rank the severity of a running injury.

Secondary regions: Regions of the leg that are uncommon sites of simple running injuries. Treated using a plan for an associated (primary) region.

Self-assessment (general): The process of evaluating one's own progress.

***Self-Assessments*:** Techniques and forms used in the *Running Injury Recovery Program Workbook* to guide you through your recovery program and to evaluate your progress.

Self-management plan: A purposeful strategy designed individually for you, used to identify and treat your specific injury.

Self-mobilization: Using physical therapy procedures on yourself to pinpoint injury regions and gain mobility.

Self-Paced Plan: A series of *Self-Assessments* in the *Running Injury Recovery Program Workbook* which allow certain individuals with less-severe injuries to proceed through the *Running Injury Recovery Program* as quickly as possible.

Set (of exercises): One continuous repetition of one exercise on one leg.

Shear forces: Rotational or diagonal exertions on the body that can cause injury.

Shod: Wearing a foot covering (not barefoot).

Simple running injury: A nontraumatic injury caused by running, which occurs within one body region, and with only one significant element.

Sprain: Injury to non-contractile tissue such as a tendon or ligament.

Stability shoe: A shoe that provides significant support to the foot to minimize undesirable movement.

Stability: The result of using muscular strength to control the movement of body parts, or to keep them still, to maintain correct form and balance.

Stabilizing muscle: Muscles that tighten so that other body parts can move correctly.

Straight posture: Standing with arms and legs straight and the body in vertical alignment in all planes. (*Example: Figure 11-13.*)

Straight-leg raise (SLR): A test of mobility. Lying down with knees straight and feet dorsiflexed, flex the hip joint and try to raise one leg straight up to a 90-degree angle with the body.

Strain: Injury to contractile tissue (muscle).

Stretch/Mobilization Cycle: Used in the *Running Injury Recovery Program Workbook*; specific techniques used to identify running injuries and to increase mobility in affected and unaffected regions.

Stretching exercises: Techniques to improve flexibility.

Strike: For different strides, the part of the foot that makes first contact with the ground during walking or running (heel strike, flatfoot strike, forefoot strike).

Strum (strumming): Self-mobilization technique using a mobilization tool with downward pressure and moving from side to side.

Submaximal level: Exercising at a level of intensity or duration below that which might cause injury or failure to perform an exercise with proper form.

Supination: The foot rolls excessively outward during walking or running.

Symmetry: Being able to perform an exercise in exactly the same way on both the left and right sides of the body.

Training habits: The way we routinely exercise.

Traumatic activity: Something that can injure you by causing movement of a body part outside of its normal range of motion. May be caused by a force outside of your body, such as a box falling on you.

Trunk: The main part of the body, not including the head, arms, and legs.

Two-Week-Interval Plan: A series of *Self-Assessments* in the *Running Injury Recovery Program Workbook* which requires individuals who have severe or complicated injuries to proceed through the *Running Injury Recovery Program* at a slower pace to allow complete recovery.

Unaffected regions: Body areas that are *not* directly impaired by a running injury, but may have issues that can be addressed during your recovery program.

Underpronation: The foot is in a supinated position during mid-stance.

Unshod: Barefoot. Wearing no foot covering.

Vasodilation: Blood vessels widen and hold a greater volume of blood.

Walk/glide program: The training portion of your recovery program in which you progressively increase weight-bearing through your injury region. Includes fitness walking and balanced running (glides) done during recovery. Your Base Schedule.

Walk/glide sets: A progressive series of five minute exercise sets consisting of various combinations of fitness walking and glides used in *The Running Injury Recovery Program*.

Weightbearing leg: While doing closed-chain exercises, the leg that is carrying your body weight.

INDEX

training shoes, **119**, 388
Twist Test, **117**
Stride. *See* Gait

T

Training habits, 6, 10, 14, 20,
24, **213**, **214**, **216**, 221

Treadmill
for exercises, 342, 344
for gait analysis, 35, 43, 122
for shoe selection, 112
when not to use, 363, 365

W

Walk/glide program, **17**, 220,
223, **301**, 302, 311, **313**, **314**,
316, 318
Workbook, 2, 18
Appendices, 224, 251
Log Forms, 186
Self-assessments, 45, 49,
146, 175, 177, 182, 186,
211, 248, 251, 302, 312,
340

ABOUT THE AUTHOR

Bruce R. Wilk, P.T., O.C.S., has been writing and lecturing about running injury management around the world for more than thirty years, teaching specialized classes for running organizations, professional associations, medical schools, and the military. He received his degree in Physical Therapy from SUNY, and is certified in Manual Therapy and Orthopedic Physical Therapy. His primary practice is in Miami, Florida, where he is the director of Orthopedic Rehabilitation Specialists, Inc.. Wilk is also a lifelong runner and triathlete, Vice President of the Miami Runner's Club, and has worked with many racers as an RRCA certified running coach. Along with his wife, Sherry, he owns and operates a running specialty store called *The Runner's High*, which has become the center of Miami's running community.

Made in the USA
San Bernardino, CA
16 May 2014